Students of sociology as well as of international law and relations will find this an illuminating and interesting analysis of the basic elements in international organization. Using the term "institutions" in its broad modern sociological sense, the author examines the beliefs, traditions, and basic rules underlying the conduct of international relations and the structure and functions of modern international organizations.

A preliminary section defines international society in terms of the accepted principles of group psychology. Part One then reviews the historical development of international relations from ancient times, and analyzes the political and legal bases of present-day international institutions. In the last two parts of the book the author discusses interstate relations and current international organizations. He describes the machinery for day-to-day relations between states as well as structural relationships; discusses the fundamental concepts and juridicial problems of today's international organizations; and presents the essential features of the structure and work of the United Nations and the regional organizations established since World War II.

MINERVA SERIES OF STUDENTS HANDBOOKS

International Institutions

THE MINERVA SERIES

Russian Political Institutions
Free Elections

International Institutions

BY

PAUL REUTER

Professor of International Law
University of Paris

TRANSLATED BY

J. M. CHAPMAN

RINEHART AND COMPANY

New York

FIRST PUBLISHED IN 1958

———

Translated from the French

INSTITUTIONS INTERNATIONALES

published by

Presses Universitaires de France 1955

PRINTED IN GREAT BRITAIN

BY PURNELL AND SONS, LTD

PAULTON (SOMERSET) AND LONDON

ABBREVIATIONS

Publications

AJ	*American Journal of International Law.*
Annuaire	*Annuaire de l'Institut de Droit International.*
BYBIL	*British Yearbook of International Law.*
RCADI	*Recueil des Cours de l'Académie de Droit International de La Haye.* (The first figure refers to the year, the second to the volume and the third to the page.)
RGDIP	*Revue Générale de Droit International Public.*

International Organisations

FAO	Food and Agriculture Organisation.
GATT	General Agreement on Tariffs and Trade.
ICAO	International Civil Aviation Organisation.
ICJ	International Court of Justice.
ILO	International Labour Organisation.
IMF	International Monetary Fund.
ITU	International Telecommunication Union
NATO	North Atlantic Treaty Organisation.
OEEC	Organisation for European Economic Co-operation.
PCIJ	Permanent Court of International Justice.
UNESCO	United Nations Educational, Scientific and Cultural Organisation.
UNO	United Nations Organisation.
UPU	Universal Postal Union.
WHO	World Health Organisation.
WMO	World Meteorological Organisation.

FOREWORD

Broadly speaking institutions are the organisations, the traditions and the basic rules of a particular society.

International institutions are therefore the institutions of international society.

It is first necessary to clarify what international society is. The Introduction to this book will attempt to define the elements of international society in terms of the accepted principles of group psychology. It should then be possible to assess the continuity and the variety of international societies as they have existed in recent history and exist in the world today. Part One will deal with the *Origin and foundations of present-day international institutions*. A historical section will be followed by an analysis of the subject from both the legal and the political points of view. Part Two will deal with *States*, their day to day relations and their structural interaction. Part Three is concerned with *International Organisations*.

Modern sociology uses the term 'institutions' in a broad sense, and it is in this sense that the phrase will be used in this book. Institutions are 'the ideas, beliefs, symbols, customs and common usage as well as the political, legal and religious institutions' (A. Cuvillier, *Manuel de Sociologie*, p. 216). The definition of an institution is consequently arbitrary up to a certain point. To be regarded as an institution, a tradition, a rule or an organisation, must be a fundamental characteristic of any given society.

The study of institutions is a matter of sociology, history and politics; but it is also a study of a legal system, and unlike international relations with its concentration on geo-politics, anthropology and the other social sciences, the study of international institutions is firmly based on a foundation of law.

CONTENTS

INTRODUCTION

The Nature and Characteristics of International Relations

The purpose of this Introduction is to define the social relations characteristic of an international society and to describe some of them. International relations today are primarily relations between States. Most of this book deals with the contemporary society of States. But there are other international societies, and there have been other societies of States.

Some degree of abstraction is necessary in the first instance in order to distinguish common features independent of particular historical circumstances; only then will the historical account in the next section be seen in its proper perspective.

To do so, however, three fundamental sociological ideas must be discussed: the notion of social relations, society, and the group; they overlap each other.

Social relations is a term used to describe the basic element of all social life; it involves contact between two people (or two groups) and can take different forms: trade, conflict, influence. Even competition and conflict are social relations: 'every conflict is a form of imitation' (Dupréel, *op. cit.*, p. 151).

A *society* is made up of a collection of individuals (or groups) bound together by continual relations so important as to give rise to common interests whose satisfaction involves a mutual adjustment of behaviour.

A *group* is an organised society in which the furtherance of common interests is ensured by a differentiation of functions and powers to the benefit of certain members of the group.

An explorer of the eighteenth century trading glass beads with savages had trade relations; the families of part of the English or French bourgeoisies of the nineteenth century constituted a society—'good society'—with its customs and habits, although it remained unorganised. A clan, a tribe, a sports club, are groups;

17

a differentiation of function can be perceived within which office-holders have power.

The most familiar and important aspects of social life occur inside the group and in the interaction between groups. The development of international life is most easily understood using the group as the point of departure. But to do so a further distinction is necessary, the distinction between primary and secondary groups.

Groups can be distinguished from each other by their purpose (family, professional, religious groups), and by the nature of the powers possessed by those in authority.

Primary groups are groups with the following characteristics: (1) a duty to defend the totality of the interests of all the members; (2) the right to resort to force. A general purpose and the use of physical force when necessary are the essential features of primary groups. Secondary groups are groups with limited objectives which are not entitled to use physical force with regard to their members unless so authorised and under the close control of the primary group. Associations, commercial companies, families, municipalities are in this category.

Primitive peoples are usually regarded as constituting primary groups encompassing political, family, economic and religious relations; secondary groups have not yet emerged, indeed they are a characteristic of advanced societies. The terms 'primary' and 'secondary' in no way imply moral judgments or scales of values.

This book will be mainly concerned with primary groups, in particular the modern State. But both primary groups and secondary groups have common features, more marked perhaps in the first case than in the second. Section I will deal with group characteristics; section II with the social order; a conclusion with the special features of an international society.

Section I

FUNDAMENTAL CHARACTERISTICS
OF THE GROUP

A distinction must be made between in-group relations determining the internal organisation and life of a group, and out-group relations affecting relations with other groups including the questions of continuity and exclusivity.

§ 1 THE ORGANISATION OF THE GROUP

(A) *General*

By definition a group differs from a society by a differentiation of function conferring authority on certain of its members: these members exercise powers in order to defend the common interests of the group; they constitute the organs of the group.

Furthermore, social relations within a group are determined by rules. Certain rules are juridical and must be distinguished from moral laws or customs.

Juridical rules are essentially rules which create an obligation, breach of which is punishable by the group.

What is the basis of a juridical rule? A distinction is drawn between formal and material sources of law. The formal sources of law are the instruments whereby juridical rules are formulated and made manifest: a law, a treaty or a custom are different formal sources of law. Material sources of law are the principles or facts which explain the fundamental origin of juridical rules: morality (natural law)—social solidarity—sense of justice. Material sources of law depend on a philosophical view of human nature, but they do not necessarily change from group to group; formal sources of law however show great differences between groups and between different periods of history.

Juridical laws can easily be distinguished from scientific laws: they create an obligation, but they are not deterministic. Even if law is accepted as stemming from social necessity, obedience is still voluntary and not mechanical. A juridical rule can be broken a certain number of times, but it cannot be constantly and consistently disobeyed without eventually losing its juridical character. Law therefore corresponds to the desires of a social group, it constitutes a guarantee and a final point.

It is therefore simple to distinguish between law, morality and custom. An ethical code has its own obligations but they can only be defined in psychological terms and are often impossible for an outsider to investigate; unlike the law it is not punishable by and in the name of the group. Customs are rules concerning social life but breach of them only entails the sanction of individual reactions and not sanctions imposed by the group.

(B) *Primary and secondary groups*

Both primary and secondary groups have their own organisations and laws, but there are numerous differences between them.

With primitive peoples, where secondary groups are few or non-existent, religion, morals and law are so confused together that it is almost impossible to distinguish between them.

On the other hand, a secondary group does have its own system of law and its own rules and sanctions. Compared to a primary group its system of law is of a lesser order and subject to control. If the law of the French State (a primary group) is compared with the law of the Catholic Church (secondary group), only the first possesses the ultimate right to have recourse to physical force; of course the law of the Church may impose severe penalties for its believers (in particular excommunication) but it does not possess the right to use force. The law of a secondary group has certain characteristics of its own: it is easier to include considerations of morality. On the other hand within broad limits a primary group (see Section II) supervises the life of all the secondary groups in it, including the formulation and execution of their laws. In primary groups the organs possessing a monopoly of force try to monopolise the formulation of law; they tend to manipulate the formal sources of law to their own advantage. To contribute to the formulation of law is a privilege of power.

Another important consequence of a monopoly of physical force is that all primary groups must have a fixed *territory*. A monopoly of physical force presupposes a fixed area within which no other authority may exercise force. In its modern form a territory includes many other factors such as demography and economics, and is affected by the change from pastoral to settled ways of existence. But a territory is rightly regarded as the basic element which States use to justify their more extreme pretensions. Max Huber has very reasonably remarked that in its purest form the concept of territorial sovereignty reflects the absolutism of the modern State.

§ 2 PROGRESS, EXCLUSIVENESS AND EXTERNAL RELATIONS

(A) *The struggle for existence*

Groups are frequently studied as if they were living creatures. Clearly this can go too far, but nevertheless from many points of view groups do appear to have a life of their own: they are born, they grow, they decline, they die. Like living creatures they have to adapt themselves to their environment. Stagnation is always a danger sign normally marking the beginning of a decline. In short, in order to survive groups are forced continually to progress. Progress is shown by the number of members, the internal solidarity, the power of invention and creativity, and the differentiation of functions within the group.

To safeguard its own future a group has frequently to meet the challenge of competing groups. *This struggle may take many forms but is chiefly evident in a tendency to exclusiveness.* The keener the competition between groups, the more marked this tendency becomes; for instance in relations between rival churches or religious orders, or between political parties. Every group is prepared to enlarge its functions, the more embracing its purpose the more a group will tend to become exclusive.

In many cases, of course, groups either cannot or do not wish to prevent relations between their members and outsiders; in certain cases such relations are useful and necessary; but they nearly always entail some risks, and are therefore subject to various kinds of rules and prohibitions.

(B) *External relations*

A group's relations with the outside world may be of two kinds:

—either a member of the group enters into contact with an outsider: these are called *direct* relations;
—or contact between the groups is entirely a matter of contact between the office-holders of the groups, and not between individual members of the groups; these are called *indirect* relations.

The tendency to protect the group from outside influence often leads to a preference for allowing only indirect relations, even up to a point of prohibiting all forms of direct relations. *Closed society*

The individual member of a group finds external relations a test and sometimes an adventure. The group supports as well as forbids; it not only limits its members' activities, it also helps them, enriches their personal lives, accustoms them to ways of thought and expression which become an integral part of their lives. All external relations present dangers and difficulties; the members of a group which accept responsibility for them are in a real sense serving the group. The members of a group capable of assuming the burden of external relations are the élite; it is therefore perfectly natural for the leaders to accept the responsibility on behalf of the rest.

The leaders' monopoly of external relations is not only a matter of necessity or a gratuitous service rendered, it is also an expression of a political consciousness to protect the group from dissolution and to safeguard its exclusiveness.

Primary groups are particularly sensitive to the effects of external relations. The group is the expression of a society which has attained a high degree of social life; its members have certain characteristics which mark them off from 'the foreigner'. External contacts, especially direct contacts, threaten the cohesion of the group and the monopoly of physical force possessed by the leaders. There is a continual conflict between satisfying essential needs through outside contacts, and defending the group. The group is menaced not only by war which is one of the commonest forms of external contacts, but also by all the indirect forms of conquest, domination, influence and penetration which exist in all forms of social relations.

There is no difficulty in citing examples of the way leaders of primary groups obtain control of external relations.

When a primary group is united by ties of blood, as in primitive families, the marriage of children is an act of major importance. The family allows exogamous marriages with a 'foreigner', but the marriage is arranged and concluded by the heads of the families, often without the consent of the children concerned. The woman then generally becomes part of the other family.

The States are the primary groups of the world, and without exception their external contacts are indirect relations conducted by specialised official machinery; they take the form of diplomatic relations, treaties and participation in international organisations. States do not necessarily tolerate direct contacts; not all of them allow exogamous marriages, and most of them restrict and control their members' attempts freely to build up contacts abroad for purposes of trade, education or relaxation. Yet of all international relations direct contacts are the richest, most stimulating, and progressive; if they are suppressed the relations between States are nothing more than frontier disputes, planned economic exchanges and alliances for war and peace. Direct relations prevent States building up closed societies, and are a vital factor in the development of all international relations.

Section II

THE QUESTION OF A SOCIAL ORDER

Common interests grow as social relations multiply; a society is born from the general realisation of these common interests. A society tends to become a group as it develops and becomes aware of its unity. This process inevitably involves an intricate pattern of relations, societies and groups. Some order may be imposed on this pattern if it is analysed from three points of view: the control of all social life by primary groups, the social order when uncontrolled by the group, and the hierarchies of domination into which the groups fall.

§1 CONTROL BY PRIMARY GROUPS

In primitive societies secondary groups are few or non-existent; they develop as people advance, although not always without opposition from 'the government'. Apart from outright prohibition which is normally restricted to particular fields, supervision of the formation and operations of secondary groups exists even under the most favourable circumstances. The public authorities exercise particular control over the steps taken by secondary groups to regulate, execute or judge their own affairs. The primary group possesses the ultimate sanctions, and it is therefore called upon to approve or annul these measures. The primary group's supervision and control rarely reach a point where the autonomy of secondary groups completely disappears.

But control over the different aspects of social life becomes stricter whenever they affect external relations. These relations also give rise to matters of great legal complexity. For instance, if a member of primary group A buys a commodity from a member of primary group B, whose legal system shall be used to settle disputes?

Each group will attempt to arrogate this power to itself: in the eyes of group A it is for group A to decide whether or not its laws should be applied to the dispute, or if it wishes as a concession on its part to allow the laws of group B to apply. Group B will argue in precisely the same way. The type of problem which arises when the legal systems of two groups come into conflict is called in the modern world a *conflict of jurisdiction* or a *conflict of laws*. *Private international law* is the body of rules which determines how such conflicts between States under these circumstances should be solved. The majority of these rules are determined by the national authorities of each individual State, and this has caused legal chaos.

This shows that the control of all social life uniquely exercised by primary groups is incapable of properly resolving questions posed by social relations extending beyond the group's limits.

How can a problem as simple as that mentioned above be reasonably solved? There are alternative methods: (i) The two groups A and B could conclude an agreement to remove the worst obstacles. They could, for instance, agree to accept the same legal rules, and thus avoid all possible conflict of laws. They could also accept common rules to determine which judges should be competent in particular cases. This method introduces the notion of an agreement between groups. It raises a more general problem: which system of law is to be used for interpreting the agreement itself. This will be discussed below in § 2.

(ii) There is another solution. If both groups A and B allow their merchants some liberty of action, merchants of the two groups will enter into direct contact. In the first instance relations between the two merchants will be full of suspicion, and they will draft in writing detailed prescriptions to govern the conditions of sale. Other merchants will follow, contacts multiply; the habit grows up of using conventional clauses, phrases and formulae. The merchants become aware of their common interests, and buyer and seller accept certain conventions. Does this give birth to a society of merchants with its own body of legal rules which supplant the rules and courts of both groups A and B? This question is different from the question above, but it has this in common that it concerns relations and societies which, by definition, transcend the jurisdiction of individual primary groups.

§ 2 SOCIAL ORDER UNCONTROLLED BY THE GROUP

So far social life has been analysed in terms of the group. But external relations concentrate attention on those forms of social life which cannot be regulated by the authority of a single group. In this way social relations and societies emerge which have to discover rules by other means.

This question will best be dealt with by first looking more closely at the terms 'social relations' and 'society', and then examining the moral to be drawn from this.

(A) *General*

'Social relations' and 'society' are briefly defined above. A preliminary comment: *there is a transition usually by imperceptible stages from the multiplication of social relations to the constitution of a genuine society.*

It is perfectly possible to imagine two distinct social groups coming into contact for the very first time: for instance the Spaniards meeting the natives of the New World at the end of the fifteenth century. Theoretically it is possible to examine these contacts in isolation. But men, irrespective of all other factors, usually recognise other men as being similar to themselves, and apply to each other the intellectual constructions, the experiences and the rules which they consider valid for all mankind. There is at least one basic lesson to be drawn from this: besides relations of violence and constraint, *there is room for freely negotiated relations.* From the first moment of peaceful relations a fundamental rule of behaviour emerges: relations can be based on agreements freely concluded. Neither words nor symbols would have any more sense if this were not true. The more alien people consider other peoples to be the more necessary is it to define agreements between them as strictly and minutely as possible. Max Huber rightly suggested that law was probably first used amongst primitive peoples for inter-tribal relations rather than for internal affairs.

It would therefore be reasonable to say that the law applicable to these first isolated relations is treaty law, generally written down, whose exact terms are regarded as the only binding obligation.

When social relations increase treaty relations also develop; the reasons for respecting treaties become more obvious, the conditions which justify a breach of a treaty begin to emerge, and the rules for interpreting them become clearer. Thus, *the basis for the observation of treaties is external to the treaties themselves.* Furthermore, a series of identical treaties fosters the view that certain rules are self-evident and *implicit.* In this way a new body of rules grows up from the practice of social relations: they are not written down but are *customary rules.* They come from continually repeated situations, and in their turn they create new rules. They are an expression of common attitudes.

Frequent social relations lead to common patterns of behaviour expressed in terms of culture and civilisation, and are the basis of *common interests.* They are dealt with by treaty as much as by custom, and often more so. Certain rules presuppose technical definitions which can only safely be written down.

A society of this kind remains *unorganised*. Much of the legal system involved is entirely based on the *voluntary* consent of the members of the society; if they refuse the rules are never created. They may refuse to accept arbitration when involved in litigation with another member, they cannot be forced to accept. When the rules are broken each member makes his own justice. Progress is already considerable when the members of a society agree to limit their recourse to force to cases where the law has been broken; but even in this case which is typical of advanced societies, each member remains his own judge and policeman.

A society of this kind can have many years of peaceful relations, but it will experience difficult moments. Every society is challenged by the contradiction between the static nature of the legal rules and the dynamism of social life. But societies which are also groups can reduce this tension more easily; legislation is simpler and more authoritative. A law can be imposed by force on a recalcitrant minority, and new laws can be speedily passed to accommodate changed circumstances. The process does not of course always work and then there is a revolution. But a society which does not form a group is perpetually liable to overthrow; its only guarantee for eliminating tensions peacefully is the good faith of its members.

(B) *Societies of primary groups*

At different periods of history societies of this kind have had as members families, clans, tribes, principalities, and States.

Each primary group attempts to monopolise the whole range of human affairs of its members in the last resort by the use of force. Each group will passionately insist that no authority is higher than its own: and this is *the original and profound meaning of sovereignty*.

A society whose members are primary groups has two social characteristics: the limited number of its members and the extent of collective interests each member represents. The fewer members in a society the more rigid its structure: unanimity or virtual unanimity can sometimes be obtained but disagreements between the members will be bitter. Each member of the society is the centre of a whole network of collective interests. A group's attitude is not therefore comparable to the egoism of an individual person, but is an attempt to safeguard collective interests in the face of other collective interests. Primary groups differ markedly from each other in size, population and power. Consequently all the reactions of a society composed of primary groups are swayed by the balance of power, and this balance of power is often cynically adjusted for temporary ends. Hegemonies and coalitions determine the future of such a society.

In fact the use of armed force is part of the normal course of events; war is no longer incidental but can be studied in itself and for itself (see Annex).

(C) *Societies external to primary groups*

Social relations also link people together in certain well-defined fields which transcend the limits of primary groups; for instance, in religion, trade and culture. The primary groups may not attempt to control them either because they cannot or because they are not interested in them.

Societies linking merchants, scholars, clerics, philanthropists, can be found cutting across the primary groups. These societies group together numerous individuals and secondary groups (business houses, communities, associations) with comparable interests. Conflicts and penalties have nothing like the same brutality as they have in primary groups. There can be no concept of sovereignty comparable to that claimed by primary groups. The relations within such a society are concerned with strictly limited objectives and they are always menaced by the threat of interference, prohibition or supervision by the primary group. The ambition of these societies is to live freely, and if possible unnoticed by the governments, rather than claim any illusory independence which would soon be wiped out.

The laws of such societies develop along the lines indicated above and their members willingly accept arbitration. Nevertheless, particularly when economic affairs are involved, the laws of these societies touch on the laws of the primary groups: the latter accept them and have them applied by their own courts. Maritime law is full of examples. At all times in any given area merchants have built up their own body of customary laws. The governments of the primary groups (cities, principalities, States) have absorbed them into their own law; sometimes they have codified them, in which case they cease to be independent sources of law.

In fact these societies are perpetually threatened by absorption into the stronger system of the primary group. *Their instability compels them either eventually to disappear, or transform themselves into groups in their turn*, that is, provide themselves with their own autonomous powers and organs.

Primary groups organise themselves slowly and with difficulty;

unlike them these societies quickly accept—at least for a time—
organised institutions to govern them. Unions of merchants, of
churches, etc., are formed to accept responsibilty for the direct
external relations of the society. Their relations with primary groups
are difficult to arrange and not infrequently their continued existence
depends on the possession of real power, or secrecy.

The best example of the first group is the Catholic Church which
remains powerful in different parts of the world because of its hold
over people's souls. It is a 'Power' and not a primary group, and
modern States treat the Church as an equal (c.f. p. 189).

The best example of the second group are the various economic
cartels, particularly in the early part of this century. Modern States
allowed some freedom for international trade; in the first instance
they allowed producers and traders freedom to manipulate international markets, particularly by means of international companies
and agreements. In their most advanced form these groups came to
have their own legislation, arbitration procedures and penalties. But
such organisations nowadays have a precarious existence, because
their interests conflict with those of the States; the hostility of the
States has been such that since 1945 some of these groups can only
exist in secrecy.

§ 3 THE HIERARCHY OF GROUPS

(A) General characteristics

The domination of secondary groups by primary groups has been
mentioned several times; it is a result of a difference of kind between
the two. *The permanent relations between groups of the same kind*
must now be briefly dealt with.

The process is similar to that described previously; various groups
keep up relations with each other, and these relations give birth to a
society. After some time this society comes to form a group, and this
unites together other groups. The question is now to fix the relations
of this new group with the founder members.

Social life shows that this can be done in various ways. In some cases
the new group absorbs all the member groups; in principle a solution
along these lines leaves no trace of its predecessors. It can come about
either by the strongest group absorbing weaker groups, or by several
groups joining together to found a new organisation which subsequently absorbs them. A more interesting case is when the original
groups continue to exist, as in the case for example of sporting

associations or federations of trade unions. Even though the original groups exist their *structures* are altered because of the *permanent* nature of the new relations. Structural relations is now a term which may be used; there has been a new division of functions between the groups, and a change in the jurisdiction of their organs. Structural relations are sometimes on a basis of *equality*, sometimes on a basis of *inequality*, most frequently a mixture of the two. The original member groups may retain their equality with each other and in addition the new group which they form together may be on the same footing as they are. A *federal* structure is one in which equality of the members is a dominant characteristic.

When one of the groups dominates the others and usurps their functions a basis of inequality has been created; *colonial* structures are of this kind. It is also possible for the new group to be superior or inferior to the original member groups; from this point of view political systems offer a wide range of examples. In the majority of cases a society is formed of primary groups in an attempt to remedy the dangers which arise when no organisation exists; the situation studied above. A rudimentary organisation is set up which gradually grows in strength, unity and universality although the original groups remain the dominant elements. If this process continues a moment comes when an attempt to strike a balance is made, after which the local groups decline and eventually have no more than a secondary and subordinate role to play. This has become a unitary structure with some degree of decentralisation. The opposite process has occurred, in which a single group has split up into several independent groups.

(B) *Technical means*

The technical means whereby these processes of hierarchisation and domination take place cannot reasonably be studied divorced from historial examples. Some of the means used are legal, some purely empirical; some examples follow.

The most important juridical procedure is the *division of powers*, which consists of dividing powers of government between the central authority and the local authorities (in federal systems), or between the dominant power and local institutions (in colonial protectorates). Another method consists of associating the local groups with the formation of the organs of the central group. The organs of one group may also act on behalf of another group; this *substitution* is normal in protectorates; it can work the other way round in the case of federations where, in order to avoid needless administrative profusion, local officials perform certain acts as agents of the central authority.

Equality and inequality may also be questions of fact and not of law. Thus if certain individuals are the organs of different groups they may unify in their person distinct political bodies (personal unions), or commercial companies may set up parent and subsidiary firms. Sometimes these methods are distinguished from legal relations by the fact that they are subject only to internal control whereas legal relations depend on objective controls. Disguised methods of control are nowadays mainly to be found where inequality exists. Thus new forms of colonisation have made their appearance, noticeable in the relations of commercial undertakings, of rival trade unions, and of States (control by a single party, by military bases, by economic and financial ties). The use of symbols and psychological factors is common in attempts to dominate other groups.

CONCLUSION

Is it now possible to say anything about 'international' situations?

In terms of strict logic these situations always appear to be definable in negative terms. To do so emphasis can be put on two slightly different features:

(1) Every situation in an unorganised society is subject to juridical rules of a special kind. They can consequently be regarded as international, whether groups or individual persons are involved. Thus, *international relations are based on the co-ordination of independent entities not subject to a common authority; an international society is the result of these relations.*

This definition is based on the criteria of legal systems which function outside the authority of a group.

(2) The primary social factor is the primary group, and it is therefore possible to consider all situations external to the affairs of the group as constituting international situations. In this view the Catholic Church is considered to be an international group, and its law, canon law, as a variety of international law. In the same way, an international union of railway networks and the regulations it lays down for its members.

This definition is based on sociology rather than on law; it ends by denying international situations any specific characteristics; they are merely a function of a particular historical situation, the primary groups.

Bearing in mind these two points of view, the social factors relevant to a study of international life are, broadly speaking:

(1) *Relations between primary groups.* Both isolated and in society they are the central element of international life;

(2) *The hierarchy and ascendancy of groups.* From a dynamic point of view they profoundly modify social structures, destroy the primary character of groups, and consequently the international side of their activity. If the whole world were a federation there would be from the jurist's point of view no international relations in the proper sense of the word;

(3) *All external relations which are outside the jurisdiction of the primary groups.* It is these which contribute to the development of international life and are at the root of international social forces.

ANNEX

The Sociology of Conflicts

Part Two, Chapter II (p. 160) contains a summary account in purely legal terms of non-pacific relations between States. But a sociology of conflicts could usefully throw light on the extent of international relations. Conflicts and tensions are a vital part of social life, and viewed abstractly contribute to the development of international society. Sociologists have already made general studies in the classification of antagonisms and the logic of conflicts (see Dupréel, *op. cit.*, pp. 134 and 140), but a general study of conflicts and tensions in international relations remains to be done.

Objective research and studies have so far been concentrated on war, which is certainly the most characteristic form of international conflict; in its modern forms it requires a more broadly based study properly to be understood. The legalism which affects so many writers when dealing with war has been rightly called 'juridical illusionism' (Bouthol, *Les Guerres, éléments de polémologie*, Payot, 1951). Nevertheless, jurists have written excellent books on the subject; the basic book is Quincy Wright (*A study of war*, 2 vols., University of Chicago Press, 1944). It contains a classic analysis of the subject and interesting statistics.

The contemporary evolution of war shows (G. Schwarzenberger, *Jus pacis et belli: prolegomena to a sociology of international law*, AJ 1943, p. 460) that the underlying conceptions of certain international actions are inaccurate. It is unfortunately inaccurate to say that peace is the normal state of affairs and war has specifically defined legal functions, or to say that war and peace are separate conditions and alternatives to each other (F. Grob, *The Relativity of War and Peace*, Yale University Press, 1949). Problems appear and re-appear. Wars are started with the object of completely wiping out a race or a people, and this has given rise to the question of war crimes and crimes against humanity (genocide). In addition there are the problems raised by weapons of mass destruction (chemical and atomic weapons). War takes on new forms: civil wars merge into international wars; behind the massive façade erected by the modern State ideological groups spring up proclaiming their unity with similar groups in other countries; war becomes a conflict between individuals as much as between political systems. The breaking down of international wars into civil wars witnesses to the development of international solidarity. The inherent logic of conflicts tends to make them universal (see Dupréel, *op. cit.*, p. 140 seq.). There are also undeclared wars, local wars, and wars with several belligerents not necessarily grouped into two blocs.

PART ONE

ORIGIN AND FOUNDATION OF PRESENT-DAY INTERNATIONAL INSTITUTIONS

CHAPTER ONE

The Historical Evolution of International Relations and International Institutions up to the Second World War

Section I

UP TO THE AGE OF DISCOVERY

In the most primitive societies the relations between tribes or villages have many of the features of international relations. Unfortunately they have never been studied systematically, which is a pity.

§ 1 ANCIENT CIVILISATIONS

Similarly there was a system of international law in ancient civilisations and also within the great exotic civilisations of America and Asia. In some cases international relations were limited to indirect contact; but in others foreign peoples were able to enter into direct relationships with each other. Primitive and even old-established cities have generally been hostile to foreigners, but in all ages traders have been treated favourably for the sake of trade which neither the seas nor deserts prevented. Cities belonging to the same civilisation have been faced at an early stage with the problems of federalism, for example ancient Greece. It is impossible to generalise about these forms of international relations; despite the undoubted interest they have for modern research in international law we shall confine ourselves to a few brief remarks.

In the first place they developed within a restricted geographical framework. This is not only true of primitive peoples. The area of the Greek, Roman, Hindu or Chinese civilisations is obviously greater, but even there we are far removed from universal relations; their international relations were limited by the boundaries of a single relatively closed civilisation. There were a few exceptions. Alexander's conquests gave rise to interesting contacts between India and the Mediterranean basin. The relations between the Roman Empire and the Asiatic or African kingdoms were based on a near-modern conception of protectorates. Similarly the manner in which the Roman Empire dealt with the question of nationality and citizenship has often been regarded as a model. Despite this it is difficult to draw conclusions from these institutions relevant to the present day.

It would seem that Rome was originally formed by the federation of hitherto isolated villages (pagi). It has been suggested that the identity of the Latin roots *pagi*, *pax* (peace), *pacifisci* (to conclude agreements), is a record in the Latin language of the earliest international relations and the benefits arising from them. Authors who have studied the process of the formation of cities in undeveloped civilisations have arrived at identical linguistic conclusions: in arabic, for instance, E. Masqueray (*Formation des cités chez les populations sédentaires de l'Algérie*, Leroux, 1886, Paris). If these conclusions are proved correct they are interesting; but we cannot conclude from them that it is possible to bring about a universal federation nowadays between political groups as important as national States.

Since the intensity of international relations is a result of material needs, relations between groups belonging to non-technological civilisations had relatively limited objects. The use of force in international relations and preparation for war through alliances constituted the greater part. Moreover, the use of force gave rise to political structures based on hegemony rather than federation. Trade also led to very intense relations; but contacts between traders were reduced to the minimum: they did not become members of the city.

The dominant ideas and the internal situation of the social groups generally made them distrustful of foreigners. Philosophy and ethics were often primitive, the foreigner was a 'barbarian', the concept of justice and the dignity of the human person had not yet made themselves felt.

Political structures were often monarchical and tyrannical; relations with the outside world tended to be mixed up with palace intrigues; they were therefore closely guarded and restricted. This was not entirely true for India and China.

§ 2 MEDIAEVAL CHRISTIANITY

The Middle Ages were much closer to the world of today. It is difficult to propound general statements for a period covering five centuries, but the following observations are generally speaking valid.

(1) Although the countries of Christendom formed a homogeneous whole clearly distinguished from non-Christian countries, contact between the two groups of countries was sustained during the prosperous period of the Middle Ages. The Islamic world and the Christian world did not cease fighting each other but neither did they cease concluding agreements, exchanging goods and knowledge. Spain was the point of contact where these two forces met. The crusades also had enormous consequences in the development of international relations. Until its fall at the end of the Middle Ages, Byzantium was an intermediary between the western countries, the Middle East (and by caravans the Far East) and the Slav countries: the Italian trading republics kept posts on the shores of the Black Sea during practically the whole of this period. While relations with the Slav countries were intermittent, they were close enough to lead to dynastic marriages.

(2) Relations between the Christian countries themselves were dominated during most of the Middle Ages by feudalism. In modern terms feudalism may be defined as the dispersal of state functions; they were distributed between territorial areas sometimes with ill-defined frontiers. The overlords of these areas, dukes, marquises, counts, and seigneurs of various kinds, were linked together by a bond of personal allegiance to make up a society in the form of a pyramid with at the apex the Emperor, heir to the title of Charlemagne. Some kingdoms, however, did not recognise this supreme allegiance. In modern terms we can say that in mediaeval society there were primary groups everywhere as a result of the dispersal of the functions of the State, and yet no such group possessed all such functions; we therefore tend to see international relations where there are none.

We can keep the term international relations for relations between *de facto* independent political groups. Thus Ganshof distinguishes what he calls 'States' from mere 'principalities' (*Histoire des relations internationales*, t. I, p. 119).

But even if its political relationships were confused and the dividing line between private law and public law seemed lost, feudal society was fluid and rich in original social, human and juridical relationships. The premises of modern international law were there and the modern State with its monopoly of power had not yet developed to the point where it was strong enough to oppose the creation of an international order as it is today.

(3) In the Middle Ages the problems and institutions of modern international law were recognised : the notion of a frontier, the theory of reprisals, arbitration, truce and armistice, territorial waters (Ganshof, *op. cit.*, especially pp. 60, 142, 287, 289, 294). Even the position of neutrality was perfectly familiar, if not its juridical theory. At the end of the Middle Ages, too, came the first permanent embassies from the Italian republics. The problems of federalism were already discussed in the working of the German Holy Roman Empire or in the leagues like the Hanseatic League.

It has sometimes been maintained that the revival of Roman law studies contributed nothing to international law. This view is clearly exaggerated. Bartole contributed to the transformation which has taken thinkers from the framework of the Holy Roman Empire to that of an international community, and G. Schwarzenberger quite rightly places Bartole and Balde as well as Succaria among the first internationalists. (*A Manual of International Law*, p. 6. For an example of a matter where Roman law can play a part in the development of international law cf. Winiarski, *Les principes généraux du droit fluvial international*, RCADI 1933, pp. 45, 79.)

(4) Never, particularly between Christian countries, have international contacts between individuals been so close as during the Middle Ages. The legal status of foreigners did not seriously handicap them although the *droit d'aubaine* did not allow them to dispose of their property in the event of death. There were many foreigners in Byzantium (especially from the Italian republics) and they lived in special districts, under a system which the Muslims were later to apply to Christians.

But the Church and certain professional groups were the principal source of international contacts.

The existence of Papal States and the participation of Church dignitaries in the feudal system could be used to put the Church on the same plane as other political authorities. But it united members of many countries, had continuous international relations, and made a solid counterweight—perhaps the only one that has ever existed—to the ambitions of the primary groups. It was through the Church that mediaeval society developed intense international relations. Connected with the Church were the universities and scientific progress. Through the great pilgrimages (St. John of Compostella, Rome) the poor, too, made international contacts.

Trade guilds were powerfully organised at this time, and some of them, particularly traders and bankers, played an active part in international exchanges. The big international fairs were well attended, bankers were internationally organised and their friendship sought by princes. For commercial reasons these groups drew up a system of international commercial law, the *jus mercatorum*, the *jus nundinarum*; it was not until the first quarter of the twentieth century that commercial law, broken up by the sovereignty of the modern States, was partially unified again by treaty agreements. Finally, the Middle Ages gives an example, not only of republics organised for commerce like the Italian trading republics, but of international political organisations whose sole justification was trade; for example, the leagues of trading cities of which the Hanseatic League is the most famous example.

(5) With Christianity the Middle Ages introduced into western society a number of very important moral values: respect for the human person, equality of human persons in the eyes of God, charity which knows 'not Jew, nor Greek, nor Barbarian,' etc. The brutality of mediaeval society continued; for example, slavery or the legitimacy of executing prisoners of war; the conversion of some non-Latin countries to Christianity was slow; Spain did not return to Christian control until after the end of the Middle Ages; the Normans let loose a tide of paganism on some European countries, etc. But Christianity was one of the elements of the western conscience, and this fact did not fail to influence international relations and the development of international law as such. International law was influenced by ethical ideals and by certain ways of thinking. Since Christianity was based on sacred books and a spiritual revelation, it could go on living and developing for some time without being systematically set down or the object of intellectual speculation. But the need to combat heresies, and the influence of Greek philosophy (rediscovered through Islam) led to the creation of great organised constructions of thought devoted to theology and philosophy. And so with the conservation of acquired wealth there developed a taste for synthesis, for universality, which has been a mark of western civilisation. There is a simple transition from theorizing about morals to practical morality and thence to international law. It was not achieved during the Middle Ages, but we shall see that it was understood by thinkers who bore the mark of Christian thinking and practice.

Thus, while the Middle Ages ended with the fall of Byzantium, the journeys of Marco Polo heralded a new age.

Section II

FROM THE AGE OF DISCOVERY TO THE TREATIES OF WESTPHALIA (1648)

This period contains two factors of major importance for the development of international relations: the great maritime discoveries and the emergence of the modern State; a remarkable achievement in the realm of thought also gave shape to international law.

§ 1 THE AGE OF DISCOVERY

The discovery of America by Christopher Columbus in 1492 heralded the era of universal international relations; international problems appeared on a world-wide scale. These discoveries left Africa untouched and Asia was only partially and temporarily affected; but the New World was the field of European expansion which transformed it, and out of it came the map of civilisations and linguistic areas as it is today. The Western European nations, Spain, Portugal, the Netherlands, England, France, began the movement which placed Europe at the centre of world history.

The sea was at the heart of the development of international relations. International law and also colonisation were greatly stimulated. Colonisation, with its abuses and defects, created problems of conscience which, although not new, assumed unexpected proportions: slavery and the slave trade, racial conflicts, all the after-effects of human inequality which were to summon up a counter-movement based on what was later known as the rights of man. By offering shelter to those who were persecuted (puritans, *Mayflower* pilgrims, French protestants, etc.) the new lands came to be the place where ideas fermented prior to rebounding back on Europe. In the economic field immense new forces were released, and at the same time there appeared a new type of international trade (colonial pact, then various forms of liberalism and protectionism). As the problems arose they were solved in legal terms fairly quickly: occupation and conquest of free lands, rights of navigation in times of peace and war, etc.

Colonisation contributed to the development of capitalism. The latter came into being with the mobilisation of wealth and the creation of symbols, particularly monetary ones, which facilitated saving and credit. All machinery which promoted the spreading of risks and the constitution of large-scale enterprise worked in its favour; its origins go very far back, certainly further back than the great discoveries. But the navigation system and the development of the new lands greatly stimulated it.

The Church's prohibition on lending money at interest was circumvented very early by various methods; it ceased to apply to loans involving risk (maritime loans); navigation was to gain from this. Since risk-sharing in a business demanded considerable capital this was to lead to the setting up of joint stock companies; these first appeared in international trade. (Introduction in sixteenth century of Merchant Adventurers for trade between England and the Russian market.)

Later on colonisation was directly undertaken by large companies. They were in the form of a modern limited company, but were subject to state control; the State (or at least the princes) often held part of the capital: they were similar to present day mixed economic enterprises. These companies acted in the name of the State, its political functions were delegated to them, and they possessed military force. In modern terms we should say that they were public utility companies. They introduced a new form of international relations: legally they treated with foreign political groups in the name of the State, but in fact they represented private interests. As soon as there was a breach between the political ends of the State and their economic interests, they were to disappear.

Even the legal status of Christopher Columbus setting out to discover new lands was that of a *concessionaire de droits régaliens.*
In connection with maritime colonial discoveries it must not be forgotten that it was in the sixteenth century that Russia started on the progressive conquest of Asian lands which, a hundred years later, put her in touch with China, and by assimilation ensured her an immense territory all in one block, from the Pacific to the Atlantic, both Asiatic and European; in the eighteenth century the Russians, coming down from Alaska, were to meet the Spaniards near San Francisco.

Finally, the greatness and splendour of a young State, the Netherlands, destined to play a big part in international law, were bound up with maritime trade and colonisation. The Netherlands always firmly supported developments in international law, partly because of their commercial interests, partly from the idealism they learnt in their struggles for liberation.

§ 2 THE BIRTH OF THE MODERN STATE

The birth of the modern State is traditionally put in the sixteenth century.

It was partly a matter of consolidation rather than innovation. In some countries like France, England, Spain and Portugal the royal power had begun to centralise the political functions previously undertaken by the nobles; this centralisation reunited lands split up by the feudal system. This policy was not pursued equally vigorously in all countries: Germany and Italy remained divided up into principalities and republics, of which the most important sought to assert their independence. The Holy Roman Empire lost all non-German lands at the end of the sixteenth century and at the same time its activities became increasingly symbolic. (G. Zeller, *La réunion de Metz à la France*, vol. I, p. 170.)

The State was strengthened by the decline of the international role of the Church and by the threat of anarchy which hung over Europe with the religious crisis of protestantism. The protestants appealed to the princes, the Catholic Church did the same. It was not only the religious schism which diminished the part played by the Church, but the fact that even in catholic countries the services rendered to the Church by the State made the former into an ally of the civil authorities. The Catholic Church did not theoretically abandon its oecumenical position, but its temporal influence diminished, although it still maintained some debatable political positions. The Papal Bull (1493) dividing up the New World, was the Church's only major contribution to international order. All the benefit went to the State; not only was it the only power capable of counterbalancing the decline of the princes, but the political group made sure of its dominance by identifying itself with a religious system, as in primitive societies. Anarchy was put down and people accepted the machinery of the absolute State.

This assertion of the dominant role of the State profoundly changed international relations. The sovereignty of the State was necessary to internal stability and it was premature to think of an international organisation. On the other hand States were in continuous contact with each other through permanent embassies. This practice started in Italy in the fifteenth century, and became widespread in the sixteenth century. Under Louis XIV France maintained twenty-five permanent embassies abroad. The principal purpose of these contacts was to keep an eye on the plans which the princes might be plotting against each other and to foil them. Commerce did not develop as much as might have been expected after the great discoveries: the colonial powers tried to make the home country and their colonies into a single closed economy. Relations between the Christian west and the Muslim countries settled down with the general application of a system borrowed from Byzantium: Christians in Muslim countries were confined to a strictly limited area and put under their own national consular authority (capitulations).

Direct contacts increased, but only in certain fields. The catholic missions built up long and fruitful contacts in the Far East between China and the West.

Every year in Europe rebellions and revolutions added to the number of emigrants who took refuge in neighbouring States: French, Italians, Germans, English, Dutch, came together through the accident of political rivalries between the princes of Europe, and recreated in exile an international *milieu*.

§ 3 THOUGHT AND INTERNATIONAL LAW

The widespread use of printing, the use of native tongues, the conflicts and rivalries of sets and clans, provoked an effusion of all kinds of works of political theory. Some of them dealt with international problems and others were completely devoted to them. Besides the works of Erasmus (1468–1536) and Thomas Moore (1477–1535) other writers outlined plans for an international organisation, for instance Emeric Cruce (1590–1648) with his *Nouveau Cynée* and Sully with his Great Plan of Henri IV. They were partly utopian visions and partly self-interested political schemes, with demands for economic freedom and the 'open door', particularly overseas.

International law made its appearance in the writings of some specialists, among whom two authors stand out, the Spanish Dominican Francisco de Vitoria (1480–1546) and the Dutch Hugo de Groot known as Grotius (1583–1646). They are very properly regarded as two of the founders of international law.

Colonies and the rights of shipping on the high seas were the major new problems demanding attention; the debate about just and unjust wars was revived as a result of the upheavals of this period.

These two authors were symbols of their time. One was catholic, the other protestant; both, deeply imbued with religious sentiment, showed great originality, de Vitoria heralding the renaissance of catholic thinking which was to come about two hundred years later:

the other, Grotius, despite abundant biblical quotations, seeking rational solutions which constitute a first definition of international law.

(A) *Francisco de Vitoria*

He might have remained all his life a respected and influential Dominican theologian, professor at Salamanca. He was tutor to Charles V. At that time the question of the Indies was highly controversial; slavery and the rights of the Indians had been the subject of polemics, some of them amongst theologians. The Spanish Government could not be expected to favour such public discussion. Everything concerning the Indies was regarded as a state secret and was kept under strict state control.

Vitoria devoted the main part of his work to the problems raised by the Indies; it was published under the title *Relectiones de Indis*. Although it was clearly preoccupied by religious considerations, this work contains, together with some obsolete theories, modern conceptions and arguments whose validity is independent of the Christian revelation. The author held that universal sociability was the fundamental principle of law. All men, by virtue of the *jus communicationis*, have the right to enter into relations with each other. The result is an international community based on the equality of men. This community is not organised but it recognises common interests; in the defence of these interests the princes are in duty bound to undertake just wars.

These are concepts which, despite their origin, remind us of the principles underlying the modern social sciences.

A general system of international relations emerges quite naturally from these principles, and the author elaborates from them a precise and vigorous theory of the duties of the colonisers. The Church preached them without success. Only in the present day have they found formal expression in the League of Nations and the United Nations.

Vitoria also expounded a theory of just and unjust wars. This part of his work was less original. For a long time Christian thought had dwelt on this question. His doctrine is formulated in ethical terms; it rests on distinctions which ultimately depend on moral judgements and are not very suitable for translating into legal formulas. It was passionately urged at a time when circumstances were against any practical solution: cavalry had been superseded by bands of mercenaries; the Church had disappeared as an international power and the States' sole concern was to maintain a political equilibrium.

The work of the Jesuit Suarez (1548–1617), especially his treatise *De Legibus ac Deo legislatore*, made a clearer distinction than Vitoria had between natural law, immutable and universal, and positive law, flexible and mainly based on custom.

Vitoria's influence was less than it is sometimes claimed to have been. He seems to have been half-forgotten until the beginning of the nineteenth century, when international law started to develop on modern lines.

(B) *Grotius*

A rich personality, poet, author of plays and epithalamia in latin, theologian, politician, diplomat, Grotius had an adventurous life which took him into Dutch dungeons and later to Paris to end his life as counsellor to the President of the Parliament of Paris, and as Swedish Minister to France.

His works were therefore not simply deductive from abstract principles, but were the considerations of man enriched by experience. Since he knew the perils of applying political principles, the numerous biblical references in his book were not always speculative but were sometimes used to disguise reflections on contemporary events.

It may be interesting to recall the origin of his major work. The ships of the Dutch East India Company had captured a Portuguese ship in Indonesian waters. The shareholders of the Company seem to have had qualms of conscience about the legitimacy of this action and asked Grotius for an opinion based on religious and ethical considerations. This opinion was not made public; one chapter was detached from the work and published later under the title *Mare Liberum* (1609) in quite a different context during the controversy between the Netherlands and England about the freedom of the open sea. Grotius' opinion in its complete form was not rediscovered and published until 1868 under the title *De jure Praedae*. Later Grotius wrote his major work, *De jure belli ac pacis* (1625), which may be considered a genuine treatise of international law.

For the first time we find questions relating to the concrete problems of the Law of Nations looked at from the point of view of a jurist.

Grotius defended the freedom of the open sea as a limiting factor to the ascendancy of the States and a powerful instrument in the development of international relations. Freedom of the open sea was the result of free trade (in the broad sense) and free trade was justified because no single State could satisfy all the needs of man.

Grotius, using different words, made a clear distinction between natural law and positive law. The first, based on general ethical considerations, was a result of deduction. The second could only be established by observing the way nations behaved; it was inductive.

On the fundamental problems of just and unjust wars Grotius' attitude was no longer that of a moralist but that of a jurist. He laid down the principle that the State may commit a crime and must then be treated accordingly, but (see Van Vollenhoven, *op. cit.*, p. 72) in international society there is no impartial judge, and therefore an international crime can only be presumed where guilt is established beyond doubt. States which undertake police action may have interests in the affair and can offer no guarantees of disinterestedness; the law may offer them scope for intervention, but it cannot bind them to do so. Consequently—expressed in modern language—for Grotius there is no fixed and certain criterion for defining wars of aggression.

In the seventeenth century Grotius had greater influence than Vitoria, although subsequently he was eclipsed by authors like Vattel. He has made a brilliant come-back since the second half of the nineteenth century.

There are slightly divergent interpretations of Grotius. That of Van Vollenhoven (*op. cit.*) may be compared with that of M. Basdevant in the symposium, *Les fondateurs du droit international*.

A complete study of the doctrine should also include Albericus Gentilis (1552–1608), who encouraged the creation of special privileges for ambassadors, and Zouche (1590–1660), who succeeded Gentilis in his chair at Oxford.

Section III

FROM THE TREATIES OF WESTPHALIA TO THE CONGRESS OF VIENNA (1815)

§ 1 INTERCOURSE BETWEEN STATES

Permanent diplomatic missions soon developed proper administrative services. However, their action was supplemented by the personal envoys, official and secret, whom the princes continued to use.

Treaties multiplied; they also increased in scope; the tangle of political interests bound all problems more closely together; at intervals major international agreements attempted to solve them. The best example was the Congress of Westphalia, with its different treaties and acts. It was important for the political decisions it came to, the length of the negotiations, and the variety of the provisions covering a wide range of topics.

Max Huber regards the Acts of the Congress of Westphalia as the first acknowledgement of the existence of an international community, a society of States; this view is a measure of how far matters had deteriorated since the Middle Ages. The Treaties of Westphalia were the forerunners of *collective* treaties; in addition to arbitration clauses and guarantees they contained clauses covering very modern problems: war criminals, reparations, prisoners, disarmament, minorities . . .

While the territory covered by the treaties was not greatly increased it was consolidated. Russia was brought into the European political system: a Russian guarantee appears in the Treaty of Teschen in 1779 giving her the right to intervene in European affairs. In the limited field of Capitulations and commercial treaties relations between the western States and Islam were placed on a firm footing; at the time of the Napoleonic Wars alliances were made as far afield as Persia.

These international relations were of political importance. Their extension made States uneasy; the rudimentary idea of a balance of power emerged as the basis of international relations; some treaties, for example the Treaty of Utrecht, recognised this new principle *justum potentiae equilibrium.* Nevertheless, trade remained an important consideration; it is seen in the conclusion of trade and shipping agreements, but above all it was the basis of the great colonial rivalries.

Maritime and colonial questions still dominated the development of inter-State relations.

The war at sea is worth looking at more closely; we can see there some of the fundamental problems of modern international law. The notion of war as defined by Gentilis was restricted to inter-State relations. In the Middle Ages there was the institution of letters of marque and reprisal: an authorisation given to private persons who had been injured at the hands of foreigners to take the law into their own hands and attack the compatriots of the offending party on the open sea. This practice had died out. But war on the open sea still involved private persons and private property was not respected. Until 1815 there was no absolute distinction between men-of-war and merchantmen. To lessen the financial burden States conceded to private persons (privateers) the right to make war on the open sea in ships fitted out privately.

The privateers seized enemy ships and often made good business out of it. In modern terms we should say that there was a delegation of sovereign rights for the purposes of war.

These practices gave rise to a variety of problems to distinguish between a ship and its cargo, and between enemy property and neutral property. It was impossible for non-belligerent States to allow their goods to be treated as enemy property; but belligerents would not give neutral shipping the enormous advantage of carrying enemy goods, nor allow them to supply enemy territory. The position of different States varied according to geographical position (insular or not), their role on the open sea (whether or not engaged in international traffic), their national traditions and their political shrewdness. Many theories, principally about contraband and blockade running, defined the rights and duties of neutrality. And so there emerged a concept of neutrality, and political alliances based on it (League of Neutrals). There emerged a new kind of warfare with a great future before it: economic warfare. Napoleon systematised the confused schemes of his predecessors in his policy of the continental blockade.

Bertrand de Jouvenel (*Napoléon et l'économie dirigée*, Brussels, 1942) has shown the importance of this attempt which, among other things, hastened the economic expansion of the United States and the advent of the *Zollverein*.

Colonisation was marred by slavery and the slave trade, at their peak in the eighteenth century, and the great European political treaties were frequently concerned with the division of spoils. In the New World the treatment of well developed white societies as colonies provoked demands for emancipation. And so the economic barriers implicit in the Colonial Pact did not stop the movement for independence in the Spanish and Portuguese colonies in South America, countries newly stimulated by the arrival of refugees from lands conquered by Napoleon. They won their freedom a few years after 1815. The confederal and later the federal experiment which developed in the United States was a model for the evolution of international relations in a closely unified society with common interests.

In the other parts of the world the great trading companies were on the decline, like all forms of delegated sovereign rights.

With the French Revolution they disappeared altogether except in England where the East India Company continued until 1857.

Strictly speaking the great companies did not disappear then. They continued for a long time in some parts of the British Empire; the last would seem to have disappeared in 1946 (cf. Agreement for the transfer of the Borneo Sovereign Rights and Assets from the British North Borneo Company to the Crown, June 26, 1946. HMSO Colonial. No. 202).

International relations were more and more the concern of Governments, but the position of foreigners did not prevent close relations developing on the literary and scientific plane. Scholars and men of letters were called abroad, travelled without difficulty and, especially in the age of enlightenment, contributed to the creation of a new Western European unity. Apart from war at sea, hostilities only affected inter-State relations: the nationals of warring States enjoyed full rights on enemy territory.

§ 2 NEW FORCES AND NEW IDEAS

Centralisation, the growth of State power and conscription revolutionised the political system by absorbing the subject into the State. England and France became democratic in different ways and at different times.

In origin democratic ideas were intimately linked to international relations, particularly to events in the New World. By asserting the rights of man the Americans laid the foundations of an international society which was not a society of States but a universal society of individuals. The utopian tradition of planning an international society continued. Leibnitz, William Penn, the Abbé de St. Pierre, Rousseau, Kant, were, in their various ways, successors to Erasmus and Thomas Moore. Hobbes, and in the eighteenth century Helvetius and Holbach, continued the tradition of Machiavelli. The search for a philosophy of history and the idea of progress developed separately; not until Marx were they brought together.

Many philosophical societies attempted to usurp the place formerly occupied by the Church. They had some influence in changing attitudes to coloured peoples, and in France they brought about the abolition of slavery (unfortunately only temporarily) (1794). Abolition eventually came in 1833 in England and in 1848 in France. Many of those societies were internationally minded, in particular *freemasonry*, whose role cannot be overestimated.

On this point see the very curious article by E. Nys, *Idées modernes, droit international et francmaçonnerie*, published in the *Revue de droit international et de législation comparée*, 1907.

The intellectual theories of the French Revolution favoured the development of international relations and the independence of other peoples. But practice fell short of principle. The modern nation, which had been slowly ripening since the sixteenth century, achieved its full political significance in France, and became a dominant sociological factor. In 1815 the modern nation had not been theorised about, as it was subsequently: it appeared as an historical phenomenon. A collective consciousness amongst all classes of the population, in particular the lower classes, imbued all members of the group with a sense of common origin, a shared destiny and a feeling of superiority towards other nations. Revolutionary wars fostered nationalism in Spain. The birth of a collective consciousness was opposed by the princes, but it benefited from the liberalisation of régimes even when it conflicted with liberal philosophy. The collective consciousness did not appreciate subtleties. The period of the nation State illustrated the obstacles to international relations. The structure of a State was that of a political-judicial-military machine. We could imagine that, with appropriate machinery, the State could be absorbed into a super-State, comparable to business houses merging or associating together into larger groups. But nations, with their own particular sociological characteristics, their individual historical consciousness, their special interests and their prejudices set a limit to the development of international society. The give and take of the princes, their policy of marriages and personal alliances, gave place to differences between national collectivities.

§3 THOUGHT AND INTERNATIONAL LAW

Among the philosophers of this period who, like Leibnitz or Kant, studied international relations historically or ethically, J. Bentham, in his work *An introduction to the principles of morals and legislation* gave a name to the discipline hitherto called 'the Law of Nations', calling it 'international law'. 'International law' was to be the work of specialists, nearly all of whom had extensive practical experience of affairs. Diplomats and politicians formed an ever increasing public for works on international law.

But apart from commentaries on treaties (for example, Mably, *Le droit public de l'Europe fondé sur les traités*, 1747) where the commentary is of a historical and political nature, what could the subject-matter of this discipline be? The rules of international law were not very numerous. Diplomats attached great importance to the formal aspects of diplomacy, particularly ceremony; in 1759, Hübner said that seven-eighths of the works on international law dealt with questions of this sort.

Theorising about international law followed two paths: one was based on natural law, the other on positive law.

'Natural law' formulates a body of ethical rules applicable to intercourse between States. It might equally well be called 'political ethics' or 'international ethics'. But it may be that tactical considerations lay behind the preference given to the term 'natural law'. In view of the slow development of juridical rules many authors took the liberty of rounding off their descriptive account with a few ethical notions. The words 'natural law' facilitated the transition from one notion to the other. The practice of some States excused this attitude. Some treaties or diplomatic acts appealed to natural law, for instance the famous decree of 16 November, 1792, promulgated by the Executive Council of the Convention. This text laid claim in the name of natural law to the right of freedom of navigation on international rivers, that is, rivers which flow through or between several States. 'Natural law' was certainly helpful in the early stages of international law. Even positivists like Max Huber consider that the development of natural law in the eighteenth century helped to build up international law.

Most of the eighteenth-century theorists did not attach 'natural law' to any particular creed. Nevertheless, the Catholic Church appreciated its importance and nearly all modern studies on natural law come from its members, for instance the classic work by Taparelli d'Azeglio, *Essai théorique de droit naturel basé sur les faits* (French trans.; 2 vols.; 1883, Paris).

But many writers of the time, like Pufendorf (1632–1694) or Wolff (1679–1754) gave absolute supremacy to natural law. A reaction was inevitable. It had not yet appeared in authors who had studied maritime law like the Dutchman Bynkershoek (1673–1743), nor is it to be found in the work of diplomats like the Swiss Vattel (1714–1767). The latter's work, *The Law of Nations and the Principles of Natural Law* (1758), met with a rapid commercial success; it set out the modern doctrines of State sovereignty and the exclusion of individuals from international law, but he occasionally appealed to natural law.

There was another school of thought directed against the contamination of natural law. Positive law was the proper field of study for a jurist. He should confine himself to the practice of States, recording it impersonally and setting it out in the most orderly way possible. The German Moser (1711–1785) is the real founder of this school, followed by G. F. von Martens (1756–1822), of a famous family of juristconsultes, author of *Précis du droit des gens moderne de l'Europe* (1788), founder of the *Recueil des Traités*. From then on-wards all jurists kept to, or tried to keep to, positive law. It is a pity that the reaction against the confusions of natural law was carried too far, with results we notice even today, particularly in an inter-pretation of the sources of law centred exclusively on the will of individual States.

Section IV

FROM 1815 TO THE SECOND WORLD WAR

§ 1 THE FRAMEWORK OF INTERNATIONAL RELATIONS

The sixteenth century marked the beginning of world history, but even so in 1815 a number of countries were still isolated. Africa was unknown, except for the Mediterranean and Eastern areas; the Far East, after some limited contacts with Europe, was almost completely closed to trade. The polar regions were unknown. The new period profoundly altered all these areas. The Far East was compelled by force to accept European ties. A semi-colonial system was imposed on China; unequal treaties ensured European States territorial rights; financial difficulties led to strict customs control; the independence of some areas was mortgaged by the building of railways. There were interesting legal peculiarities about this system but it lasted until the Second World War and prevented a normal relationship which would have absorbed China into the western community.

In contrast to this Japan adopted the legal and technological methods of the western community; she won all her wars and rapidly expanded politically, demographically and economically.

Africa was rapidly explored and colonised by the European nations in circumstances which offered diplomacy the chance of complex, tortuous and frequently unscrupulous bargaining. The General Act of the Conference of Berlin (1885), which solved some of the most difficult problems of apportioning African territory, laid down a number of international rules. The African kingdom of Ethiopia was the cause of one of the crises international organisation experienced in this period leading up to the Second World War (1935).

Although their strategic importance was not then recognised, open and unrestrained competition for the polar regions began in the first quarter of the twentieth century.

Not only were all parts of the world brought into contact with each other, but the relations between them became so intimate that major events had repercussions which involved all countries in the world.

In fact, this new world unity benefited Europe. It possessed colonies, was the seat of international bodies and conferences, a centre of technological development and what is known in general as 'civilisation'. Whatever name is given to international society: 'the society of civilised nations', 'international community', it is inspired and dominated by Europe.

In former times European countries had international relations with a good many countries without becoming part of a 'society' which included them. Typical of this is the formula used in the Treaty of Paris of 1856 which extended to Turkey the advantages of European public law (Wood H. McKinnon, *The Treaty of Paris and Turkey's status in international law*, AJ 1943, p. 37). On the eve of the First World War a standard German author, Liszt (*op. cit.*, p. 2), still excluded from the international community semi-civilised States, among which he counted China, Persia, Siam and perhaps Liberia and Ethiopia.

§ 2 THE GROWTH OF INTERNATIONAL ORGANISATIONS

(A) *General features*

The increase in new wealth as a result of technical progress, and the exploitation of new and vast sources of energy greatly widened the field of all kinds of international relations.

This can be shown in purely quantitative terms by, for example, the increase in the number of consulates (Nussbaum, *A Concise History of International Law*, p. 210), or by the growth of international postal traffic (Ruyssen, *La société internationale*, p. 15).

These relations gave rise to common interests and encouraged the creation of international organisations. To return to the terminology used in the Introduction, a multitude of individual international societies arrived at a point in their development where, for specific objects and specific regions, they made themselves into 'groups'.

This was a constant trend from 1815 to 1930, except during the First World War. Thereafter it declined until the Second World War.

A distinction must be made between private and public organisations.

(*a*) *Private organisations*. A number of private organisations sprang up both for economic and non-economic purposes. Scientific associations, propaganda leagues, religious, sports and tourist associations, etc., became international in scope. Particular mention must be made of the humanitarian and pacifist societies which brought pressure to bear on States to make them support international institutions, particularly those movements to safeguard the rights of man and human values. These organisations played a large part in the abolition of the Eastern slave trade (General Act of Berlin, 1885; General Act of Brussels, 1890), in the creation of the Red Cross, and later of the League of Nations.

International associations inevitably ran into legal difficulties when they tried to acquire international status. But even without this status they were able to obtain facilities by the favour shown them by certain national legislatures, notably in Belgium. On this question see the report of Mme Bastid to the *Institut de Droit International* on *Les conditions d'attribution d'un statut international à des associations d'initiative privée* (*Annuaire de l'Institut de Droit International*, 1950, vol. I., p. 617, and vol. II, p. 335).

They set up a central office of international associations whose publications make it possible to follow the growth of the movement since 1907. The League of Nations kept up to date an index of international organisations.

The growth of private organisations for economic purposes was connected with the capitalist expansion of this period. A large number of commercial firms assumed an international character by extending their activity to all parts of the world. And so international companies came into being; international competition was regulated by agreements, *ententes* and cartels between private organisations, which at times took on a quasi-public form.

The international standing of some of the great international enterprises is shown in arbitration cases where their co-litigant is a State (for example, China *v.* Radio Corporation of America, 13 April, 1935, AJ 1936, p. 334); and also in the direct participation of certain private groups in international agreements, for example the Chadbourne Plan or the Rubber Agreement of 28 April, 1934 (Cino Vitta, *La coopération internationale en matière d'agriculture*, RCADI, 1936, pp. 56, 304).

(*b*) *Public organisations.* The 'common interests' of international society forced States to pay them some attention. A wide-spread movement began; 'collective' treaties recommended to a growing number of States standard rules to protect these interests; one of the first treaties of this kind was the *Convention Sanitaire* of 27 May, 1853. But the need for permanent organisation gave rise to 'international bureaux', which acted as secretariats, issued publications, exchanged documents, facilitated contacts. Under the title of 'unions' some very rudimentary international organisations emerged in this way in the field of communications and commerce (1865, International

Telegraphic Union). Most of these 'commissions' or bureaux (there were 14 on the eve of the First World War) had restricted powers.

However, the problem was how to govern the affairs of international society. In the nineteenth century it was solved empirically: the Great Powers met together at a Congress and by their preponderant weight settled the most urgent problems; this practice was known as the 'Concert of Europe'. The end of the nineteenth century saw the birth of a regional organisation in the New World in the modest form of a commercial 'bureau': it was the beginning of the Pan American Union. Finally, in 1919, the first universal political organisation appeared: the League of Nations. These three institutions confirmed the importance of international organisations, and need to be studied separately.

(B) *The Concert of Europe*

Immediately after the collapse of Napoleon's Empire the four victorious Powers divided Europe into zones of influence by the Final Act of the Congress of Vienna, 9 June, 1815, completed by the recession of the territory of Frankfurt on 21 July, 1819. They also laid down a number of juridical rules constituting 'European public law'. The Treaty of 20 November, 1815, consolidated an alliance directed against France for the maintenance of peace in Europe. This treaty made provision for meetings of sovereigns or their ministers to settle disputes, if necessary by intervention. The Protocol of 15 November, 1818, associated France with the policy of the Congress, and the counter-revolutionary bias of the Congress was due to the Holy Alliance, signed by the heads of State between 14–26 September, 1815. But the question of Belgian independence was dealt with by principles which differed from those agreed to in 1815. The treaties of 19 April, 1839, settling the status of Belgium were imposed by the five Great Powers and guaranteed by them. It was the beginning of the 'Concert of Europe', which was maintained throughout the nineteenth century and up until the First World War. It was based on the distinction between small powers and great powers, to whose number Italy must be added after 1859. Extra-European States only appeared at international conferences dealing with non-European questions: the United States only took part in the Berlin Conference in 1885 (she did not ratify the General Act) and the Algeciras Conference in 1906 (with reservations). Meetings of the Concert of Europe were in fact frequent; until 1914 there were only 36 different years in which no meeting was held, and only rarely did more than two years elapse without a meeting (1833–1838;

1842–1845; 1887–1894; 1907–1912). This only emphasises the number of major diplomatic reunions. The Concert of Europe remained un-organised: in principle the meetings were not compulsory; there were no rules governing the conduct of the meetings nor how to carry out its decisions. The influence of the large States on the small ones was variable; the small States occasionally took some part in the meetings; sometimes the large States required them to obey their decisions, sometimes they protected them. The States never in law gave up their sovereignty. Nor should some of the apparent successes of the Concert of Europe be overestimated. In some cases the States agreed to set up internationalised bodies or services, but these temporary solutions were rarely inspired by any regard for inter-national organisation as such. For instance, international organisa-tions were set up to administer and re-organise the finances of certain countries in financial difficulties (Greece, Egypt, Turkey, China); and an international military organisation administered the affairs of Crete for a time.

Not until the Hague Conferences of 1899 and 1907 did the Con-cert of Europe concern itself with humanitarian and idealistic con-siderations. Formally, the Conferences drafted several conventions for the purpose of codifying the rights and duties of belligerents and neutrals. But they reflected a far deeper pacific instinct. The first conference, called at the suggestion of Tzar Nicolas II, brought together the United States, Japan, Mexico, Persia and Siam as well as the European States; the second was attended by 44 States: the newcomers were 17 of the 19 Central and South American States. The conferences moved on from war to the pacific settlement of international disputes, in particular to arrange a system of arbitration now assuming some importance in international practice. The creation of a Permanent Court of Arbitration sketched the outline of a per-manent organisation for this purpose. The conferences were to meet at regular intervals, and the third conference was to be held in 1914. Some people have seen in the Hague Conferences a genuine inter-national organisation, but this is going too far. The conferences were, like the Concert of Europe, no more than an intensive use of the traditional methods of diplomacy. The Concert and the conferences were the *occasion* for forming specialised, temporary and strictly limited organisations; they *paved the way* for the League of Nations.

(C) *Pan Americanism*

Latin America was a particularly propitious ground for an attempt at international organisation, because the emancipation of the ex-colonies at the beginning of the nineteenth century had led to the establishment of an excessive number of successor States. These States, bound together by cultural and economic ties, formed a single society which could not remain unorganised. Simon Bolivar understood this; a treaty was signed at the Panama Congress in 1826 setting up a 'Union, League and Confederation', but it came to nothing: its aim was to reunite some of the South American States.

Unification on a continental scale, to include the United States (but not Canada), was delayed by divisions between the Latin American republics and by their periodic disputes with the United States.

Nevertheless, from 1899 onwards there were, at the suggestion of the United States, periodical Inter-American Conferences. They followed the pattern of traditional diplomacy, and drew up a great number of agreements, several of which were only partially put into effect. The nucleus of a permanent organisation was formed with the creation of a commercial bureau and a governing board (Mexico 1901), composed of American diplomats accredited to Washington. In 1910 the bureau assumed the name of Pan American Union. In 1923, at Santiago, it decided that the president of the executive committee should no longer be the United States representative, but one of the elected delegates. In 1928, at Havana, it was decided that the representatives on the committee might be specially chosen for this purpose. The role of the Pan American Union was confined to making 'recommendations' addressed to the States; an agreement was actually prepared in 1928 which would have given the Union a more solid legal basis, but it was never put into effect. As it stood, the Union could not in principle deal with political questions; however, the evolution of American policy under Franklin Roosevelt (good neighbour policy), the conclusion of political treaties like the Saavedra Lamas Pact (1933) led to the American States tackling these problems openly at Montevideo (1933), Buenos Aires (1936) and at Lima (1938), where meetings of Foreign Ministers were held.

The Pan American Union then, had administrative and political functions. It had some success in cultural, administrative and technical matters, and so justified the flimsy permanent structure which distinguished it from the Concert of Europe. But it never had any real political role until the eve of the Second World War (perhaps because of the threat of war), while the political role of the Concert of Europe was clearly stated from the beginning but deteriorated steadily through the policy of alliances.

We must also take into account the existence of the League of Nations, to which, with the exception of the United States, the American States belonged. The role of the League of Nations, particularly in the Leticia and Chaco affairs, lessened the urgency of strengthening the Pan American Union.

(D) *The League of Nations*

Set up just after the First World War at the suggestion of the United States, the League of Nations marked a new phase in the history of international relations. In principle it set out to be a *permanent universal* organisation with general competence to encourage the development of international relations of all kinds and the peaceful settlement of international disputes, and to provide guarantees against aggression. The universal character of the League of Nations fluctuated: the United States refused to join from the beginning; the delayed entry of the USSR in 1934 did not make up for the departure of some States against whom the League had taken a stand or who had not obtained satisfaction for their demands: Germany (1933), Japan (1933), Italy (1937) and a number of American republics. The State remained sovereign, the League of Nations did not directly discharge any functions of the States, and most decisions had to be unanimous.

The fundamental purpose of the League of Nations was to maintain peace. It has been judged on these grounds. The mounting aggressions which led up to the Second World War marked its failure. On the whole the League of Nations never managed to bring effective pressure to bear on a major power. Its successes were confined to questions between small and medium-sized States.

However, the League of Nations altered the problem of international organisation. It generally acted as the centre of all the other organisations which it sought to co-ordinate without annexing them; its existence helped the creation of a large number of international institutions in all fields, particularly an international court (Permanent Court of International Justice, 1920). It provided an unrivalled arena for negotiations and study groups and it had some notable successes. After the League of Nations it was hard to imagine a return to the old conditions. A body of international officials had grown up, technical services were created which worked even during international crises. In law, the League of Nations did not disappear until it was replaced by the United Nations in 1946.

§ 3 COLONISATION

(A) *The partition of the world*
Up to the eve of the First World War the more technically developed
States resumed their conquests which had so far spared black Africa
and some islands in the Pacific. England and France were joined in
this venture by Germany, Belgium, Italy, Japan and the United States.
The legal basis of colonisation ranged from annexation to various
forms of protectorate. New techniques of colonisation appeared
to neutralise charges of colonisation while conserving its advantages:
the acquisition of military and trading rights, the pressure of public
loans and large-scale private firms, the open-door policy, etc.

The continuance of capitulation systems meant a quasi-colonial
position; they did not disappear until the eve of the Second World
War and even then not completely. Indirect and disguised forms of
colonisation applied to some Central American republics, the Ottoman Empire, Egypt and China. In view of its historical importance
particular mention must be made of the 'open door' policy. The
'civilised States' compelled certain countries to agree to treat all
foreign nationals without discrimination in economic matters; in
addition, these same countries were generally forbidden to intervene
in economic life in any way which would have made this equality
purely nominal; some States (Morocco, China) were compelled to
lower their tariffs. These measures were often defended in the name
of liberalism, but the States who benefited from them were not
prepared to suffer the consequences of liberalism at home. It was this
which gave them their clearly colonial character. In fact, this system
was only to the advantage of countries whose economic position was
so strong that they could do without tariff protection (Belgian
Congo).

(B) *Disinterested idealism*
The horrors of slavery and the slave trade provoked the Conference
of Vienna to pass a resolution recommending the abolition of the
slave trade, and the slave trade later disappeared through the efforts
of national politicians. England managed to get many States, though
not France, to recognise her right to put down the slave trade on the
open sea. After the abolition of slavery (1833, England; 1848,
France), international efforts were made to improve the lot of un-
protected peoples. The immigration of unskilled labour to supplement native labour in tropical colonies gave rise, after some abuses,

to international treaties which marked the beginning of the international protection of labour. The General Act of Berlin (1885), the General Act of Brussels (1890), and the Convention of St. Germain (1919) contained clauses abolishing the last traces of African slavery and protected backward peoples. New currents of thought and practical assistance were largely instrumental in humanising life in the colonies (missions, trade unions, etc.).

(C) *International organisation*

Colonial systems could eliminate inequalities by one of two means: by assimilating the overseas populations with the metropolitan country or by granting local autonomy leading eventually to federation. The Portuguese in their colonies, and the French in Senegal and the West Indies pursued the first course. The second course was followed by the British in the white colonies of the British Empire. Eventually this became the British Commonwealth of Nations. The treaties of 1919 confirmed the international character of their relations with the United Kingdom. But the new system inaugurated by these treaties had even greater influence.

Article 22 and the following articles of the Covenant of the League of Nations made special provision for the territories and colonies taken from the defeated States after the War. The new principles went, at least in spirit, beyond the particular issue at hand. According to Article 23b the members of the League undertook to 'secure just treatment of the native inhabitants of territories under their control'. 'The sacred trust of civilisation' analysing the rights of colonising powers had already been developed by Francisco de Vitoria; it also justified the occupation of lands not under the dominion of any State (*terra nullius*). Later specialised international organisations like the International Labour Organisation developed the doctrine to its logical conclusions in the field of labour and economic life.

Nevertheless, it is in the limited context of the machinery for international mandates that the new doctrine was asserted most effectively. The management of territories placed under mandate was to be directed towards 'the well-being and development of such peoples'. For the more advanced nations (A Mandates) the Covenant specified that independence was the final aim of this tutelage. It was laid down that the less advanced territories (C Mandates) should be administered by the mandatory power as 'integral portions of its territory'. Between these two there was an intermediate category (B Mandates). The A and B Mandates were bound by obligations laid down in the interest of the territory and of the other members of the League of Nations (the open door policy and equality of commercial opportunity). The management of these territories was entrusted by the League of Nations to the mandatories, 'advanced nations who by reason of their resources, their experience or their geographical position, can best undertake this responsibility'. In fact, the territories taken from Germany and Turkey were divided up between the United Kingdom, France, Belgium, Japan and some of the Dominions. The League of Nations acted through the 'Permanent Mandates Commission' which examined the annual reports of the mandatory powers and also petitions which they were bound to transmit to it. Although it encountered many obstacles the League of Nations action in colonial questions proved very useful. Some Mandates ended with the appearance of new States like Iraq. But the evolution of territories under mandate was retarded by the introduction of indirect or disguised forms of colonisation.

§ 4 ECONOMIC ASPECTS OF INTERNATIONAL RELATIONS

Apart from recessions due to wars or cyclical fluctuations of no great magnitude, international trade developed steadily from 1815 to 1929. The fall in the volume of trade between 1930 and 1939 has been attributed to various causes. It was not unconnected with the Second World War.

Trade had important economic consequences; it gave rise to capital transfers, and increased investment led to the migration of specialists and technicians.

During the greater part of the period under consideration, indeed until the world crisis, capital transfers were the work of private enterprise. States only intervened by means of tariffs to adjust trade fluctuations in their own interests. These seriously hindered increased transactions, but they never stopped them altogether. Many countries, in particular England and the Netherlands, adopted free trade. This liberal doctrine reached its peak in 1860 but there were still traces of it in world relations after the First World War. According to a famous maxim liberalism in international relations reflected liberalism in internal affairs. The young South American, Balkan and Mediterranean States and China left the construction and management of their public services (ports, lighthouses, railways, tramways, gas, electricity) to private firms (English, French, Belgian). The exploitation of new countries was naturally in the hands of private enterprise.

A vast community of economic interests was born in the civilised world; labour and investment found an international market; the interdependence of all nations had never seemed so strong as on the eve of the First World War. The freedom and unity of the world economic system were symbolised by the existence of gold as a universal medium of exchange. In Europe, up to 1914, all population problems were solved by mass emigration which peopled the United States at a prodigious rate.

And yet the economic machinery on which this solidarity was based bore within itself the seeds of destruction. In general it doubtless raised national standards of wealth. But as it was based on private interests, not only theoretical socialists but also the States receiving foreign investments questioned the nature of its benefits. These States feared the political influence of foreign capital in their territories and considered that the profits, real or imaginary, reaped by this capital were excessive. Although the revenue of some of the countries being developed increased, that of the lending countries increased even more, and the gap between rich and poor countries seemed to widen all the time.

Consequently, as soon as difficulties arose as a result of the First World War, States like Turkey, who had not wiped out their debts by making a fortune at the expense of the belligerents, took steps to expel foreign capital. The sharp recession in international trade in 1930 hastened this trend; by imposing monetary controls States broke up the economic unity of international society. State intervention in economic life brought about growing structural differences between national economies; the destruction of the old international society was complete by the eve of the Second World War after the international organisations had shown their ineffectualness.

These economic changes greatly affected international law. Trade agreements multiplied during the nineteenth century and used interesting new formulas, for example, most favoured nation clauses or guarantees of non-discrimination. Some international organisations were directly concerned with economic problems, and lending abroad exposed foreign interests to local political hazards such as revolutions, civil wars or arbitrary measures. These risks led to armed intervention, and to the continuation of the system of capitulations. They also led to some advances in international law, particularly with regard to diplomatic protection, legal responsibility, methods of arbitration (mixed arbitral tribunals), and the use of force (peaceful blockade, embargo, and the Second Hague Convention on the limitation of force for the recovery of contract debts).

§ 5 NEW FORCES

Europe still occupied a dominant position in nineteenth-century international society. But the First World War, which was in fact a purely European war, ended her dominance. After 1919 the United States had a growing effect on world affairs, despite its political and economic isolationism. Russia, after 1815, patiently built up her immense Asiatic empire, and the impetus of European capitalism started her off on the path of expansion on the American pattern. The 1917 Revolution cut Russia off from Europe. Japan anticipated the awakening of the whole of the Far East.

But the transformation of international forces between 1815 and 1939 was as much the result of political doctrines and structures as of changes in the geographical framework.

The States' machinery of government became increasingly ponderous, but while this unified social life it presupposed and at the same time fostered a collective consciousness. This collective consciousness was the basis of the 'nations'; it thrived on memories and hopes, realities and myths; it became indispensable to the State. From nations States were born: Germany, Italy, and the States which succeeded the break up of the Turkish and Austro-Hungarian Empires.

Social life within each State was intense, but this only emphasised the fragmentation of world society. The nation States, which had begun long before in England and France, spread, but the scope of international life was correspondingly reduced.

The identification of the State with society once begun could not be overturned. Democracy added to the powers of the State, and the democratic State demanded even closer identification between the State and society. Socialism provided this. The practical results of all the important democratic and socialist doctrines were very different from their aspirations. They all hoped to defeat tyranny and foster universal harmony; they all, by acting through the State, increased the weight of the machinery of government and contributed to national isolation. The poorest classes were the most 'nationalistic', and inevitably fought the hardest for their own interests. Leaders who are thrown up spontaneously rarely appreciate foreign civilisations and culture.

In this way the State acquired unparalleled strength. This is no judgement of the value of democracy or socialism, it is a statement of fact: you cannot unite without separating, all integration hardens frontiers; by identifying itself with society each nation cut itself off from other groups.

Some international organisations continued to function, however, but none of them was strong enough to prevent the First World War. Opinions vary as to their real influence. In the business world no international union was able to obtain lasting political results; only a few international agreements were made during the depression. The Churches could reasonably claim to be more active than they had been, but none of them had an effective political role. On the other hand socialism was a new force, international in origin but later degenerating into national units. The various workers' 'internationals' were important from the end of the nineteenth century up to the Second World War, but had little influence on the course of international affairs.

Nevertheless, after 1917 a socialist system of thought and action triumphed in one of the largest empires in the world. One form of socialism therefore had at its disposal substantial armed forces which, if it were tempted to expand, would raise the problem of international relations. How far Russian communism was 'national' and how far an international revolutionary force is open to question. The question of co-existence between the USSR and the capitalist world was raised by Marxist-Leninism. Whatever the answer, a new force existed which, after a period of fluctuating foreign policy, appeared in international affairs.

The new forces in the world were not only groups of States, but also systems of thought and action, and indeed the States tended to identify themselves with such a system. The two-fold claim to furnish an explanation of the world and to solve actual political problems was a mark not only of Marxism but in some degree of other less important doctrines: fascism, national-socialism.

The division of the world into diametrically opposed systems of political thought created new problems both for international politics and for international law.

§ 6 DOCTRINES OF INTERNATIONAL LAW

During this period different schools of thought appeared and became as we know them today. International relations were the subject of all kinds of studies and published works: utopians, historians, essayists, politicians, vulgarisers, pacifists, jurists, sociologists, all devoted much attention to international problems.

The work of the jurists calls for some basic comments.

All juristic writings now contained descriptions of the positive law whose substance increased enormously during these 150 years.

At the beginning of the nineteenth century positive international law was still European in character; scholars and diplomats tended to talk of 'European public law'. A note of 24 June, 1919, addressed to M. Paderewski by M. Clemenceau still refers to 'European public law' (quoted by Güggenheim, vol. I, p. 197, n. 1).

International law rapidly assumed its modern universal character, although there were of course some regional groupings whose relations were sometimes governed by special rules, as for example on the American continent.

How can we distinguish between these schools of thought?

A first alternative is to divide the authors into two groups: empirical writers and systematic writers.

(A) *Empirical writers*

They were the first in the field. They carefully enumerated the rules recognised in intercourse between States, and only after that did they discuss definitions and principles which might make international law into an organised body of law. The empirical approach persists on a higher level to the present day among authors anxious to avoid encumbering accounts of international law with too many abstractions and hazardous hypotheses. Modern empiricists are aware of all the difficulties of attempting to synthesise. They voluntarily restrict themselves in order to be more scientifically rigorous. In their view, public international law is first and foremost a matter of observation: the jurist must accept the juridical rules of a society as they exist; his task therefore is not to deduce the rules from general principles, but on the contrary, as Grotius had already seen, to proceed from the particular rule to the general principle. Most Anglo-Saxon jurists and some French belong to this school.

(B) *Systematic writers*

What they have in common is their belief that public international law is subordinate to certain general rules which give it its value and provide it with a logical framework and internal unity. Nevertheless these general rules vary from author to author and their attempts at synthesis are based on very different conceptions.

First there are those who deny the existence of international law; this tradition persists to the present day. They start from definitions of law, justice, power, the State, from which it follows that an international public law is a contradiction in terms and therefore impossible. Although they discount the evidence these writers have a very useful function; they make us realise the imperfections of

c

international public law and stop people from expecting too much from it. People have thought that a body of law (or even a single facet of it such as arbitration) would be sufficient to ensure peace. These writers warn us that this is an illusion.

Next come those who subordinate law to another discipline: ethics (natural law) or sociology.

No one since the beginning of the nineteenth century has confused morality and law or refused to recognise the existence of an international code of morality or its importance in international law. Authors as different as Max Huber and N. Politis agree on this point. The dividing line is whether the notion of legal obligation can be divorced from ideas of moral obligation, and whether, if the moral law is the source of legal obligation, positive law should not continually draw upon it. Supporters of this view have been criticised for allowing natural law to invade positive law. The quarrel is therefore more concerned with defining what the professional jurist should do than with the 'nature of things'.

Other authors, reacting against the abstractions of natural law, have sought to establish scientific laws concerning the existence and growth of human societies. Juridical rules would be dependent both for their existence and their binding force on sociological laws. These authors have been criticised for confusing the nature of scientific laws where impersonal forces behave according to a fixed pattern, and human laws which operate through a voluntary restriction of choice. Their reply has been to show that scientific laws are statistically determined and human laws are fairly similar to this: if a law is violated by everyone it ceases to exist but it can tolerate a limited number of violations. The disagreement between the natural law schools of thought is not as important as would at first sight appear. The general rules for the evolution of human societies are very often basically the same as those of natural law, and both trends often seem to foster a similar idealism. But it is difficult to extract from either of them a valid notion of obligation.

There is a final school of thought mainly consisting of German and Italian authors. It vigorously reacts against treating the study of international law in terms of ethics, sociology, diplomacy or any of the other moral or social sciences. The essence of a juridical rule is its normative and positive character. On the other hand to avoid contradictions they try to make all juridical rules fit into a coherent whole, and therefore seek to unify the rules of international law into a single body of law. If we accept the idea that the binding force of a juridical rule depends on another juridical rule, the sum of these rules (and situations) is seen as an ordered whole which some authors have called the juridical order. There is therefore one fundamental juridical rule from which all the rest stem.

At this point the authors divide. For some the fundamental principle cannot be the same for municipal law and for international law: in the first it is the constitution of the State, in the second it is the *pacta sunt servanda*. For others, amongst whom Kelsen, there is a single fundamental rule, municipal law and international law form a single whole, and the rule uniting them is of a hypothetical character, that is, it must exist but its existence is not susceptible to legal proof.

These schools of thought have purified law and made it more rigorous. They have, however, confused its vocabulary and raised problems which would not arise were they not implicit in the original premises. They have complicated the relations between municipal law and international law by refusing to recognise a large part of social reality: monism and dualism in all their forms reflect a certain stage in the evolution of international relations and are of only relative value. No legal theory, however elegant and beautiful in itself, is of any value divorced from social and human realities, for these are its justification. In a society in the process of being organised like the international society of States the pure logician can only stand at the point of departure or at the point of arrival, he cannot help being either ahead of his time or behind it. In contemporary international law, more than in any other branch of law, logic and reality are profoundly divided from each other.

CHAPTER TWO

International Relations after the
Second World War

Section I

THE STATES

The present population of the world is divided up between about 80 States.

The figure is 90 if we include the Vatican, Muscat and Oman, and Nepal, and by counting China and Korea each as two units.

Strictly speaking some peoples do not live within a State, but in territories under international administration; but their importance in the general picture is slight.

States are not identical. There are profound differences which affect international relations: size, national income, geographical position, homogeneity, ease of access, propensity to expand.

(A) Size

Size may be a matter of territory or of population.

The size of a State's territory varies greatly from a few to several million square miles.

We find the same variations in population. In 1949 there were States where populations varied from (in millions): China 463, India 346, USSR 193, USA 149, Indonesia 79, Australia 8, New Zealand 2.

Alternatively population and territory can be taken together: there are very densely populated States like the Netherlands, and others with a very low density such as Canada.

We may wonder whether, at any given moment—today, for instance—there is an optimum size for States. The notion of the optimum size of a State is borrowed by analogy from economics where it has been worked out for firms (Meade). The notion cannot be applied to States without further qualification, since their size may be optimum for one purpose but not for another. Nevertheless, while physical size is not sufficient to make a State a Great Power, it must be admitted that all States with a growing part to play in international relations are large and often very large. Size is therefore fundamental; some States are historical survivals, others may become so, but large populations and extensive territories affect modern forms of production, defence, art and civilisation.

(B) *National income*

The comparative wealth of States varies enormously. But it is not easy to give a simple definition of comparative wealth, nor to support it with figures. Reliable data could be established only by an intricate system of national accounting; but few States have a reliable system of national accounting, and some only publish extracts. In addition, on the most favourable assumptions national accounts are rough approximations.

Three factors should be distinguished: the total national product (gross or net) which gives a measure of the total mass of production, the average income per head of population, and the distribution of the national income between consumption, productive investment and non-productive investment (national defence, political expenses).

Some international organisations publish studies on the national incomes of various countries. The United Nations published the following figures as the average national income per head of population for 1949, in dollars: US 1,453, New Zealand 856, UK 723, Australia 679, France 482, USSR 308, Indonesia 25, China 21. But the interpretation of these figures is a very delicate matter if you want to draw conclusions from them about, for example, the standard of living. For western countries the reader is referred to the study published by OEEC in 1954: Milton Gilbert and Irving B. Kravis, *An international comparison of national products and the purchasing power of currencies*; for the Soviet countries Bergson and Heymann, *Soviet national income and product*, 1940–48 (New York, Columbia University Press, 1953); Romeuf, J., *Le niveau de vie en URSS* (Paris, PUF, 1954).

There is a good deal of very interesting information to be had from national income and expenditure. The first practical application of this information has been made in the field of international organisations (contributions to expenditure according to size of national income, *infra*, p. 256). From another point of view, the role of the individual in the modern world can be measured objectively by this method. The share of wealth left in the hands of the individual is in some sense a measure of his freedom, and the discretion allowed him to allocate his own savings gives him an opportunity to express his philosophy of life. Modern States have adopted widely differing attitudes towards the quantity of consumer goods to be available to the individual, and towards his freedom of choice between present and future consumption.

(C) *Geographical position*

Geography is overwhelmingly important in international relations. It affects problems which cannot be studied here; we shall confine ourselves to a few essential points.

If we consider States in isolation, marked differences appear as regards the continuity of their territories. Most States today have a single comprehensive area; the only major exception is Pakistan, divided into two parts after the partition of India in 1949. However, we must bear in mind the development of the colonies. The Second World War undoubtedly hastened this development, and the system of international trusteeship has been extended, but in addition former colonial territories have become independent and are new States (Indonesia, India, Pakistan, Burma, Lybia, Syria, Israel, Jordan, Korea). Other overseas territories on the other hand have been completely assimilated by the home country, or seem to be developing within its general framework. This is the case of France and its territories in America and in the Pacific, Reunion, and some African territories. The United Kingdom also has kept territories in all parts of the world, but looks at them differently from France. The United States has added a widespread network of bases to her colonial territories. There is therefore a difference between those countries made up of a single continental area and States with scattered territories. The latter see their future bound up with the use of the sea; they are therefore less independent than other States and they have interests in all parts of the world. Political systems with maritime interests are the moving spirits in international life.

If we now look at States from the point of view of their immediate frontiers, we can see that who their neighbours are vitally affects their interests. This may explain the moderation with which victors frequently deal with the vanquished: their disappearance might lead to major upheavals and their replacement by equally undesirable neighbours.

Geography determines that certain States shall have particularly close contacts and these relations constitute a type of magnetic field. There are many examples in the world today; they are to be found in treaties, and above all in international organisations: the names of agreements or organisations are often taken from geographical regions. Inside international organisations there are traces of geographical decentralisation : it is very noticeable in the World Meteorological Organisation, the World Health Organisation, the International Telecommunication Union, the International Civil Aviation Organisation, etc. The same kind of regionalism can be seen in a more flexible way in the daily work of the United Nations; votes are taken and nominations put forward on a regional basis (sometimes by a statutory requirement).

Traffic and communications are practical aspects of international relations. A State's interests change according to its place in relation to international lines of communication; the States most influenced by international relations are those through which the greatest number of lines of communication pass. On the other hand those at a terminal point are more favourably placed for undertaking through services. Today air communications introduce new elements: air traffic across the polar regions will no doubt cause fresh changes.

There are also certain boundaries which can be used to mark off the lines of political tension across the globe; they are important in determining the strategic position of States. They are easy to establish by reference to conflicts over territory and major political rivalries. By this method the political analyst can indulge in the simple game of describing the position of States in terms of the rivalry between the USSR and the United States.

(D) *Homogeneity*

States are more or less homogeneous units. Climate, soil and general economic and social conditions may be studied from this point of view. Some variety seems to make for a better overall balance than uniformity; the position of States like France in Europe, or Colombia in America has often been admired in this respect. But these are only considerations connected with physical geography.

As far as population is concerned the problem assumes different proportions. Some States are more or less ethnically homogeneous, with the same language, and identical ways of life. Other States are made up of different ethnic groups. The term 'ethnic group' is not very accurate here. If we substitute the term 'nation' for ethnic group and describe some States as 'plurinational' we are resorting to a term which, as we have already seen (*supra*, p. 50) is still very vague. Some people define a 'nation' by reference to the State, and make the fundamental factor the will to live together; others define it objectively by race, language or religion, etc.

In this chapter we need only point out that most States today contain within their boundaries human groups whose differences affect social solidarity. The United States, Canada, the States of Central and Southern America, Ethiopia, Morocco, India, Switzerland, Belgium, France, Spain, Jugoslavia, the USSR, Italy, etc., are all in different ways and to different degrees made up of heterogeneous human groups. It is necessary to decide how much tension there is between these different groups. Not only is internal tension a source of weakness and international difficulties, but the attitude which States adopt towards foreigners in international relations is necessarily influenced by the attitude they adopt internally towards their own national elements. A State which does not allow discrimination despite having a very mixed population can treat foreigners very cordially. Russia, even under the Tzars, treated most of the peoples who lived there on a basis of equality. The USSR has condemned racialism outright, she is therefore free to preach racial equality in international relations and to uphold universal human rights in international institutions—at least up to a certain point. Switzerland's part in the development of international institutions has not only been due to her traditional neutrality and her geographical position, but even more because the fact of belonging to the Swiss nation is defined in such terms that no free man feels completely a foreigner in Switzerland.

No extreme conclusions should be drawn, of course. The reception given to foreigners depends on other factors as well, as the examples of the USSR and Switzerland very well show. The most liberal States often refuse to allow foreign workers into their territories. In some countries political ideologies have assumed such prominence that the position of individuals depends less on nationality than on sharing a particular ideology. This is true of communism and the ideologies related to it.

If a totalitarian ideology divides the world, then the internal homogeneity of a State in relation to that ideology affects its position; it determines how far it is free to fight the ideology or attempt a policy of co-existence.

(E) *Ease of access*

National societies are more or less accessible to each other. Natural conditions no longer have the role they once did; instead the freedom of States to determine how far they shall have external contacts has had considerable importance for the freedom of international relations and the formation of societies and secondary groups. The extent to which a State is accessible may be reflected in exchanges of persons, goods, information and religious and cultural ideas. Technical progress has abolished physical barriers, but ease of access to other national societies has seriously diminished.

(*a*) *The movement of individuals.*—Facilities for immigration have almost completely disappeared today. The need for manpower which is still felt in undcrdcveloped countries is confined more and more to specialists ; new countries can attain high living standards if they are not weighed down with too large a population. Numbers are no guarantee against new weapons. Immigrants are refused entry to vast empty territories like the high African plateaux for political reasons. At the same time it is not unusual to find countries, like Egypt and Java, where the population doubles in twenty-five years.

The after-effects of the Second World War have thrown, at least in Europe, a more tragic light on the problem of international population movements ; the Council of Europe countries have accepted nearly 12 million refugees, of which only a small number have been able to emigrate to other continents ; in 1949, 660,000 Europeans were accepted abroad (145,000 British in the Commonwealth countries, 135,000 Italians in South America, 326,000 displaced persons taken over by the International Refugee Organisation).

(*b*) *The exchange of ideas.*—The exchange of information and cultural ideas is equally variable. Some techniques have overcome political barriers: radio, for instance. Others, like the cinema, can have widespread effects. But in many countries controls and ccnsorship reduce foreign influence to a minimum. The most universal means of expression like music and the plastic arts no longer escape political censorship. The exchange of scientific information is hampered by official secrets acts as a result of its use for military purposes.

(*c*) *The exchange of goods.*—The exchange of goods should be easier, but the situation is not simple. The world war, followed by a period of shortages which lasted five years, adversely affected international trade.

Some States must have a large volume of trade, others can if they want to ; not all countries have the same freedom of choice. Here the size of the State is very important. Small and medium-sized States cannot produce all they need either for geographical reasons or because some products may not be an economic proposition for a

7474747474747474747474747474747474747474747474747474747474747474747474747474747474747474747474747474 INTERNATIONAL INSTITUTIONS

small market. States like Switzerland or the Netherlands are therefore obliged to resort to international trade to satisfy many of their needs. This is not the case for the United States or the USSR; the share of foreign trade as a proportion of total output is very small for these countries. Contrary to some appearances their interest in expanding international trade is limited. On the other hand, because of their great size these States (and particularly the United States) have an overwhelming effect with decisive consequences on the economic equilibrium of other States. Other States then have two alternatives: either join with other small and medium-sized States in a common market with preferential treatment, or secure the market for a very specialised product (for example, Swiss watches).

There are also States for whom a considerable volume of international trade is indispensible but yet not possible. These are the so-called underdeveloped countries. These States need a great variety of commodities, but goods are traded for goods, and these States have no goods to trade with. First they need capital and credit. The effects of the economic depression of 1929 were made worse by the Second World War. State financial commitments were not honoured, and private capital suffered such losses from confiscation, monetary operations and nationalisation that the prospects offered were not good enough to persuade it to take new risks. Moreover, even assuming that there was a certain volume of capital seeking profitable investment, it is sometimes necessary in the most backward countries to make very long-term investment (communications, schools, hospitals) such as can only be undertaken by public authorities. The example of the USSR shows how complete control of the economy can, by sacrificing consumption to investment, succeed in producing capital even in a backward country. But apart from its harshness, this method is only technically possible in a country with at least one highly productive sector. This condition is not generally fulfilled except in States which are very large and technically advanced. Otherwise the situation is insoluble without foreign aid. *The problem of assistance to underdeveloped countries has therefore become the central problem of present-day international society*; to solve it, while yet avoiding the difficulties encountered in the past, calls for a changed conception of capitalist methods, a modification of the position of foreigners and an effort at international organisation on many fronts. But the problem cannot be divorced from the position of trade in general, for capital is only repaid in goods; there are therefore only two rational forms of foreign capital aid: by gifts or by arranging for repayment through trade. It is a paradox that international gifts should have made their appearance in the postwar world which is otherwise so bitter and divided. The performance of activities in international relations entirely free of charge is revolutionary. It may be of course that indirectly gifts are politically and economically profitable.

Because of all these differences between States, the closeness of international contacts in the modern world greatly depends on the grouping of States. In addition to a general network of trade between all States, which cannot reach a very high level, there are groups of States which accord each other preferential treatment. The closeness of these contacts encourages a kind of federalism if the States concerned are of comparable size, or leads to the hegemony of one of them if they are not.

Whatever features we study, therefore, we come to the conclusion that international relations do not tend only towards increasing world solidarity, but also to individual solidarities which cut across each other and threaten world solidarity.

(F) *Propensity to expand*

Some national societies are in a period of progress and expansion, others of decline and contraction. The impetus to expand and the reasons for doing so vary, but they always seriously affect international relations. It is rare for expansion to be confined to the interior of a country, or for a country to be flexible enough for expansion not to affect other States. It is rare to find countries like the United States and Russia whose uninhabited hinterlands were fertile enough to support a two-fold demographic and economic increase. Furthermore, when the drive to expand is the result of a collective psychosis, it inevitably affects international life.

For a long time the life of States was marked by phases of decline, stagnation or growth which were evident in the continuous progress of historical development; only in a few States was there rapid (and often precarious) growth during the same period of history. The drive to expand shown in a rapid rate of growth and activities affecting other States seemed at any given moment to be confined to a few powers.

In the world today the impulse to expand seems to affect many more States. There are several reasons for this; in essence it is due to the rapidity of technical progress and the more systematic and deliberate management of social affairs by the State. The fantastic manpower potential of the poorest States had for centuries been hidden by the lamentable effects of disease. A few medical discoveries have wiped out great natural scourges and suddenly provoked an unprecedented growth of population. Rapid technical advances can suddenly make some forms of natural wealth comparatively unimportant and increase the importance of entirely new ones. Still more marked is the rapid rate at which industrial plant and materials can become out of date. This means an economic burden which no system can stand up to unless it is very large and renews its equipment gradually. The intervals between introducing new equipment inevitably mean that medium-sized States have an advantage over each other in turn. In the world today the race for progress is no longer a luxury but a condition of survival. Even the most liberal States keep a close watch on investment at the highest level. In the global terms of a national economy figures are irresistibly eloquent; every State tries to expand economically and uses propaganda and direction to impress the need for it on the public.

International relations today are between expanding units, and this makes the competition, whether peaceful or violent, much greater.

Section II

INTERNATIONAL SOCIETY

§ 1 THE GROWTH OF TENSIONS

Today society is still dominated by the after-effects of the Second World War. First, then, we must see how, and if, the War has ended. But there are other tensions which were disguised or held in check by the World War, but which have been developing since the armed conflict more or less ceased.

(A) *The conclusion of the World War*

This conflict was formally a war, although not all the States at war actually declared war on each other. Moreover, not all the States at war were at war with each other, the most notable case being that of Russia at war with Germany but not, until the very end of the war, with Japan.

Normally hostilities, once ended, should have been followed by peace treaties to settle the situation on an international plane. Peace treaties were signed on 10 February, 1947, with Italy, Hungary, Bulgaria and Rumania, and on 8 September, 1951, with Japan, but up to now no peace treaty has been discussed with Germany and the treaty with Austria was only finally agreed upon in 1955.

This is not the place to discuss the legal problems involved in this position, nor by what methods, short of a peace treaty, the most urgent difficulties have been solved, but one simple fact remains: the political balance which is the object of peace treaties after a war has not yet been established. The future of Europe is uncertain while the fate of Germany is undecided. The position of Germany, which has always in the past been settled by the great peace treaties (Westphalia, Vienna, Versailles), is today simply an *ad hoc* arrangement which satisfies none of the interested parties.

The other treaties have only been partially put into effect. Serious disagreements over the application of the treaties with the Balkan States have divided the Allies (Advisory Opinion of the International Court of Justice, 3 March, 1950, Reports, p. 65). It took until 1950 to give effect to provisions of the treaty with Italy concerning the Italian colonies; the fate of Trieste was decided, at least as regards Italo-Jugoslav relations, by the Protocol Agreement of 5 September, 1954.

(B) *New political tensions*

The most important cause of new political tension was partly disguised by the Second World War, but it rapidly assumed international proportions after the war. It is the rivalry between communism and its opponents, reflected in the rivalry between the USSR and the USA. This hostility was already noticeable before 8 May, 1945, during the conflict with Germany; there were two governments claiming to represent Poland, and this prevented her participating in the San Francisco Conference. The struggle between communists and non-communists has led to various changes of fortune in various States: civil war in Greece, a *coup d'état* in Prague (1948), communist domination in Hungary and Rumania, complete disagreement between the allied military governments of Germany (blockade of allied sectors of Berlin by the Soviet authorities in 1948). The same fundamental rivalry was evident in insurrectional movements in Iran, in China and in the armed conflict in Korea, as well as in other revolutions. The point about this situation is that it did not develop to its logical conclusion, a world war, but had periods when tension relaxed and gave rise to a great deal of diplomatic activity. A new kind of international relations came into being. Nothing appeared to be irreversible, even at the worst moments. At the international conferences preceding the German armistice (8 May, 1945) the Great

Powers laid the foundations for what has become the United Nations Organisation, the successor to the League of Nations. The political belief underlying the structure of this organisation was that everything was possible in international organisation provided the Great Powers preserved close unity between themselves, and that nothing was possible if they did not. In these terms events should have sterilised all efforts at international organisation within the framework of the United Nations; but close inspection modifies this pessimistic view. After the refusal, in 1950, to admit representatives of the Chinese Peoples' Republic, Russia left the United Nations and a number of international organisations, but she was only absent from the United Nations for a short time, and after 1953 her representatives returned to the other international organisations.

Since 1945 other tensions have developed in dealing with colonial problems. The emancipation of the sub-continent of India led to hostilities until 1948; Indochina was the scene of armed conflict which was only provisionally solved after nine years of fighting; other outbreaks have occurred in various forms in other territories (Madagascar, Kenya, North Africa). The growing influence in South and Central Africa of the Union of South Africa, a State with a clearly stated racial policy, has also raised problems.

Territorial adjustments between young States born of colonial emancipation are still sources of tension and conflict. The friction between Pakistan and India, notably over the future of Kashmir, continues despite the efforts of the United Nations. The future development of the State of Israel and her co-existence with her Arab neighbours is still unsettled.

§ 2 THE DEVELOPMENT OF PEACEFUL RELATIONS

(A) *Their variety*

International relations vary according as to whether or not they involve totalitarian States. In principle totalitarian States accept only inter-State relations; between non-totalitarian States a richer, more varied international life facilitates or paves the way for more intimate contacts.

In inter-State relations, the gulf between the very large powers and the others seems to have widened compared with former times. This has made international relations much more rigid. If there are only two dominant powers, the other States group themselves in political systems round them, or try laboriously to free themselves by organising separate systems. Present-day society records several attempts to do this, but it is clear that regrouping is sometimes for reasons not always calculated to foster peaceful international relations. But the existence of very extensive political systems raises the question of whether international unification will be brought about simultaneously on several different planes; the partial attempts to give Europe a political structure illustrate this point very well: they seek to unify territories already united by many social ties, and to constitute a political mass strong enough to escape from the attraction which the great systems which surround her inevitably exercise. Between non-totalitarian States the intensive development of direct relations and the prospect, however distant, of unification, reflect the existence of a similar social reality.

International relations at the present time then are extraordinarily varied in form, in the level at which they operate, and in their results.

(B) *The development of a moral conscience*

Tension has been too great and conflicts of interest too numerous and too violent to allow international morality much chance of success or much influence on government practice. But it is noticeable today that people are demanding a more exacting code of morality than in the past. People have concluded from this—rather hastily—that the gulf between the principles which nations professed and their practice was widening, and that hypocrisy too was expanding. But in every human society there is a gulf between moral precepts and practice, and the moral level of a society's actions was never raised by accepting a lowering of moral standards. The elevation of moral standards opens up new chances of perfection to a society: it is not unimportant to take this risk, even if it does not succeed. The enormity of the crimes committed during the Second World War revolted peoples' consciences. The trial of war criminals by international and national courts, the appearance of new crimes like that of genocide, the whole trend towards agreed definitions of 'crimes against humanity', and the institution of a proposed international criminal court, are limited and imperfect attempts to create institutions to meet a deeply felt need. Similarly, the work of the International Labour Organisation in improving workers' conditions, provisions to protect racial, linguistic and religious minorities (too rarely inserted in peace treaties), led to a general movement for the protection of human rights which has assumed great prominence in the work of international organisations. Objection can be made to the verbalism of many of the texts, and to ulterior political motives of the power politicians found here as elsewhere. But it is not a question—for the moment—of passing judgement on a legal work, but simply of stating that in a time which sometimes seems to be dominated by material inertia, the human conscience, or more particularly the individual conscience, is not sleeping. Not only is the wealth of the world on the whole more justly distributed now than a hundred years ago, but women, children, the sick and the destitute are on the whole less neglected.

The sensitivity of the public conscience today can be shown in several ways; there have never been so many cases to illustrate the conflict between the individual conscience and State authorities. It is a sign of the times that the question of the legitimacy of tyranni-cide was raised with the abortive attempt on the life of Hitler, the worst of them all, and despite the fact that the fatherland was in danger.

(C) *Common interests*

In the international world today the interests States have in common appear to be very marked and this has aroused a wide movement of collective consciousness. Common interests develop principally as the result of material progress, of the speed of communications and of the identity of technical civilisations. The masses have woken up to the situation as an indirect result of the war: serious military crises tend to become world-wide, like economic crises only to a lesser degree; it is easy to infer from this interdependence and many common interests.

International organisations have multiplied during the last twelve years as they have never done before. They are both intergovern-mental and private organisations, and the latter are called upon to collaborate more and more with the former.

The Yearbook of International Organisations, 1954–55, mentions about 1,200 organisations, governmental (about 150) and non-governmental, excluding organisations whose object is financial gain.

A comparison between the two 'post-war periods' would probably bring out the fact that infinitely more care was taken in 1944 than in 1919 to envisage world economic development as a 'whole' with all the parts interdependent. Thus the nations at war imagined, following the lead of the United States, that world economic relations would be restored by a return to free convertibility of national currencies; and so in 1944 the International Monetary Fund (IMF) and the Inter-national Bank for Reconstruction and Development were created by the Bretton Woods Agreements. But even before the non-ratification of the Havana Charter (1948) had put off (at least provisionally) the creation of an International Trade Organisation, it had already become clear that the first problem was international reconstruction through mutual aid and disinterested assistance. The first form of this was American aid, and particularly that known as Marshall Aid. Then, from 1949 onwards, came technical assistance, in a more universal and in principle a more permanent form: it consisted of all kinds of aid, in principle free of charge, distributed to underdeveloped States through international channels. The creation in 1955 of the International Finance Corporation marked a new stage in the development of international investment; at the same time trade was increasing with the general economic expansion.

But in this field it is particularly necessary to keep a sense of proportion. Interests are *common* only up to a certain point, and therefore they can never be fitted completely into a convenient organisation. For instance all States have a common interest in adopting uniform standards of measurements and scientific terms. There has been substantial theoretical progress here. Yet very few States have actually adopted the metric system; for those countries with industrial equipment based on another system a change over to the metric system would be expensive and complicated. Again, any attempt to regulate internationally the production and transport of certain goods meets with the same objections as are raised by individual firms against similar proposals at the national level. Some countries demand free trade for one commodity, some for another: the strong demand freedom, the weak protection. Economic interests are only 'common' in desperate circumstances or from a long term point of view; this view is not common even by governments.

Moreover the fact that States have common interests does not mean that they will adhere to an international organisation to defend them. International action must fit in with the internal structure of individual States. The internal structure of some States prevents them from joining in efforts to defend interests which they share. Thus, as will be seen later, federal States are not as free as unitary States to enter into international engagements. Differences in internal economic structure are also obstacles to the conclusion of universal agreements. The International Labour Organisation provides a simple example of this. It is laid down that the Conference of this organisation shall be composed of government, employers' and workers' representatives. This arrangement was originally made to fit the economic structure of free enterprise systems, but it does not make much sense for countries where the entire economy is in the hands of the State. This led to discussions in the ILO as to whether representatives from some countries could justifiably be called representatives of workers or employers. This is once again the problem of international relations between totalitarian and non-totalitarian States, between countries with a State-controlled economy and private-enterprise countries.

CONCLUSION

International relations in the world today are not solely relations between powers or between States, but inter-State relations are the dominant element. International society consists of relations between large-scale units whose solidarity is mainly conditioned by material and mechanical factors. The main characteristic of such a society is its lack of flexibility. On the surface at any given moment international society seems rigid; but there are countless subterranean movements, which give rise to periodic readjustments in the form of sudden, resounding jolts—the revolutions and wars which are increasingly intimately connected.

A prominent feature of the contemporary world is its ambivalence: there is a logical continuity in the most contradictory sequence of events which is not always evident at first sight.

What are the general rules of law which govern such a society?

We must not be disconcerted by their variety. First the degree of abstraction to be found in the juridical rules which govern international society varies considerably. Some, though not many, are both universal and permanent, e.g. the sources of law. Others, on the other hand, are only the practical application of those general rules, and deal with more concrete, and in some ways more temporary problems; the more abstract and general a rule, the more stable it is, and vice versa.

At first sight there is a formalist side to international law: diplomatic relations or the conclusion of written undertakings are conducted with certain formalities. But this is a purely superficial impression; the problems of international law are too serious and too important to be settled by empty formalities; the wills of States must be able to make themselves felt within a legal system without being subjected to useless rites and procedures: international law is one of the least formalistic branches of law.

International law is partly voluntary, partly compulsory. In practice the solidarity of international society and the permanent ties which bind States together are inescapable facts from which a number of fundamental rules follow. On the other hand, however, alternations in the pattern of international trade are the voluntary acts of particular States, and these are often sources of the most concrete engagements. But to speak of 'voluntary acts' is not necessarily the same as 'acts arising out of wills all equally free and equally strong'. States are inevitably aware of the weight they are likely to exercise in comparison with the weight of other States. This is why there are so many international agreements in a post-war period, which then generally fall off as the losers regain their place in the world or make new alliances leading to a new balance of forces.

Law in international society is therefore a secondary phenomenon reflecting other forces, and at the present day it is impossible to go beyond this and claim for it a position it has never had. Law is a result rather than a cause of peace, since in the last resort in order to function it must needs be an expression of preponderant power.

ANNEX

The Atomic Age

The development of atomic energy and the uses to which it has been put have made many people look at international relations in a new light.

So far atomic energy has been used for three main purposes: the construction of military engines of destruction; the production of electrical power; and the creation of new substances with beneficial biological qualities (medical uses and fertilizers). Only the military use of atomic energy is genuinely revolutionary. Electrical power produced by atomic power stations will probably hasten the development of regions lacking other sources of power; but this can only be done by easy stages, since it requires a great deal of capital.

The military application of atomic energy ultimately means that it will be possible to destroy at one blow the whole population of any highly urbanised country.

This possibility poses in the first place a moral problem. In 1945 only Pope Pius XII protested against the use of the atomic bomb. Since then others, often with ulterior political motives, have tried to stir up public opinion. Since there is nothing to prove that other arms—particularly biological warfare—are not just as much to be feared as atomic weapons, the problem is more general and covers the use of all forms of non-selective weapons and weapons of mass destruction. Unfortunately it is by no means certain that the people of the world as a whole are fully convinced on this point; perhaps only the threat of reprisals will help them to make up their minds.

States with the atomic bomb find themselves in possession of considerable means of pressure over other States. The possibility of making and using atomic weapons becomes a new criterion for distinguishing the relative power of States and for deciding which States are entitled to be called 'Great Powers'. Nevertheless this new criterion should not be exaggerated. To create an atomic industry a State needs considerable capital, a team of expert scientists, and, for military trials at least, large open spaces. The three States who have so far produced atomic weapons in any case are the three largest world powers. Perhaps atomic industry will only develop in States which are already powerful and will simply increase their margin of superiority over the rest. This may persuade other States, who are too small at present (from all points of view), to unite to form a wider political system. But atomic energy cannot do more than tip the scale and is not by itself sufficient to bring about a closer union. Such, at any rate, is the impression one gets from the setting up of the European Council for Nuclear Research at Geneva (1954).

For a democratic country atomic weapons raise serious constitutional problems; there is the question whether the decision to employ atomic weapons should be entrusted to special organs of State. So far the question has been discussed only in the United States.

Will state control of atomic raw materials and state monopoly of atomic industries lead to a general state control of the whole economy? It seems as if it only strengthens an existing trend; the same could be said of the increase in security services which seems to go with the possession of large-scale atomic industry.

On an international plane the United Nations has tackled only the military aspects of atomic power and has not achieved much success. In President Eisenhower's declaration to the United Nations General Assembly of 8 December, 1953, he proposed the creation of an international organisation to put at the disposal of all countries fissionable materials for peaceful uses. During 1954 there were discussions on the subject between the United States and the USSR. A conference on the peaceful use of atomic energy met at Geneva on 8 August, 1955.

CHAPTER THREE

General Notions of Contemporary
International Law

International law is defined in terms of the *subjects* of international public law: international law is then 'the body of rules which governs intercourse between the subjects of international public law'. Section I of this chapter will therefore deal with the subjects of international public law.

These subjects constitute a society. International law is the law of that society; the term usually used to describe it is the 'international community'. Section II will deal with this notion.

It should then be easy to determine the characteristics of international public law and the differences which exist between it and municipal law and the relations between them. This will be the purpose of Section III.

Section I

THE SUBJECTS

§ 1 IN GENERAL

To say that any entity is a 'subject of international law' is to say that it has: 1. Rights and duties which are *directly defined and enforceable* by international law; 2. The capacity to participate in some measure in formulating the rules of international public law.

The subjects of international public law are States and any other entities the States may recognise as subjects.

From this definition several very important facts follow:

(a) States are not only the original subjects of international law, but in present-day international relations they are still the principal subjects. It is to a study of them that Part Two of this work is devoted;

85

(b) Within certain limits and under certain conditions States have recognised international organisations as subjects of international law. These organisations are therefore subjects of international law only by derivation. International organisations may conclude agreements which are regulated by international law, recognise the existence of a custom, and present claims under international law. They possess the two essential characteristics of subjects of international law: they have rights and duties defined and sanctioned by international law and they take part in making the rules of international public law. Part Three of this work will deal with them;

(c) the subjects of international law vary in their nature. The International Court of Justice has said categorically (Advisory Opinion on reparation for injuries suffered in the service of the United Nations. Reports, 1949, p. 178):

'The subjects of law in any legal system are not necessarily identical in their nature or in the extent of their rights; their nature depends upon the needs of the community.'

It is the international community which is alluded to in this quotation; it will be seen later (Section III) what is meant by this.

(d) Are private persons subjects of international law? This question has given rise to innumerable controversies, much of which is entirely a matter of language. It depends on what is meant by 'subject' of international law. The definition given above helps to clarify the term and shows how it applies to individuals.

International rules can easily *define* the rights and duties of individuals. Rules to this effect have existed for a long time, and as will be shown later they are becoming increasingly common. Here is a simple example: in a law-making treaty two States make a reciprocal agreement to authorise each other's nationals to exercise certain professions on condition that they observe certain regulations. The nationals of each State are thereby accorded rights and made subject to duties.

But are these rights and duties of individuals directly enforceable by international law? Let us suppose that one of the signatory States refuses to recognise that a national of the other State has the right to settle within its boundaries. There are three ways open to this individual to defend his right. He can, after having referred the matter to all appropriate administrative authorities, first of all apply to the local courts of the offending State; this procedure uses municipal law; whether it succeeds or fails depends on the municipal law of that State. Second, the individual can turn to his own State and inform it of the treatment he has received; that State can then take action against the offending State. This action will be between two States, two subjects of international law; it will be regulated by international law. But even if it succeeds in securing observation of the treaty, this result will not have been obtained *directly* by the individual, but through his State. It cannot then be said that the rights of the individual are *directly* enforceable by international law. But there is a third possibility. If there is an international organisation, with power to enforce an individual's rights, he can apply to it to defend his right. In this case we can really talk of a direct sanction through international law.

But such organisations only exist if they have been created by the States; they are exceptional, and their powers of enforcement generally ineffectual.

To sum up, the rights of individuals *may* be directly sanctioned by international law; but only when an appropriate international organisation exists. If this is so, individuals are subjects of international law twice removed: they are subjects of international law only when they resort to an international organisation which has itself been created by the States.

As for having some part in making the rules of international law, the individual's role must depend on the answer to the preceding question. If individuals have no rights and no duties directly sanctioned by international law, they do not in a private capacity take part in the intercourse regulated by international law; they therefore have no opportunity of participating in making the rules of international law. This gives some measure of how far, and under what circumstances individuals may be acknowledged to be subjects of international law.

This is the answer from a systematic and abstract point of view. We must now examine from a practical point of view the actual position of private persons in the world today.

There is no agreed vocabulary on the subject. If, in accordance with general practice, we take the expressions 'international law' and 'law of nations' as meaning the same thing, there are important differences in the use of the terms 'subjects of law' and 'juridical personality'. Some writers make a distinction between juridical personality which consists in having certain titular rights and duties, and subject of law, a quality reserved to States, which are the sole makers of international law. The view put forward here lays the main emphasis on defining international law by its institutional characteristics.

§ 2 THE POSITION OF PRIVATE PERSONS IN PRESENT-DAY INTERNATIONAL LAW

(A) *In general*

Private persons have an important place in modern international law. There are two distinct ways of looking at this. As far as our sense of values goes, it is clearly encouraging to see a movement towards closer direct contacts in international relations (cf. p. 23). This is a reflection of greater human solidarity; the State and international organisations are only technical machinery, and the purpose of law must be the fuller expression of individual human beings and not of abstractions.

On a technical level however the movement must be considered in the light of our previous remarks. It is then seen to have three characteristics: the growth of conventional law, the institution of diplomatic protection, the appearance of a direct sanction under international law of the rights and duties of private persons.

(*a*) *The development of international conventional law*. There have always been international rules defining the rights and duties of private persons. Foreigners are protected against certain kinds of flagrant discrimination within a State's territory; and individuals have certain duties to that State; in peacetime they are forbidden to commit acts of piracy against foreign ships; in war-time they are compelled to observe a number of rather complex rules concerning trade with the enemy. These rules, which are long-established, are on the whole based on custom.

But the distinguishing mark of modern law is the development of conventional law. The position of foreigners has for a long time been the subject of bilateral agreements contained in law-making treaties. This kind of treaty is still found in modern law, often broadened by the inclusion of the most favoured nation clause: a State undertakes to confer on the nationals of State A all the advantages it may in the future confer on the nationals of State B. There have also been attempts to conclude more general treaties between a number of States defining certain rights to be granted to private persons, for example a passport system or customs formalities. But in modern conventional law there are also more ambitious collective treaties. Efforts have been made to safeguard personal rights not only against a foreign State but also against a private person's own State. This movement began with the international ban on slavery and the slave trade; it has continued with the conventions concerning labour and the protection of public health. It protects racial and religious minorities against the power of the State. But it is difficult to generalise. This type of convention occurs frequently after major wars to ensure a peaceful settlement in certain States, in Germany after the Treaties of Westphalia, in the new States which emerged after the First World War; but to impose common rules for all States protecting the rights of individuals against their own government is a direct attack on the absolute authority of the State. The movement now operates under the title of 'protection of human rights'; in view of its importance it will be studied separately later.

(*b*) *Diplomatic protection.* When the rights of one of its nationals have been violated by a foreign State, a State can take action on his behalf. It can turn to the offending State and demand reparation for the violation of an international rule. There are several points about this machinery:

(i) The victim's State is absolutely free to endorse its national's claim; if it does so it may merely protest through the diplomatic channel, in whatever form or tone it pleases; *a fortiori*, it is for the victim's State to decide whether it will resort to more solemn procedures (arbitration), or take steps to enforce its claim. Experience shows that questions of private interest are settled by States in the light of general political considerations. Private interests are protected to a greater or lesser degree depending on the relative strength of the States and on the general diplomatic situation.

(ii) If the claim is endorsed by no matter what kind of pacific action, the disagreement remains one between States, in which, with some exceptions, the individual has virtually no part at all. His claim has undergone the legal transformation needed to make it into a State claim.

(iii) If the victim's State is awarded any form of reparation, the victim is not automatically entitled to benefit from this reparation; it is a purely domestic matter between him and his government.

This process shows the uncertainty of the indirect protection of the rights of private persons.

(*c*) *The emergence of a direct sanction under international law of the rights and duties of private persons.* In international law as it is today this is an exceptional case. There are however some examples:

(i) International jurisdictions have been created to enable individuals to assert their rights against States which have injured them:

the International Prize Court (XIIth Hague Convention—not put into effect), Central American Court of Justice (Washington Convention 20 December, 1907—in force for a few years), Mixed Arbitral Tribunals, at least for part of their jurisdiction (by virtue of article 304 of the Treaty of Versailles during the years following the First World War). The Court of Justice of the European Coal and Steel Community is, to a certain extent, open to private persons, but to safeguard their interests against an international organisation rather than against States.

(ii) Provision has sometimes been made for a right of *petition* to enable private persons to put their case before an international organisation with vaguer, more flexible powers than a court.

The right of petition was granted by individual conventions concluded after the First World War to guarantee the rights of racial, linguistic or religious minorities in certain States; the petitions were addressed to the League of Nations Council. The same procedure was adopted for the inhabitants of mandated territories, it still operates for the inhabitants of trust territories; they can send petitions to the Trusteeship Council concerning their rights under the trusteeship agreements (cf. p. 281).

(iii) While some rules of international law were binding on private persons it is much rarer for these duties to be sanctioned by a special international legal process. Usually the injured State (or the State whose nationals have been injured) sanctions the violation through its national authorities, in particular through its courts. The only major (and imperfect) example of sanctions by a special international legal process is the trial of certain war criminals by the international military court of Nuremberg. There are several proposals for international criminal courts on this pattern.

(B) *International protection of human rights*

(*a*) *In general.* The protection of human rights postulates two conditions: that human rights be defined in rules agreed to by the States, and that there is international machinery for enforcing them. If the second condition is not filled the only method of enforcement is the machinery of ordinary law, which means only diplomatic protection. The uncertainty of diplomatic protection has been mentioned; if diplomatic protection worked perfectly it would mean that foreigners were better protected than nationals; if a private person's rights are violated by his own State he has no international protection at all. The special feature of the protection of human rights is that its purpose is to protect people *against their own State*.

The legal definitions of human rights are worded in such a way as to confer rights on individuals irrespective of nationality; they doubtless have repercussions on the status of foreigners, but the boldness of an international system of protection of human rights lies principally in this intrusion into the domestic affairs of a State and its nationals, and in providing an alternative to the national authorities. In a perfect international system of protection of human rights there is no room for State sovereignty in the usual sense of the word: all important questions are subjected to a superior authority: in a perfect system of protection there is no longer a State but a super-State which enforces the observance of individual rights.

This explains why a perfect system of protection has not yet been achieved. But it would be a mistake to think that a beginning has not been made. While there is no call for easy optimism, we must be careful not to underestimate the influence of ideas and the weight of the interests which seek to make use of them. Although the absolute nature of State sovereignty must decline in the long run with the growth of the international protection of human rights, States which lay down the necessary rules and institutions think more about the limitations this protection will impose on the sovereignty of neighbouring States than on the limitations that will be imposed on them. Each State expects to profit from the right to look into other people's affairs, hoping at the same time to escape interference in his own business. The protection of human rights gives rise to keen political competition and it can only progress slowly and painfully.

If we look at the way this problem was first raised, we are forced to distinguish between two things:

(1) A certain number of particular human rights were defined and protected in the first place by separate conventions, while at other times the problem has been treated as one of protecting human rights in general.

An example of the first case is the international machinery of the Labour Conventions, which is still by far the most advanced method for protecting human rights. The proposals are voted by a Conference which is not composed solely of government delegates, but for each country there are two government delegates, one representative from the most representative employers' organisations and one from the most representative workers' organisations. The proposals are adopted by this conference by a two-thirds majority, and the governments must submit them to the national body (in principle the parliament) which has authority to ratify them. If they are ratified, international machinery is set up to control the way the conventions are put into effect. Each State must report on how the conventions are carried out (article 22 of the constitution). The reports are examined by a committee of experts, then by a special commission which submits its conclusions to the two principal organs of the Organisation; these contain representatives of the parties concerned. In the event of a breach of the convention claims may be submitted by either employers' or workers' organisations, or by governments. A complex procedure may then begin, with conciliation, enquiry and finally, if need be, intervention by the International Court of Justice. To assess the practical results of this part of the work of the ILO, see: *The International Labour Code*, 1951 (Geneva, 1954).

(2) The area in which human rights are protected varies in size. Sometimes it is only within a single territory, usually where a territory is under international administration or control, such as mandated or trusteeship territories (pp. 60 and 281). The distinction, however, is between universal machinery and regional machinery. In fact one of the most delicate questions is how abstract to be in defining those rights and freedoms considered to be fundamental. The more abstract the definition is the greater the possibility of universal application, but the vagueness of such a definition then deprives the undertaking of much of its significance. It is easier to conclude a convention which applies only to a few States who already belong to a single regional society, with a common culture and civilisation. Yet popular idealism likes to think of human rights as universal and moreover if the States united under regional machinery for protecting human rights share the same general features anyway, protective machinery will be simple but at the same time relatively useless. The value of an international system for the protection of human rights lies above all in the progress likely to result from bringing dissimilar systems of society squarely face to face with each other. The most important regional example of the protection of human rights is that provided by the Council of Europe; it constitutes an arrangement which is at the same time more sharply defined and more effective than the first efforts of the United Nations in this field. For the time being it is unlikely to affect other groups.

(b) *Protection of human rights by the United Nations.* The United Nations Charter mentions human rights several times (in the preamble and also in articles 1, 13, 55, 62, 68, 76). Apart from provisions concerning the trusteeship system, probably the most precise legal obligation in the Charter comes from articles 55 and 56; members are pledged 'to take joint and separate action in co-operation with the organisation' to obtain 'universal respect for, and observance of, human rights and fundamental freedoms for all without distinction as to race, sex, language or religion'.

This provision would no doubt enable the United Nations to take useful action if it were faced with a flagrant and persistent violation of human rights, but it is not in itself sufficient to ensure continued progress in this field.

Apart from individual cases which have been referred to it within the framework of its general competence (Convention on the crime of genocide), the United Nations also tried to work out an overall solution to the problem of human rights.

The Economic and Social Council set up a Human Rights Commission under article 68. This commission divided its work into three stages: to draft a Declaration which is really a political and moral manifesto, to incorporate precise legal commitments into a Pact to be submitted to the States for ratification, and finally to prepare the machinery necessary for putting the Pact into effect. The whole was to constitute a Charter of Human Rights.

The first stage was passed fairly quickly. The General Assembly of the United Nations adopted the 'Universal Declaration of Human Rights' on 10 December, 1948, with 48 States in favour (8 abstentions and none voting against). The other stages have been the subject of profound studies which are still going on.

The Declaration contains a list of rights and freedoms, with definitions, arranged roughly into four categories: personal rights (life, liberty, safety and dignity of the human person; equality before the law: prohibition of slavery, torture and arbitrary imprisonment), social rights (marriage, property, asylum, right to a nationality), public and political freedoms (freedom of belief, expression, peaceful assembly, association, election), economic and cultural rights (right to work, to form and join trade unions, to education, leisure, social security, etc.).

The political debates on the Declaration confirmed the obvious truth that in modern declarations of rights there is a conflict between the rights of liberal democracy which tries to protect the individual's freedom of choice, and the rights of social democracy which aims to provide certain positive benefits. Inevitably the different political systems within the United Nations each seek to insert into the Declaration of Rights the conceptions which most favour its own outlook ... and which are most likely to give it the right to criticise other systems. The Declaration has not indicated any order of precedence between the different rights, but has mentioned them all; the problem has been postponed until the Declaration is put into effect. The so-called 'social' rights do not lend themselves to any easy definition nor specific legal action under traditional legal procedures, still less to enforcement in the courts.

It has been said that strictly speaking this declaration has no legal value; it is simply a resolution of the Assembly, whose terms show that these rights are not regarded as being enforceable in every detail: the preamble to the Declaration simply puts them forward as 'a common standard of achievement'.

But it would be going too far to regard it as empty words; the Declaration is a model for the United Nations to follow and therefore all other States too. It is a text which can conveniently be referred to when an international agreement or action involves human rights. The United Nations refers to this text when questions arise about its supervision of trusteeship territories and of non-self-governing territories. The Declaration is also referred to in several international agreements, for instance the Agreement on Trieste of 5 October, 1954. Some national courts have even considered that the Declaration was directly applicable to the internal system of their State.

It was in the United States that the famous decision of Fujii v. California of 24 April, 1950, directly applied provisions of the United Nations Charter concerning non-discrimination; there was a strong reaction against this interpretation, which raised very serious issues as far as the United States Constitution was concerned: cf. especially studies by Manley Hudson (AJ 1950, p. 543) and by Quincy Wright (AJ 1951, p. 62). As M. René Cassin has rightly pointed out, (RCADI 1951, pp. 79, 283), the Declaration might be the basis for a complete transformation of the position of foreigners.

The Universal Declaration of Human Rights may be the beginning of a long-term development in the field of both customary and conventional law.

Section II

INTERNATIONAL SOCIETY

§ 1 ITS JURIDICAL NATURE

The subjects of international law, principally the States, have relations with each other; or we might say, in the sense proposed in the Introduction, that an international society of States appears when common interests emerge and when States become aware of them. The question is how this position is reflected in juridical institutions.

It would be possible to regard international law as simply dealing with particular and isolated relationships, each involving its own rights and duties. International law would then consist of a body of unconnected relationships, a mere collection of 'monads'. If this is so the expression 'international society' may perhaps make sense in terms of sociology, but it has no legal significance. Some order may be discernible in this accumulation of isolated relationships, but this order has no legal results, it is not a *source of obligation* but the consequence of a series of individual obligations. It merely states a fact: States voluntarily and freely adjust their relations with each other. International law is simply a law of *co-ordination*.

From another point of view, in the present state of international relations, international society appears to be something more than a secondary phenomenon drawing its origin from the States. It appears rather to be a concomitant fact whose existence must itself be postulated since it serves as the fundamental basis of the existence of the States. In this case international society is not only a sociological fact, it is also a legal reality, which creates and provides a certain legal order. This legal order may be imperfect and incomplete, international society is not organised into a 'group', and it does not have its own organs. Yet this legal order exists more or less independently of the attitude of this or that individual State. To emphasise the fact that international society is not simply a collection of individual relationships, the expression 'international community' is sometimes used.

The practice of international relations shows two forms of activity. The first comes from the fact that international relations are co-ordinating functions; the second shows States acting as members of an international community. Co-ordinating functions still constitute the major part of international life, but the others, though limited, are growing in importance.

(A) *Co-ordinating relations*

In some ways international law is still a law co-ordinating the relations between States. Since there is no organised international society, there is no authority superior to the States; there is no international legislator, no judge, no police force, no international executive. States are bound by certain rules, disputes between them are referred to a judge, and under certain circumstances there may be strong international pressure. But when these situations arise they are basically the result of a *voluntary* act of a State. Co-ordinating relations therefore show both State sovereignty and the voluntary nature of international relations: they are two aspects of the same thing.

(*a*) *State sovereignty.* It is still current international practice to use the expression 'sovereignty' to denote the specific character of the power of the State.

Sovereignty does not mean that the State is not bound by international law; neither does it imply that States have the right freely to determine their own jurisdiction, or more accurately their own competences; it simply means that, in the pyramid of human groups as it is at present, the State is at the top. Looked at in this way as a statement of fact, there will always be a sovereign power however international society may develop; if the world should one day be under the authority of a single State, that State will be sovereign.

From this doctrine it follows that all States must be equal.

A sovereign State may delegate some of its functions to another State, but it is still sovereign with respect to the other States since these functions are carried out in its name.

This simple situation of fact has given rise to inadmissible claims, notably that of not being subject to law. Politicians and even jurists have used the term sovereignty to mean something more than this, and have confused a perfectly simple notion. There are therefore overtones to the word 'sovereignty'. The term 'independence' has been suggested as an alternative (Rousseau, RCADI 1948, pp. 73, 171) since this implies that State jurisdiction is exclusive, independent and autonomous. Sovereignty has also been used as the criterion for a State (p. 148).

(*b*) *The voluntary character of international relations.* International law is still strongly impregnated with the idea that international relations are entirely subordinated to the wills of the States.

(i) The formal sources of international law are for the most part sources which assume that legal obligations are simply manifestations of the will of a State. As will be shown, international agreements are the most abundant source of international rules and they are generally manifestations of the wills of States.

(ii) To maintain contact States send permanent agents to other States, and this is the most tangible expression of intercourse between the States; these 'diplomatic relations' depend entirely on the will of the States.

(iii) In international law there is no authority which can lay down that a certain rule or situation of fact exists for all subjects of law. Hence the importance in international law of the different kinds of *recognition*. No doubt the term 'recognition' implies that the rule or the situation exists, quite apart from whether the State recognises it, but since there is no authority which can compel the State to recognise it, it is usually exactly as if the State were free to choose

whether or not to recognise it, and this has the same practical effects
as if the State's will was alone effective.

This has one very important consequence: the *relativity* of juridical
rules and situations. A situation may exist in law in the eyes of one
State but not of another. Incompatible commitments, each perfectly
valid in its own sphere, are common. A State may have more than one
government recognised as legitimate by other States. The situation
may be regrettable, absurd, or even excusable. One can only note that
it corresponds to contemporary international practice.

It is a pity that international society is not better organised, but it must not be
forgotten that 'recognition' in international law is not concerned with the relatively simple *de facto* situations of private life. To recognise a power (whether
recognising a State or recognising a government) is always in some part a creative
activity. Power rests on collective psychology, and to 'recognise' from outside an
internal situation as existing helps to make it become a reality. Where there are
'situations' of this importance and of this kind, one cannot simply say that
recognition is a juridical act of a purely technical nature.

It would be very interesting to compare this with general practice in private
law, the relativity of contracts and the development of the notion of conflict of
interests.

(B) *Subordination to the International Community*

Most of what has just been said is obviously incompatible with the
existence of a 'legal order'. The question here is how far practice has
been prepared to accept some of the consequences of this 'legal
order', this reflection of an 'international community'. States often
use expressions such as 'international community' or 'international
law' in international treaties, in diplomatic correspondence or in
internal affairs; they often proclaim that 'international law is the
standard of conduct of States in their reciprocal relations' (article
5a of the Bogotá Charter). But the implications of these principles
are only gradually reflected in practice. We shall give some of the
most important of them.

The growth of arbitration and international jurisdiction must play a leading
part in this. We can now see one of the most important technical reasons for this:
only reference to a third party placed above the parties concerned can help them
to escape from their relative positions.

(*a*) *The paradox of co-ordination.* Georges Scelle has expressed it
admirably. If it is claimed that the validity of a State's legal order
does not rest on a higher legal order, then its limits cannot do so
either; every State, then, has a universal competence and exists

D

without reference to other States. International jurisprudence denies this emphatically. There are many examples to show that a State draws its competence from international law. Two examples will be given, both of the greatest theoretical and practical importance; from them certain general considerations will follow.

(i) The first concerns the delimitation of territorial waters. Outside coastal waters the ships of all States can use the high seas freely; in coastal waters, on the other hand, coastal States have individual rights, but there is no general rule of international law which determines the extent of what is known as territorial waters. Can a State extend this area indefinitely on the grounds that there is no express rule? If the reply is affirmative there is a possibility that the high seas will be completely eliminated. Here is a passage from the judgment of the International Court of Justice in the Fisheries Case between the United Kingdom and Norway:

'The delimitation of sea areas has always an international aspect; it cannot be dependent merely on the will of the coastal State as expressed in its municipal law. Although it is true that the act of delimitation is necessarily a unilateral act, because only the coastal State is competent to undertake it, the validity of the delimitation with regard to other States depends upon international law.

'In this connection, certain basic considerations inherent in the nature of the territorial sea, bring to light certain criteria which, though not entirely precise, can provide courts with an adequate basis for their decisions, which can be adapted to the diverse facts in question.'

(ii) A second example concerns the question of nationality. Each State lays down by law the conditions which must be fulfilled before an individual can claim to be a national. This does not mean that a State can lay down any conditions it likes (cf. p. 143). Let us suppose that a person in fact satisfies the various conditions laid down by law in State A and in State B, and that he has at one and the same time the nationality of State A and State B. In certain cases a third party (a judge from State C or an international arbitrator) must decide which of the two nationalities shall be taken into account with regard to a particular issue, usually whether State A or State B is to be responsible for diplomatic protection. These third parties have not in general recognised the absolute sovereignty of the States concerned in this field. Here is a passage from another judgment of the International Court of Justice (Nottebohm Case, 6 April, 1955, Reports p. 21):

'If the arbitrators or the courts of such a State should confine themselves to the view that nationality is exclusively within the domestic jurisdiction of the State, it would be necessary for them to find that they were confronted by two contradictory assertions made by two sovereign States, assertions which they would consequently have to regard as of equal weight, which would oblige them to allow the contradiction to subsist and thus fail to resolve the conflict submitted to them.'

But the Court, following arbitral practice on this point, has ruled that a State could not claim that the nationality it had conferred on an individual was overriding unless it was effective, that is to say, taking into account various elements 'whose importance will vary from one case to the next: the habitual residence of the individual concerned is an important factor, but there are other factors such as the centre of his interests, his family ties, his participation in public life, attachment shown by him for a given country and inculcated in his children, etc.'

In this case the Court laid down a number of fundamental general principles:

'The character thus recognised on the international level as pertaining to nationality is in no way inconsistent with the fact that international law leaves it to each State to lay down the rules governing the grant of its own nationality. The reason for this is that the diversity of demographic conditions has thus far made it impossible for any general agreement to be reached on the rules relating to nationality, although the latter by its very nature affects international relations. It has been considered that the best way of making such rules accord with the varying demographic conditions in different countries is to leave the fixing of such rules to the competence of each State. On the other hand, a State cannot claim that the rules it has thus laid down are entitled to recognition by another State unless it has acted in conformity with the general aim of making the legal bond of nationality accord with the individual's genuine connection with the State which assumes the defence of its citizens by means of protection as against other States.'

These two examples, whose importance cannot be overrated since they concern two fundamental State competences, territory and population, lead us to conclude that, according to the International Court of Justice, *a State's jurisdiction is based on international law.*

It is certainly a mistake to regard international society as simply a secondary form of social intercourse, subordinate to the States and covering only those points which the States have of their own free will agreed to surrender.

It is equally a mistake to regard the international community as a social entity which existed prior to the States and established a coherent pattern into which they fit.

The truth lies between the two: in Charles de Visscher's phrase (*Théories et Réalités*, p. 127), the international community establishes a 'framework of power'.

Once the existence of a State is postulated (unless it be a universal State) it must conflict at points with other States, and so its jurisdiction must be defined to prevent encroachment on the other States. In other words, *the co-existence of States presupposes an allocation of functions between them, and this by definition can only be arranged by an international order*. International law, the formalised expression of the life of an international community, allocates functions between States; the area of a State's jurisdiction within the international community must be fixed.

At present this is done unsatisfactorily and is full of ambiguities and contradictions. But when a third party, such as an international arbitrator, has a difficulty referred to him concerning the allocation of State functions, he has to decide the problem according to international law, and the principles of international law are the very basis of State sovereignty.

More general, but also more significant, is the proclamation made by governments of the principle of non-intervention in the 'internal affairs' of another State. This principle, which has been applied since the beginning of the nineteenth century, of leaving every State free to choose its own political system and later on its own economic and social structure, is the result of the free determination accorded by international law in this field. It is sometimes called domestic jurisdiction (cf. p. 235).

We may now distinguish between two categories of rules in international law:

Those which allocate functions between States;
Those which lay down conditions for the discharge of functions allocated in this way.

It may (and frequently does) happen that, for a particular question, there are no rules in international law of the second kind; this means that the State exercises its jurisdiction at its own discretion. But there cannot fail to be some guiding rules in a case which involves the allocation of functions. If these directions are not crystal clear it is for the arbitrator or judge in a particular case to find what they are.

It has been said with justification that an international judge could not pronounce *non liquet* when he was confronted with a question of allocation of functions, and that it was up to the State claiming the jurisdiction to furnish proof. J. Basdevant,

RCADI 1936, p. 58, 471, and counsel's argument in the Lotus Case, PCIJ, Series C, No. 13, II.

(*b*) *Collective pressures.* Are international institutions (with the major reservation just mentioned) solely dependent on the will of the States? It would be incorrect to go this far. Examples show that international practice does not always recognise the will of States as the sole source of law.

(i) In the following chapter the formal sources of international law will be described. The will of the States is the most important element. But the rules are far from rigorous in this matter, for if they were they would condemn many universal laws to disappear, since it would be necessary to prove that each one had been approved by every State in the world. A customary rule can be proved by finding enough precedents to leave no doubt of its universal character, *even if none of the cases cited is taken from the State against whom it is to be used.* Furthermore, the theory of international agreements is in many ways incompatible with a theory of the will of States: for instance, the validity of treaties imposed by force, as all peace treaties are, and clauses which allow for the revision of collective agreements by a majority of the signatories; and all provisions which tend to make treaties more closely comparable to legislative acts (cf. the following chapter).

(ii) Situations grow up in international law which may be described as 'objective' because they may be applied to States which have not been asked to approve them or even grant them recognition. There is always a possible theoretical explanation which avoids resorting to the notion of an 'objective' applicability (for example, the hypothesis of tacit consent). Once there are international institutions as 'disinterested third parties' to verify the existence of a situation, it becomes 'objective', that is to say applicable to third States with or without their consent. But the political interests of States are so far involved in this that the international community can make only very slow progress in this direction. The most straightforward examples of the existence of situations which can affect States even without their consent are concerned with territorial status. Cf. the dissenting opinion of Judge MacNair in the Case of the International Statute for South West Africa (Reports 1950, p. 154), also references quoted in the Report of the Committee of Jurists on the Status of the Aaland Islands, Official Journal of the League of Nations, October 1920, special supp. No. 3.

Certain opinions of the International Court of Justice would suggest that when a situation is brought about with the consent of the majority of the members of the international community which does not interfere with the rights of other States, this situation applies to them too. This is what the International Court of Justice said concerning the international personality of the United Nations (Advisory Opinion, 11 April, 1949, on Reparation for injuries suffered in the service of the United Nations. Reports 1949, p. 178):

'The Court's opinion is that fifty States, representing the vast majority of the members of the international community, have the power, in conformity with international law, to bring into being an entity possessing objective international personality, and not merely personality recognised by them alone . . .'

(iii) Nineteenth-century diplomatic history shows that even before proper international organisations had been created, there appeared to be a *de facto* government composed of the great powers. This was the Concert of Europe. The solutions imposed on the smaller powers by the Concert of Europe doubtless caused them to protest, and many governments only agreed to those solutions because they were weak. But this is not the deciding factor; the vanquished only agree to peace treaties because they are weak, and they often protest. The truth of the matter is that these *de facto* governments meet an urgent need and it would be a pity if the law refused to take account of it. Since the Concert of Europe there have always been *de facto* governments, except when they have been legally consecrated in the form of an international organisation. During the 1914–18 War a genuine international *de facto* government was set up by the Allies; it was continued after the war by the Conference of Ambassadors. There are serious drawbacks to these *de facto* governments, and no doubt they are only tolerable in the absence of an international organisation capable of discharging their functions. They are a sign that an international community exists.

The continuity of international *de facto* governments throws special light on the emergence of international organisations. The latter are always founded by treaty, or at least with the express consent of the member States, but this really seems to be recognition that such an institution was unavoidable rather than a genuinely free act of will. Moreover, the powers which have to be granted to international organisations, and those which have to be accorded to them in practice, make serious inroads into any principle of international law based on State sovereignty. They will be examined in more detail in Part Three of this work; but the creation of international organisations introduces the distinction between governors and governed in international society which tends in this way to form itself into a 'group'. This revolutionary transformation is a slow process; international law moves gradually further away from the conception of co-ordination.

§ 2 THE SIZE OF THE INTERNATIONAL COMMUNITY

(A) *In general*

(*a*) *From the geographical point of view.* The international community must historically and logically be universal.

Today all States belong to the international community; reference to the brief historical outline earlier in this book shows how recent a development this is.

But logic also insists on this universal quality, in that to postulate an international community with general rules which nevertheless excludes certain States, is really to refuse to recognise the excluded States. It is difficult to see what would be the basis for co-existence with the groups excluded from the community.

Franz von Liszt, who has examined the problem of the international community in a particularly interesting way, has carried this to its logical conclusion (*Le droit international*, French trans., p. 5). He considers that besides the States who are full members of the international community, there are semi-civilised States, which only belong to the international community in so far as they are bound by treaty to civilised States. Moreover, 'in their relations with the "semi-civilised States" in matters not covered by treaty, and also in all their relations with uncivilised countries, the international community may use its *de facto* power; it is only bound by moral principles, based on Christian and humanitarian sentiments.'

The universal nature of the international community is therefore a reflection of the fact that the whole of the earth's surface is divided into territories administered by States or groups of States.

(*b*) *Its legal consequences.* The international community finds expression in the rules which allocate functions between the States; it makes co-existence possible. In the present state of international relations this is undoubtedly its major importance. But what else does it imply?

Would not an international organisation, representing nearly all the States, be able to claim to be an organisation of the international community? If the question is put in this general way, the jurist, in the present state of international relations, can only answer in the negative. Put in terms of the theory of *de facto* international government, the answer is certainly affirmative. Since it is sometimes possible for an international government to be set up by a meeting of the principal powers, *a fortiori* this must be possible by a meeting of the great majority of the States. Put even more precisely, does an international organisation, which includes the great majority of States, enjoy certain privileges as representing the international community? The answer seems to be yes. This is the essence of the opinion of the International Court of Justice that the United Nations has an international personality to be recognised even by non-member States.

We may well ask whether the legal order of an international community does not include rules other than those allocating functions between States. The term 'international community' is very often used in a much looser sense that it is here. 'International community' is used to imply not only that States are united in a legal order which divides up jurisdiction between them, but also by a common civilisation, common views on the fundamental principles of the life of nations, etc. One would then mean by 'international community' that a number of rules of international law which simply limit the exercise of State jurisdictions were common to all States. There are certainly rules of international law common to all States which fix the conditions within which States exercise their jurisdiction, and these may be considered as part of the legal order established by the international community.

But these rules are not as binding as the first; their purpose is not to lay down the conditions of co-existence, but to reflect a further step in international relations, a common standard for civilised behaviour. These rules are naturally less advanced than may be desirable, and it would be a grave mistake to manipulate general terms and vague conceptions into giving these common rules a strength they do not possess.

On the other hand, a legal rule, while it is not universal, may often be common to several States with similar cultures, internal structure and economic and social philosophies. One may therefore accept a certain amount of regionalism in international law. But regional systems (for example on the American continent) differ from a universal system in size and also by the kind of rules which form their constitution. General international law, which is the expression of the international community, is primarily made up of rules governing the co-existence of all States, that is, rules determining State jurisdiction; regional systems, apart from details concerning these same rules, are mainly rules concerning the conditions for exercising jurisdiction.

(B) *The co-existence of communist and non-communist systems*

Co-existence between communist countries (or similar régimes) and non-communist countries, poses several problems, the most important and most difficult of which are not legal questions; the problem, must be examined with this in mind. The existence of communist countries is not the only threat to world unity today, but it is the most typical. Is an 'international community' compatible with the existence of these States? If it is not so there can be no international community. It is impossible to apply to these States the radical solution of the nineteenth-century authors regarding 'uncivilised countries' and to exclude them from the international community.

Two preliminary remarks are necessary.

There can be no question of an intellectual exercise constructing a theory based on personal views about the communist system, and then proceeding to see whether or not the communist countries, so defined, will fit into it. The question is whether the two systems, communist and non-communist, as they are and not as we should like them to be, have compatible attitudes towards co-existence within the international community. The communist and non-communist views of co-existence must roughly coincide if co-existence is to be possible. Communist and non-communist views must be compared with each other.

The USSR and some of the popular democracies are members of the United Nations and other international organisations, and have taken an active part in their institutions. But this does not solve the problem. Normally an international organisation is the expression of a society which already exists, which gives it its purpose; but an organisation can be too deeply and irrevocably divided to constitute a genuine society.

There is no definitive, long-term answer. Not only does international law evolve, as we have said, but Marxist (or so-called Marxist) conceptions are liable to the most rapid shifts and changes of front. Soviet conceptions of international law cannot be divorced from the general theory of Soviet law; there can be no separation of law and politics in a system where law is the expression of the interests of the ruling class.

The question can only be answered, therefore, in its present context; the attitudes of the USSR are the most typical, and these will be used here.

The official Soviet attitude to economic, political and human relations within the Soviet system is based on fundamentally different

principles from those of other systems, indeed is positively opposed
to them. Moreover, the Marxist view of the way in which the so-
called 'capitalist' countries must develop means that their interests
must conflict and these conflicts will sometimes take the form of
international wars. Finally, the balance of forces in the world, at
least until very recently, has not been in favour of the communist
countries.

Since the purpose of international law, like municipal law, is to
protect the ruling class, the Soviet attitude has been one of distrust
and hostility to outside intervention. The personality and sovereignty
of the State, therefore, occupies a central position in Soviet doctrine.
International organisations can be accepted, and may even be
endowed with a personality, but since they are based on treaties, in
the last resort they are created by the will of the State. The individual,
for the moment, has a very small place in international relations. To
defend its interests, the dominant class must have absolute control of
the State's external relations. International relations between the
Soviet countries and the rest are almost exclusively indirect relations,
inter-State relations.

The control of direct relations between citizens of Soviet countries
and foreigners, and the absence of foreign business houses in these
countries, simplifies several problems which loom large in relations
between other States.

The role of international law then is principally to allocate jurisdiction to the States, but it is not to lay down common rules for
communist and non-communist countries for the exercise of that
jurisdiction. Soviet doctrine does not normally make use of the notion
of an international community, but prefers to discuss the matter in
dialectical terms.

Here are some typical passages from I. D. Lévine translated and quoted by Ivo
Lapenna (*Conceptions Soviétiques de droit public*, p. 234): 'From the point of
view of formal logic, the opposition between sovereignty and international law
cannot reveal the true, dialectical relationship between them. In one sense international law means a negation of sovereignty, but this negation is dialectical
and does not abolish sovereignty. It only serves as the basis for a higher synthesis
of sovereignty and international law.

'. . . Thus the interests of class domination personified in the State require that
parallel to, and in strict liaison with the consolidation of sovereignty, international
law should be recognised as one of the indispensable means for consolidating
sovereignty . . .

'Sovereignty does not mean the right to override international law . . . If the
State relies on sovereignty in order to violate international law, it loses by that
same token the right to appeal to international law to justify its sovereignty.'

It would seem that on the whole the USSR envisages the place of States in a system of international law in a way not very different from other countries. But the fact that communist countries belong to the international community lessens the possibility of international rules becoming universal; many of them are in fact only valid between non-communist countries, who agree that the way they exercise their sovereignty shall be brought under stricter control.

An international community which includes the Soviet States, therefore, is likely to have an increasing number of rules which are valid only between a number of particular States.

Of course, this is only true as long as the communist countries are not in a dominant position in the world. If they were, a marked development in international law would be a means of winning over the proletariat and the position would be completely changed.

Among the problems hardly ever posed in Soviet law today is the relationship between international law and municipal law, in particular the possibility of a conflict between them, and those which affect individual rights.

In the theory of the sources of international law, there is not much difference between the account given by Soviet authors and that given in other countries. It is clear, however, that Soviet authors are encouraged to stress the *voluntary* nature of international commitments. Treaties are the most important source of international relations, and they must be very carefully drafted. As regards custom, there is no doubt that the Soviet States would not allow a custom to grow up to which they were not a party and which might be turned against them. On the whole Soviet authors express serious reservations about the general principles of law, both on account of their vagueness and their origin in municipal law.

Section III

MUNICIPAL LAW AND INTERNATIONAL LAW

§ 1 A COMPARISON BETWEEN MUNICIPAL LAW AND INTERNATIONAL LAW

Few questions have given rise to so much theoretical discussion as the conflict between international law and municipal law. It has no place in an elementary work. We shall simply show briefly their common and their conflicting features, using the terms analysed in the Introduction.

(A) *Their points of conflict*
The expression 'municipal law' is ambiguous, and this ambiguity, for a long time hidden, has become obvious today.

Here 'municipal' is co-terminous with 'national', and we are concerned with the differences between international law which applies to the international community, and the various systems of law which apply to each of the countries belonging to that community. This brings out an elementary difference between national systems of law and international law: the geographical area each covers.

'Municipal' does not only mean 'national' however; municipal law is the law of a society organised as a 'group' with differentiated organs and powers; 'international' law is the law of an unorganised society. The two systems of law are therefore structurally different.

These differences may not be inter-related. The difference of structure is certainly most important, but it may gradually diminish as international society becomes more organised.

(a) Structural differences. The fact that international society has no legislator, judge or government is obviously important; in particular the absence of a legislator means that the drafting of rules of law and their formal sources are different from municipal law. As will be seen in the following chapter, the importance of custom and the conventional form of written rules are typical of international law.

But the differences must not be exaggerated. There is no reason to ascribe different material sources of law to international law and municipal law; one cannot deify the State in external relations, and then subject it to law in internal relations. Whatever is held to be the material source of law (social-ethical necessity, etc.), that source is the same for both internal and external relations. Municipal law differs from international law in very many respects, but they are technical differences.

The difference is therefore not absolute; there are many examples of municipal law using similar methods to international law, and vice versa.

During the nineteenth century some people in western States considered that the State had only limited authority to deal with relations between workers and employers. Since then, labour law has developed on similar lines to international law: the importance of custom and treaty law (collective labour conventions), recourse to arbitration, prohibition of the use of force, use of indirect pressure, distinction between legal conflicts and non-legal conflicts, etc.

On the other hand, since international organisations have grown up, a type of legislative process has made its appearance in international law; it is possible to talk of a 'municipal' law of international organisations (rules of procedure, direct jurisdiction over international officials or users, p. 263).

(b) *Differences of extent.* International law applies to intercourse between States, whose number varies according to which rule is being considered: sometimes between all the States in the world, sometimes only a certain number of them, with a minimum of two. The rules therefore apply to the legal systems of several States. Municipal law, on the other hand, applies only within a single State.

The primacy of international law over municipal law is based on this simple fact: international rules reflect interests superior to national ones; and the States concerned have agreed to recognise this.

(B) *Their points of contact*

The features common to municipal and international law are mainly due to the fact that all branches of law have the same material sources and the same kind of techniques. In societies which apply both municipal law and international law the two are closely intermingled; both sets of rules are couched in the same language, and they are both applied either by the same men, or by men with similar training.

Public international law has been to a large extent built up from notions borrowed from various systems of municipal law, especially from those which have had a world-wide influence. In passing from municipal law to international law these notions usually undergo some change to take account of the special nature of international relations and the influence other systems of municipal law might have. In international law one may well come across notions like abuse of rights, the effect of juristic acts, abuse of power, nullity of an act, etc. This does not mean that these notions were simply borrowed from one particular system of municipal law, but they are often derived from one. This is no doubt why article 9 of the Statute of the International Court of Justice reminds those who appoint the judges that 'persons to be elected should individually possess the qualifications required, but also that in the body as a whole the representation of the main forms of civilisation and of the principal legal systems of the world should be assured.'

Quite another matter is whether the influence of municipal law on international law can properly come about through direct and deliberate borrowing. It is not certain whether an international judge has the right to borrow from municipal laws a principle which is common to several States and apply it to inter-State relations. This question will be examined in the following chapter in connection with the sources of law.

§ 2 RELATIONS BETWEEN THE TWO SYSTEMS

(A) *Reference back*

It often happens that legal system A borrows a notion or a rule from legal system B. There is then said to be reference back from system A to system B.

Thus, in putting Catholic places of worship at the disposition of the ministers of the Catholic faith, the French law on the separation of Church and State refers back to canon law; only canon law can say whether a person is a properly instructed minister of the Church; a conflict between several ministers is settled by administrative law by reference to canon law.

There are many cross-references from municipal law to international law, and vice versa. For instance French law provides special protection for foreign heads of States; it refers to international law to determine which are foreign States, and to the constitutional law of those States to determine who are their heads of State. Article 21 of the Treaty of 18 April, 1951, setting up the European Coal and Steel Community, lays down that the Assembly of that organisation shall be composed of delegates chosen by the parliaments; it refers to the constitutional law of the member States to decide which organs are the parliaments.

(B) *Reception*

The rules of international law bind States; even those which create rights and duties for the benefit or at the expense of private persons bind those organs of State which will be chiefly responsible for enforcing them.

But the duties assumed by the State may be formulated in various ways. Before the State contracts an engagement there is in existence a given body of juridical rules forming its municipal law. Does the State then simply contract an obligation to modify its system or does the contract itself modify it automatically?

This must turn in one sense on the interpretation of the agreement, but though very simple in principle, it is very delicate in practice. A State may quite explicitly agree to take steps to enforce an agreement whose terms are couched in general terms. For example: 'The

States signatory to the present treaty undertake to take all steps necessary for the suppression of the consumption of diacetyl-morphine.' This text does not *ipso facto* suppress the consumption of diacetylmorphine within a State; it simply lays upon the competent organs of each State the obligation to take those measures necessary (legislation, enforcement) to suppress the consumption of diacetyl-morphine. This type of agreement allows a reasonable delay for putting it into effect; at the same time it is sufficiently flexible to allow each State to frame its internal regulations to suit its own institutions. In many circumstances it would be impossible to go further than this because of the need to set up or abolish complicated legal provisions and enforcement machinery.

Sometimes, in American terminology, these engagements are said to be 'self-executing'. The situation is exactly comparable to the provision sometimes found in municipal law for making regulations under an Act.

Other engagements are drafted so that they may be immediately effective. This is the case in law-making treaties with a most favoured nation clause, which confers on the nationals of a foreign State all the advantages and privileges already conferred on nationals of other foreign States, generally in matters relating to the position of foreigners.

Here there is no technical obstacle to prevent the direct and im-mediate application of the treaty; the administrative authorities, private persons, and above all the courts can apply it without any further steps being necessary. There is however one necessary for-mality: the proper publication of the international engagement in accordance with the constitutional, legislative or administrative rules laid down by municipal law.

Yet, in this case it may well be that instead of publication meant simply for the information of those concerned (if necessary by an international organ, cf. French decree, 14 March, 1953), a complex procedure may be required involving the interposition of a State authority between the terms of the treaty and those affected by it.

We shall use the word 'reception' for the procedure whereby an international agreement is made applicable to administrative authorities other than those charged with external relations, the courts and private persons, provided that it goes beyond the simple form-ality of providing for publication. Hence, when a municipal system requires 'reception' defined in this way, it reflects that hostility which primary groups have to allowing direct intercourse with an element outside the group (explained at length in the Introduction). Reception formalities are generally to be found at a certain phase in international relations. At the present moment many States do not have reception formalities; the national authorities only insist on simple publication—and not always that (cf. France, Decree 14 March, 1953).

This question has been pointlessly complicated by all the theories which make an absolute distinction between municipal law and international law; if, in fact, you postulate two totally unconnected systems, there will always have to be reception for a rule to pass from one system to the other; then, in order to reconcile theory with practical necessity one has to say two things simultaneously: that reception transforms the juridical nature of the rule, and also that reception can be tacit.

Another aspect of these problems is that the application of treaties often involves the courts of a country. Different political systems have very different conceptions of the role of the judiciary, especially in public affairs. The constitutional law of each country defines the role of the courts regarding the rules of international law. *The problem must be treated not so much as the relations between international law and municipal law, but as the relations between the judiciary and the executive.*

An international convention, even when published in accordance with municipal legislation, remains an international convention; it may be full of specifically international clauses; for example concerning the conditions for reciprocal treatment or litigation; the rules may be differently interpreted in different countries without the jurisprudence of a supreme court to unify them. When political interests are involved the intervention of national judges may lead to consequences which they are not in a position to appreciate.

The prudent attitude of the courts is therefore understandable, even if it is open to criticism (especially in France where the civil courts are only prepared to interpret treaties concerning private law, and the administrative courts categorically refuse to do so at all, so that interpretation is left to the Ministry of Foreign Affairs).

(C) *Conflict between municipal law and international law*

Assuming an affirmative reply to the two questions just examined, that international rules retain their international character even when they are applied by the judge, and that the judge accepts that he has the right to interpret them, should he hold that international law takes precedence over municipal law when they conflict?

International law is superior to any municipal rule, even a constitutional law. Here again, it depends on the constitution of a particular country whether a judge is empowered to depart from the constitution or the law, and recognise the primacy of certain rules of law.

This will depend on the traditions of each country and practice is not necessarily based on logic.

In England, for instance, where courts deal with many cases involving maritime law, a famous maxim, 'International law is part of the law of the land', has always authorised British judges to apply international customary law directly; the British judge is also prepared to give preference to an international custom, except when it would mean overriding an Act of Parliament. The new provisions of the French Constitution of 1946 (articles 26–28) laid down the principle that treaties 'take precedence over laws'. Parliament cannot modify rules contained in a treaty by subsequent legislation and in the event of conflict between a treaty and a law the judge must give preference to the treaty.

In practice judges avoid stressing conflicts between a treaty and a law, and when they apply a treaty instead of a law it is usually on the grounds that they are interpreting the real intention of the legislator.

CHAPTER FOUR

The Formal Sources of International Law

The formal sources of international law are international conventions, international custom and the general principles of law. This enumeration comes from documents of great theoretical and historical importance whose purpose was to set up international jurisdictions: the XIIth Hague Convention, 19 October, 1907 (not put into effect) establishing an International Prize Court, the Statutes of the Permanent Court of International Justice and the International Court of Justice (article 38).

It is supported from several other sources: all jurisprudence—treaties and individual acts—decisions of various international institutions like international courts and tribunals. An example from this last group is the Administrative Decision No. 2 of the German-American Mixed Claims Commission (Witenberg, *Commission Mixte de réclamations germano-americaine*, Paris, 1926, p. 12).

A study of the formal sources of international law must then be based on this list. Two points must be born in mind:

(1) Each source must be separate and distinct from the others; difficulties which arise will be dealt with in turn under each head, in particular under the general principles of law;

(2) The list must be exhaustive; the question whether other sources of international law should be mentioned raises another question: are there *original* sources of international law and *derived* sources? The answer must be in the affirmative: custom is the original fundamental source from which all the others are derived. But there remains the question of the relative importance of the different sources of international law: international agreements are, nowadays, by far the most abundant source of international public law. We shall therefore take custom, treaties and the general principles of law in turn; in an annex we shall examine the other sources derived from these.

The order in which these sources are dealt with is no reflection on their relative importance. The first obvious step when examining a question is to refer to the *written law*, that is to the treaties, and only afterwards to deal with the body of *unwritten law*, that is custom and the general principles of law. It is in fact rare to find unwritten laws which cannot be over-ridden by written laws; it is therefore simpler to refer to the written sources in the first place.

The problem of conflict of rules between different formal sources cannot be settled by giving systematic preference to one or other source; it depends on many complex considerations which will not be dealt with in an elementary study like this. A hierarchy may be established by convention between the various formal sources for the use of a particular court, for cases falling within a well-defined branch of international relations, such as the XIIth Hague Convention already quoted.

Section I

CUSTOMARY RULES

§ 1 DEFINITION AND BASIS OF CUSTOMARY LAW

A customary rule grows out of general practice (consuetudo) in which that rule is recognised and observed (opinio juris).

There are therefore two elements in customary law: the one material (repetition), and the other intentional (recognition of the rule).

This definition has a very important negative aspect: *A customary rule is not formulated in a precise and authenticated form: it can only be deduced by building up a body of precedents.*

In more advanced countries (except those influenced by the United Kingdom) juridical rules are authenticated by a written text, whose terms taken together constitute the rule in question. To anyone accustomed to modern written law, customary law seems strange: any person who invokes, applies or discusses a customary law can re-state it by using precedents.

This difference should not be exaggerated. Once a customary rule has been formulated in clear, incisive terms it remains virtually unchanged. On the contrary, a written rule is rarely so clear that those who apply it have no chance to elaborate it and enlarge upon it.

A customary rule comes from the individual conscience as the expression of a legal obligation imposed by social life. It is formulated by people acting sometimes individually, sometimes in an official capacity. It is not done in the abstract, divorced from circumstances; it is formed in a strictly legal context. The recognition of a customary rule is called a 'precedent'. Every legal system establishes its own usage as to when an act constitutes a precedent, and in particular who can set a precedent. *Customary rules are therefore made unsystematically, varying with the social context.*

Customary law is more uncertain in its content than written law, but it is less rigid. More precisely, customary law develops more easily than written law. Written law, like customary law, may be modified through judicial interpretation; it is also liable to radical changes from time to time through legislation. In some societies, especially at the present day, this happens at frequent intervals.

The real difference between a customary rule and a written law is that a customary rule appears as a spontaneous inorganic acknowledgement of a legal obligation without passing through formalised machinery of government. The importance of customary law therefore varies considerably from one society to another and from one epoch to another, and affects external and internal relations differently.

As has already been shown (Introduction p. 25) customs appear in international relations as soon as there is a genuine international society; but the States, which have secured a quasi-monopoly of law-making internally, play an important part in making customary rules in international law.

§ 2 PRECEDENTS IN INTERNATIONAL LAW

Precedents to establish an international customary rule must have a special origin, content and form.

(1) *Precedents can only be established by organs, institutions and persons normally engaged in international relations.*—We have said that on the whole precedents must not be made in the abstract, but must be elaborated in a definite legal context. They are laid down by persons with jurisdiction in that particular field.

Precedents in international law are therefore created chiefly by organs of State, in particular by those responsible for international relations: heads of States, governments, diplomatic services. Nowadays, there are new organs of State participating in international relations (*infra*, p. 166) and we may expect them to establish precedents. Decisions of municipal courts are regarded as precedents when those courts have traditionally been prepared to apply international customary law.

International institutions or organisations can also create international precedents. This has long been recognised in the case of international arbitrators, courts and jurisdictions; it is now extended to the expanding organs of international organisations, particularly those with a universal competence.

It is natural that individuals should not create precedents since as such they do not play any direct part in international relations. Legal experts may do so, in so far as their opinions make it possible to weigh the importance and significance of precedents; article 38 (2) of the Statute of the International Court of Justice refers to the opinion of legal experts in the list of formal sources of law.

The exclusion of individuals from this list is not, as is sometimes suggested, *yet another* sign of the hostility of international law towards private persons, but simply a reflection of the fact that individuals as such do not have international competence. This is inevitable, as M. de Visscher (*Théories et Réalités*, p. 182) recalls resignedly: 'Every international custom is created by power . . . there is no customary law with which individuals have so little to do as international customary law.' Of course, if we turn from inter-State relations to a society outside State authority, it is the persons making up that society who would be called upon, if need be, to create precedents (cf. *supra.*, p. 27); for a discussion of canon law, whose evolution is extremely interesting from this point of view, see Wehrle, *La Coutume dans le droit canonique* (Paris, Sirey, 1928).

(2) *A precedent must be based on recognition of a juridical rule.*—A juridical rule is invoked as a means of provoking a decision on law or facts.

It has been argued that a precedent may be only a personal opinion. This contention seems to be based on a misunderstanding: a precedent is always created by a particular human being, with human imperfections, including the ability to make mistakes. But a person creating a precedent never feels he is expressing a personal opinion; the precedent is a *recognition* and assumes the objective existence of a rule.

It is essential to know whether the juridical rule implied in a precedent is regarded as universal or only valid between certain States. Let us suppose it is held to be *universal*; if it appears in enough cases spread over the whole world, we may assume the existence of a universal custom, *even if it has to be applied in a country where there is no precedent for that custom*. This is accepted in many judgments, as well as in article 38 (b) of the Statute of the International Court of Justice: 'International custom as evidence of a general practice accepted as law.'

This is a very important point; it shows that theoretically a customary rule does not depend on tacit consent; and that international law is not entirely voluntary (cf. p. 101). In practical terms this makes it possible to apply customary rules to new States.

If a rule is held to be valid only between certain States, there must be precedents affecting each of those States.

This requirement comes from the notion of regional or non-universal custom; it does not change the nature of a custom nor make it any easier of proof, for the existence of a universal custom is not lightly admitted. The International Court of Justice clearly stated in its judgment of 20 November, 1950, Asylum Case: 'The party who invokes a custom of this nature must prove that it is constituted in such a way as to be binding on the other party' (cf. Suz. Bastid, *La Jurisprudence de la Cour Internationale de Justice*, RCADI, 1951, p. 628).

(3) *Precedents can take many forms*—unilateral declarations, court decisions, material acts whose motivation is in some way made public, conventional acts, etc. The only factor indirectly governing the form of precedents is that the motives of the act shall be obvious. In fact the authors of a precedent, be they representatives of States or of an international organisation, may act from motives other than legal obligation: courtesy, personal interest, pursuit of a general or particular political objective.

An unmotivated action can only create a precedent if the circumstances which surrounded it clearly indicate that there was implicit recognition of a legal rule.

We shall give two examples.

It is difficult to rely on a precedent of abstention. By legislation or the practice of their courts, States abstain from asserting criminal jurisdiction over foreigners responsible for a collision on the open sea in which a national has suffered damage. Is this abstention based on the belief that there was a rule making abstention obligatory? The question was discussed in the famous Lotus Case (PCIJ, A/9).

Another example is found in treaty practice. A rule is written into a treaty (which has nothing to do with codification); this rule does not exist in law outside the treaty. Then the same rule appears in nearly all treaties over a particular period of time. It is then found that this provision, which has become a 'common clause', is applied even when it does not appear in treaties. Can we then assume that a customary rule has grown out of precedents contained in treaties?

The answer must be affirmative if there seems to be firm belief in the objective existence of the rule (On this matter see G.-F. von Martens, *Précis du Droit des Gens Moderns de l'Europe*, 1831, p. 43.)

§3 customs

When does custom begin? When does it end?

(1) The repetition of precedents is generally held to be of major importance in a custom.

But what does repetition mean?

Different legal systems recognise different degrees of repetition; there are immemorial customs, thirty years' customs, etc.

In the absence of any formal indication the amount of repetition necessary depends on the authority and the value of the precedents. Thus, in international law there must be sufficient precedents to indicate a general practice over a given period.

If a precedent is an act recognising a legal rule, and if several precedents are needed to make a rule, then logically there can be no first precedent, and consequently no customary rule.

But several other factors must be taken into account.

A precedent never stands by itself; the first recognition of a customary rule has inevitable social repercussions. If there is a reaction against recognition the precedent is annulled: if in favour it is confirmed. Repetition reflects the continuity of the rule in a discontinuous series of precedents.

Customs can only grow up in a stable society. A long-established custom can withstand contradiction, but a newly-established custom is vulnerable.

If a State refuses to recognise a custom, one of two things may happen, depending on the circumstances: either it does not come into being at all, or it is established, but only regionally, and it does not apply to the State which refuses recognition (ICJ, Asylum Case, Judgment, 20 November, 1950, Reports, p. 277).

On the other hand customs grow *progressively*. Just as the authority of precedents varies according to the *representative* character of the person who enunciates them, so customs vary in authority. Anyone who holds that the notion of a doubtful or uncertain custom is a contradiction in terms denies the existence of customary law.

(2) Customs are better established when they are based on numerous precedents and when they are embodied in a fixed formula. They then lose their dynamism and their flexibility, and the problem of their codification arises.

'Codification' means two different things.

Scientific codification is the theoretical work of legal experts, who seek to state customary rules clearly, soberly and systematically; it has a purely informative value. But even private codifications may influence future official codifications; well-phrased formulae suggested in a private codification may well be adopted.

Some private codifications in international law, such as those of Fiore and Bluntschli, are quite often quoted.

Legal codification is the work of the competent authorities. It consists in formalising customary rules into either a law, in the case of municipal law, or an agreement in the case of international law. Codification changes the character of legal rules: their binding force depends on the formal source on which they are based. Nowadays codification is done in *treaty form* so it only binds States parties to the treaty. It confirms existing customs, but also modifies and adds to them. This is the practical result of the rule according to which treaty and custom are of equal standing, and treaty can modify custom, and vice versa.

There have been several attempts to codify sections of international law, particularly the Hague Conferences on the laws and customs of war. The League of Nations (Codification Conference, 1930) as well as the United Nations (Resolutions of 11 December, 1946 and 3 November, 1948, setting up the International Law Commission). Such attempts have always been the occasion for scientific work of great value, but so far they have only been moderately successful, because formal treaty-making allows political considerations to override legal considerations; unsuccessful codification weakens the customary rules more than it strengthens them.

4 CUSTOM IN INTERNATIONAL LAW

Despite the growth of treaty-making, custom undoubtedly occupies a prominent place in international law. Even today custom still dominates whole sections of international law: maritime law, international responsibility, jurisdictional privileges and immunities of States and their representatives.

It is not true that the number of customary rules is diminishing; at the beginning of the nineteenth century, when modern international law was expanding, authors did not attribute the importance to custom which it is given in modern doctrine (cf. for example H. Wheaton, *Elements of International Law*, 4th Ed., vol. I, p. 25). This was an unreasonable but understandable reflection of the hostility to natural law which grew up as a reaction against the excesses of the eighteenth century.

The relative *volume* of customary rules is clearly diminishing but custom still occupies a central position in international law, in the sense that it is the source of the most important rules of international law. In fact the obligatory force of the other sources of law (treaties and the general principles of law) rests on custom.

It alone can be the source of fundamental notions; it alone, in the present state of international society, can bring about a system of universal law, because there is probably no treaty which covers all the States in the world.

Nevertheless, we must not look to custom to work profound changes in international law in the future; this is far more likely to come about through the development of international organisations and the new formal sources attached to them.

Section II

INTERNATIONAL AGREEMENTS

§ 1 GENERAL NOTIONS

(A) *Definition and vocabulary*

The subjects of international law, principally the States, are bound by agreements registering their common wills.

International agreements, like all juristic acts, are of two kinds:

(1) The instrument (*instrumentum*) which embodies the engagements, in the form of written documents;

(2) The legal engagements which vary in purpose and intrinsic character.

The vocabulary used in international practice is usually taken from the nature of the instrument, or from the circumstances under which the instruments were drawn up. The historian or the text-writer may derive much useful information from the use of terms like convention, declaration, protocol, treaty; but they are not on the whole important to the jurist except in so far as the form of the agreement affects its interpretation. (Ambatielos Case, preliminary objection ICJ, 1 July, 1952, Judgment and dissenting opinions, in particular that of M. Basdevant.)

It is commonly held that there are no tests of form for the validity

of international agreements. This is only partly true; there are tests
as regards the persons who can conclude agreements and certain
rules regarding approval. These rules must be observed.

There is a procedure for concluding agreements as for any other
juristic act; one State may even have several different procedures.
In the present state of international law, there is broadly speaking a
distinction between formal and informal procedures. It would be
useful if there were recognised terms to distinguish between these
two. The following will be used here: the term 'agreement' will be
used for all undertakings which a subject of international law can
enter into; the term 'treaty' will be reserved for formal undertakings
concluded by States, and the term informal agreement for informal
undertakings.

(B) *Principal problems*

In this brief examination we shall deal only with problems essential
to the law of international agreements concluded by States (for concordats cf. p. 191 and for international organisations p. 240). There
are three problems: methods for concluding agreements (§ 2), the
connection between agreements and the constitutional law of States
(§ 3), and the possible modifications to an agreement while in
operation (§ 4).

The method for concluding agreements is the most important
aspect of international agreements, for it is essential both in theory
and practice to know how international agreements are made. This
point will therefore be treated in some detail. More difficult questions
concerning conflicting agreements or the revision of international
agreements will only be touched upon. It may therefore be useful if
we mention some of the main points.

One of the outstanding features of our time is the extraordinary
proliferation of written undertakings; but it is utterly haphazard.
In law the whole system of international agreements and their binding force comes from international customary rules which are uncertain, often disputed and do not provide that simplicity to a general
theory of international engagements which we—mistakenly—expect
from written law.

We shall only mention here the principal contradictions in the
system of international agreements.

As juristic acts, international agreements are classified according
to the methods by which they are concluded rather than by their
object. There are commercial treaties, peace treaties, boundary
treaties, law-making treaties, arbitration treaties, guarantee treaties,

etc., but although these are diplomatic terms they do not fit into legal categories. There have been various attempts to classify treaties; one classified them into law-making treaties and particular treaties, to solve such problems as the interpretation of treaties and the effects of State succession. But in international law there is no theory like that of 'contrats nommés' in civil law; international agreements are not divided into 'categories' according to the legal operations they give rise to.

Unfortunately the methods for making international agreements are, as will be seen (§ 2), changing rapidly.

The law of international agreements is formal rather than material, but it is not as formalistic as logically it should be.

International agreements are an expression of the will of States; if they bind the States they are also an expression of their sovereignty. But here again there is a serious contradiction. For the sake of order in international society some rules have to be established and some established rules have to be modified. To do the latter conflicts with State sovereignty. There are two forces at work. When they conclude agreements the sovereignty of States admits some concessions: the methods used for working out agreements, particularly concessions over form, reflect the need felt for some kind of real imposed legislation; but so far there has been no important change. As for revising agreements already entered into, international law remains as backward as ever: there is no peaceful procedure for the revision of international agreements except through the voluntary good sense of the governments concerned.

§ 2 PROCEDURE FOR THE CONCLUSION OF INTERNATIONAL AGREEMENTS

(A) *Drafting the text*

Apart from a few agreements concluded orally and recognised as valid in practice, nearly all international agreements are based on written texts, which are established in the course of discussions and meetings which constitute the 'negotiations'.

Negotiations vary greatly according to whether the agreement of many States, a few States or only two must be obtained. In the first case they entail an international conference properly so-called, in the last more or less direct 'conversations'. Negotiations generally involve conversations at all levels; experts, members of specialist committees, heads of delegations; these posts are nearly always held by officials, usually belonging to the Ministry of Foreign Affairs. Negotiations are therefore conducted on an administrative level. Sometimes, however, in the last stage, members of the governments of the States are called in to deal with the most difficult questions, or questions of particular political importance.

Whatever the details of the negotiations, there comes a moment when the texts are drawn up *ne varietur*. This moment is determined in one of two ways, one informal, the *parafe* (affixing the initials of the heads of delegations), the other formal, the *signature* (full signature of the heads of delegations). The parafe only represents definite consent, either to the form or the content, when it is a question of authenticating an annex to a main agreement; it may alternatively be used in the course of negotiations to authenticate an incomplete text or to gain time to arrange more formal signature.

In principle a person must be properly authorised to draft the text of a *treaty*. According to a long-established conception, the head of the State had the right to bind the State and he delegated powers to negotiate and sign. The authority of the delegates was confirmed by a document known as 'full powers'. They deposited this at the beginning of the negotiation. Today authority is simply communicated through the diplomatic channel. Nevertheless *treaties*, strictly speaking, are always signed by accredited plenipotentiaries of the heads of States and the preamble to a treaty usually mentions an 'exchange of their powers in due and proper form'.

In many States these formalities are conducted without reference to constitutional provisions; the French Constitution of 1875, for example, provided that 'the President shall negotiate treaties' (art. 8, L. 16 July, 1875), but he never did so except by delegation; the Constitution of 27 October, 1946, says he shall 'sign' treaties, but he has done so only in quite exceptional circumstances.

(B) *The effects of signature*

The effect of signature depends enormously on whether it is only to an agreement or to a treaty properly so-called. In the case of informal agreements the State has agreed to be bound by the mere fact of the signature. This is usually the signature of the Foreign Minister. But the extraordinary growth of informal agreements has given rise to widely different forms of procedure. They may be concluded by military authorities, members of governments not responsible for foreign affairs, etc. Informal agreements often take the form of an exchange of letters or notes; the agreement is therefore contained in a collection of documents.

It is very important to know what subjects can be dealt with by informal agreements. Constitutional law in most countries only deals with treaties in the full sense of the word. In others constitutional practice rather than law tries to lay down general directives on this point, but it is clear that the universal development of international relations is leading to the greatest confusion in the methods for concluding international engagements.

Even when they are signed, treaties in the full sense of the word are still no more than proposals. They may, however, have legal consequences if the signatories decide to apply them provisionally. This is often done on grounds of practical necessity, as happens with ordinary administrative contracts when a lengthy procedure is necessary before they become fully valid.

(C) *Authority to ratify, ratification, and exchange of instruments of ratification*

Only treaties properly so-called have to be ratified after they have been signed.

Ratification is the formality by which a State expresses its consent to bind itself by a treaty.

The meaning of ratification has changed: originally it was the control of a mandate by a mandatory; nowadays it only reflects the mutual desire for a delay for additional reflection before becoming completely committed, and also to allow each State to obtain support from organs which did not take part in the negotiations, particularly the political assemblies.

This definition of ratification implies that the right to ratify belongs to the person who is authorised to make the treaty (the treaty-making power). Constitutions, each in its own way, designate the organ or organs charged with this function: public opinion consulted by referendum, parliament, head of State. In some countries the constitution requires the participation of parliament and the head of the executive, at least for certain kinds of treaties.

In France, ratification is by a decree of the President of the Republic, but treaties in the following categories can only be authorised by law: treaties concerning international organisation, peace treaties, commercial treaties, treaties involving state finance, those concerning the personal status and property rights of Frenchmen abroad, those which modify the internal laws of France, and those which involve cession, exchange or annexation of territories.

Both in France and in other countries there are controversies over treaty rights contained in the national constitutions. As soon as the organ of the executive responsible for external relations considers that a treaty has been duly ratified, it proceeds to exchange or deposit the ratifications. A *procès-verbal* is drawn up and this act often stipulates the date when the treaty comes into force. Ratification does not legally bind a State up to the moment when it is deposited or exchanged.

But there remains the problem of the exact legal value of a treaty which has been ratified without fulfilling the requirements of the constitutional law of the State. This is known as imperfect ratification, and will be examined later (§ 3).

(D) *Registration and publication of international agreements*

Up to the end of the First World War, there were secret international agreements, and most of the major political agreements of the nineteenth century and the beginning of the twentieth century contained secret clauses. On the other hand States had to make internal provisions to enable the courts to apply the agreements where necessary; most countries published treaties in an official gazette.

Secret diplomacy was condemned during the First World War (1° of President Wilson's message of 8 January, 1918, known as the Fourteen Points), and the Covenant of the League of Nations provided that international agreements concluded by members of the League should be registered and published by the Secretariat under penalty of being unenforceable. This rule was interpreted to mean that unregistered agreements could not be invoked before the organs of the League. The United Nations Charter (article 102) makes the same stipulation.

(E) *Special features of multilateral law-making treaties*

Multilateral law-making treaties lay down general and objective rules of conduct applying to any number of States.

These agreements, like all international agreements, only bind those States which are parties to them; but their *object* is very often reflected in the *way they are prepared* and in the *form* they take; these have certain features in common with the procedure adopted by political assemblies in municipal law for laws and rules concerned with the operation of associations and corporate bodies.

These special features relate to the *negotiations* and the rule of State *equality* which in principle governs *conventional* procedure (the procedure for signing which reflects the freedom and equality of States and the procedure for allowing non-member States to *adhere* to an agreement). As against this States may limit the legislative character of agreements by specifying their *reservations*.

(a) In multilateral agreements, State equality is often purely formal during the course of the negotiations. When a text has to be drafted and there is no hope of giving satisfaction to all parties, it is often necessary to resort to majority voting; dissatisfied States are left with the remedy of refusing to sign the agreement as it stands. But this too is frequently a purely academic possibility. Particularly is this so if a draft agreement is being prepared by the assembly of an international organisation using this voting procedure; for instance in the case of some United Nations agreements, and the International Labour Conventions prepared by ILO.

(b) Certain draft agreements do not bear the signatures of States (the Labour Conventions and a number of other agreements). Even in the days of the League of Nations, the General Act for the Pacific Settlement of International Disputes was authenticated by the signature of the President and the Secretary General after a vote on the text in the League of Nations Assembly.

(c) Some multilateral agreements come into force in those States which have been parties to the negotiations and they are later joined by other States. The agreed text is not simply the result of bargaining between the original parties, but it has general objective features which from a material point of view stress its legislative character. States may become parties to an agreement already in force in two ways: deferred signature and adhesion. A State may be authorised to become party to an agreement by deferred signature: every agreement stipulates the States who may do this. By adhesion (in its present form) a State becomes party after notifying the State or organisation with whom the agreement has been deposited.

(d) States find it difficult to accept the restrictions imposed by the uniformity of multilateral conventions. To resist majority pressures they have devised a method for making reservations. At the moment of signature, ratification or adhesion, a State makes it known that it declines to be bound by one or more provisions in the agreement, or that it agrees to them only under certain conditions. A reservation breaks the unity of the legislative system established by the agreement and creates a special system for the State concerned. The Opinion of the ICJ, 28 May, 1951, relating to the validity of reservations to the Convention of 7 December, 1948 for the Prevention and Punishment of the Crime of Genocide, was that reservations were permissible if they were compatible with the aim and object of the agreement. In practice, to avoid difficulties, there is a tendency

towards making provision for reservations in actual treaties combined with international control of their validity.

§3 INTERNATIONAL AGREEMENTS AND STATE CONSTI-
TUTIONAL LAW

(A) *Practical reality*

The validity and forms of international agreements rest on customary rules of international law. It is however for the constitutional
law of each State to determine which organs are competent to negotiate, sign and ratify treaties.

There are two historical trends: the general and necessary development of international relations, and the growing complexity of the
structure of the State, in particular the growth of parliamentary
and democratic institutions. These two movements are not basically
contradictory, but there must be some compromise if they are not to
come into conflict. Constitutional rules and international practice
must sometimes each give way to the other to find a *modus vivendi*.

In monarchical systems, despite some famous precedents to the
contrary, there cannot be much difficulty when the treaty-making
power and law-making power are vested in the same person.

The emergence of political assemblies with legislative powers
makes it necessary to consider their role in treaty-making. If the
executive is all-powerful in external relations then external relations
are thrown out of balance with internal relations. Assemblies have
therefore acquired the power to ratify treaties in France since the
Constitution of 1791; in the United States it lies with the Senate as a
survival of local State powers.

For various reasons the executive seeks to evade parliamentary
control: assemblies are not well-informed about international life,
they work slowly and are often over-worked; if States are to conclude
agreements only with the consent of their legislative assemblies their
part in international life, especially the Great Powers, would be
seriously hampered. It is also convenient for the executive to have
an excuse for avoiding foreign policy debates which always weaken
rather than strengthen a State's international position. Federal States
are at an additional disadvantage: in international relations the
powers reserved to the local States are an enormous handicap to
federal States unless the demands of international life are given
precedence over local liberties.

Extra-constitutional procedures therefore grow up, for example, recourse to informal agreements, and various practices which compromise between the letter of constitutions which cannot be strictly applied and the practical demands of foreign policy. Parliaments know about these practices; but while jurists are unable to sympathise with the ambiguities of these compromises, they suit politicians very well, and it depends on the time, the circumstances, the men and the problems whether there are parliamentary outbursts or tacit surrenders.

There have been attempts to impose some order by constitutional reform, as in the Netherlands in 1952. But there are two difficulties which can never really be circumvented; first the slowness of parliamentary procedure, and parliament's lack of interest in non-political agreements; second the difficulty of subordinating international life to involved internal conditions for determining the validity of agreements. The only really satisfactory solution is still far off, except in the special cases described in Part Three: it entails a supra-national legislative power. Democracy, with its unavoidable discussions, must be transferred to an international plane by setting up representative assemblies within the international organisation.

(B) *Its legal interpretation*

There have been many attempts to find a satisfactory theoretical explanation of the relations between constitutional law and international law. They are outside the scope of this study.

We might point out many other aspects of the relations between treaties and constitutions: such as the fact that many treaties have defined or limited the constitutional status of certain States, for example, Germany in 1648, 1815, 1919...

Without being too abstract, the present situation might be summed up as follows:

(1) International customary rules lay down the law in a general way;

(2) International law authorises State constitutions to designate those organs competent to conclude international agreements;

(3) State constitutions, even the most advanced of them, generally contain only fragmentary provisions concerning international agreements. They implicitly allow international customary rules to be applied when they make good a gap in law. They therefore rarely contain provisions about the constitutional regularity of armistice

E

agreements or capitulations. International rules apply where the constitution is silent;

(4) Constitutions have an undoubted right to contain rules modifying the customary rules of international law, since these rules only make good gaps in the law. Informal agreements, therefore, bind States according to international law. But international law in no way prevents a constitution from forbidding representatives of that State to conclude informal agreements.

There are two limits to this freedom of action allowed by international law:

(a) If a constitution contained over-strict or over-complex provisions it would probably prevent the conclusion of any international agreement. Then the constitutional provisions would fall into disuse and would not be applied;

(b) In principle the executive power of a State is responsible towards foreign States for the proper observance of constitutional forms and procedures. This leaves room for a reasonable solution to the problem of imperfect ratification. A treaty concluded without observing constitutional procedure would not bind a State, but the rights of other parties to the agreement are not diminished, so long as the violation is not flagrant and the executive power of the State concerned has assured the other signatories to the treaty that the constitutional procedures have been duly observed. It is not possible, without fundamentally prejudicing all international relations, to allow a State continually to alter the interpretation of its constitution at the expense of the engagements it has concluded with its co-signatories.

Until recently discussion on this point nearly always concerned the relative rights of the executive and political assemblies over ratification. A new notion has emerged in connection with treaties for European integration. Some treaty proposals would involve amending national constitutions, and their ratification would be possible only after a previous amendment to the constitution. Their validity has been challenged in countries like France, whose constitution contains written national guarantees. But some constitutions have introduced a more elegant formula by allowing treaties to modify the constitution but at the same time requiring larger constitutional majorities for their ratification. This is the position in the Netherlands and in Denmark (cf. p. 233).

§4 INTERNATIONAL AGREEMENTS IN PRACTICE

Once in force agreements are liable to modifications affecting the areas to which they apply, their provisions and their duration. They may be modified in two ways: in application of the conventional provisions themselves, or as a result of external causes.

(A) *Modifications provided for in the agreements*

International agreements contain clauses concerning their duration, and particularly in the case of multilateral agreements, clauses concerning adhesion and denunciation. There is a tendency nowadays for agreements to contain provisions concerning revision. If there is no such provision revision is difficult. States who are parties to a convention can revise it in a different sense by a new convention; but if only ten out of twelve member States agree to conclude a new one, then to keep the two texts operating simultaneously in two different spheres of legal relations often leads to insurmountable difficulties.

Conventionally, procedures for revising an agreement are different and generally simpler than those for concluding one. In its most advanced form agreements may be modified by majority instead of unanimous decision; the minority States generally have the right to denounce the agreement, but in its old form it ceases to exist (postal conventions of the UPU). This formula is indispensable in practice for there to be revision of the charters of international organisations. It is from this point of view that some treaties in existence come closest to a legislative procedure.

(B) *Modifications not provided for in the agreements*

External events can suspend, paralyse or modify international agreements. There are no perfect answers in the present state of international law to the problems then raised; they can only be solved satisfactorily by using the legislative process, namely majority voting.

We are here concerned with conflicting agreements, with the effects of war and with the result of a vital change of circumstances.

When two contradictory treaties bind the same States, to reconcile them is a problem of interpretation; the clauses of the more recent agreement will be interpreted as abrogating, suspending or leaving intact the previous agreement. But if the two agreements do not apply to identical groups of States but to groups which contain common elements (one including the States A B C D, the other States A B E F) the conclusion of the subsequent agreement seriously affects the previous one. Contractually they are equally valid; but the execution of one constitutes a violation of the other. There is no satisfactory solution to this problem.

Does war abrogate or suspend agreements binding the adversaries? After much hesitation practice has recognised that some treaties are abrogated, some partially suspended (in relations between belligerents) and some remain in force. The problem can only be discussed in the context of the laws and customs of war; it often depends on the interpretation of the agreement in question.

Does a vital change of circumstances modify agreements in force? The question has often been put as a question of contract. International agreements would then be concluded with the tacit condition (*rebus sic stantibus*) that they lose their binding force in the event of a vital change of circumstances. This view should not be given more weight than it deserves. Every case must be taken on its own merits. If the parties agreed to such a clause, even by implication, it must be applied; but most agreements do not contain a clause of this kind. Defined in broader terms it might be regarded as a customary rule of the law of nations. Nevertheless, neither expert opinion, diplomatic practice nor jurisprudence have done much to settle the uncertainty. Change of circumstances can only be invoked if their balance is seriously altered. But there remain many outstanding points; for instance, should emphasis be laid on the *unforeseen* character of the change? on the dominant influence of a particular factor (since disappeared) when the obligation was entered into? We can argue in objective or subjective terms. Objectively we need to know what constitutes an obligation (purpose, cause, contract, circumstances attending the engagement). Subjectively, we have to consider whether a State can stir up sufficient tension to give the appearance that to uphold an obligation will endanger peace. It is not simply a question of why international agreements have ceased to be valid, but whether denunciation may be unilateral or only in virtue of a decision of all parties to the agreement. Each solution has its drawbacks. If you require the consent of all the parties it will probably be unworkable; if only one party suffices you leave the way open for unilateral denunciation of treaties. The solution is to submit the matter to a third party: to a judge if it can be dealt with solely in legal terms, otherwise to a political body.

The solution might be to let an international organisation revise treaties which have become inapplicable. Article 19 of the League Covenant contained a clause of this kind, but it was never applied. The only perfect solution to the problem would be an international legislature, that is a world State.

The unsatisfactory way written law is adapted to the changing state of the world is a major failing of international law, a failing which sums up all the others. The gulf between law and reality causes tensions and conflicts. Pacific settlements of international disputes fail if they do not give rise to a new system of law; otherwise necessary changes will be brought about by force. This is incompatible with the condemnation of wars.

Section III

THE GENERAL PRINCIPLES OF LAW

The XIIth Hague Convention lists general principles of law as a secondary source; they appear in the list in Article 38 of the Statute of the International Court of Justice in the following form: 'The general principles of law recognised by civilised nations.'

The definition and the real nature of general principles of law have been the subject of many controversies.

(A) *General characteristics*

The general principles of law, common to all or most state systems, must be distinguished from the general principles of international law.

The general principles of law common to all or most state systems are more or less the common basis of national legal systems. There are some very general rules which are common to all systems. For instance, most national legislations contain analogous provisions for the interpretation of juristic acts (statutes or contracts).

These rules are very general and very few.

Moreover, if they are to apply to intercourse between States these common rules must not conflict with the rules and institutions peculiar to international law. Thus, it may be that in municipal law every legal dispute must have a judge; but in international law, since there is only judgment by consent, disputes are only brought before a judge when States expressly undertake to do so. Principles of municipal law can therefore only be transferred to international law with considerable caution.

The general principles of international law are rules peculiar to intercourse between States, but they are so important that it would be impossible to imagine international law without them.

The courts apply rules described as 'general principles'. This has been demonstrated by courts and tribunals whose statutes allow them to apply general principles of law, and by those so authorised by agreement, but there are also cases where they are applied without such sanction. This stresses both the antiquity and the general nature of general principles, as a distinct source of law, but it sets limits to their practical importance.

An example of the way courts apply general principles of law will illustrate this.

In the Corfu Channel Case (Judgment, 9 April, 1949, Reports, p. 18) the International Court of Justice twice relied on general principles of law; in one part of the judgment it seemed to draw conclusions from principles of municipal law, in another part from international law. The Court had to examine the following question: can State A establish by circumstantial evidence, a violation of international law committed by State B within the territory of State B, given the difficulty of State A obtaining direct proof of what has happened within the territory of State B? The Court replied affirmatively to this question: 'This indirect evidence is admitted in all systems of law, and its use is recognised by international decisions.' On another point the Court based its decision on 'certain general and well-recognised principles, namely: elementary considerations of humanity, even more exacting in peace than in war; the principle of the freedom of maritime communication; and every State's obligation not to allow knowingly its territory to be used for acts contrary to the rights of other States'.

(B) *Critical observations*

The frequent reliance of international courts on general principles of law has failed to convince many jurists, who state frankly that those elements usable in international jurisprudence are 'completely irrelevant' (Rousseau, *Droit international public*, p. 71).

The real point at issue is not whether the courts invoke general principles of law but whether they do so as if they consider them to be practically and theoretically distinct from custom.

This distinction has a certain limited interest.

General principles of law, whatever they may be, might be distinguishable from customary rules in that they are fundamental, and in some ways compulsory. This is a tenable view, but if true seriously reduces the number of general principles of law.

For one thing, it implies that the repetition of a precedent is necessary to form a customary rule but not a general principle of law. This seems rather extreme and is not borne out in practice. Repetition is required only to establish proof of the conviction that a particular rule exists; it has in fact no mechanical significance. Let us consider separately the two kinds of general principles of law. General principles of international law are like immemorial customs: in point of fact they have never 'begun' since they were 'compulsory' from the start; in this case we cannot hope for any marked progress in international law. Or we can say they 'develop', and then they become very much like customs. On the other hand to authorise the judge to use principles common to several systems of municipal law is more revolutionary; but even that hypothesis, looked at practically, shows how limited is its practical interest.

It is more a matter of making explicit rules implicit than of creating new formulae, and the study of 'precedents' to justify transposition will always be much the same as the judge's task when faced with a customary rule. (For this see De Visscher, *Théories et réalités*, p. 426).

We can therefore conclude that the distinction between customary rules and general principles of law is only of secondary practical importance in the present state of international relations.

It would be different if international law were to introduce the international protection of human rights. This is not imminent in the present divided state of international society; the threat of it may perhaps explain the reticence of Soviet doctrine concerning general principles of law (cf. Ivo Lapenna, *op. cit.*, p. 170).

On the other hand it is possible to imagine that in a more limited homogeneous international society an international judge might draw more extensively on the municipal law of member States to interpret a treaty and build up doctrines which are only stated abstractly: there are several examples of this in connection with the European Coal and Steel Community (cf. Paul Reuter, *La communauté européene du charbon et de l'acier*, p. 41).

It is just possible, from the preparatory work on the Statute of the Permanent Court of International Justice, that it was intended that 'general principles of law' should be given more prominence than they have been. Some people wanted to give the judge the means of filling the 'lacunae' in international law by reference to general principles of law. Others said there were no lacunae since everything that was not forbidden was allowed; others said there could be lacunae in certain cases and in certain circumstances. According to the highest authorities on the subject (S. Basdevant, *La jurisprudence de la Cour Internationale de Justice*, RCADI 1951, p. 632), the International Court of Justice has been confronted with real lacunae in international law, and has said that it cannot solve them in accordance with the law. International practice does not accept that there are no lacunae in the law. Cf., for example, article XVII of the loan contracts between the European Coal and Steel Community and French firms: 'The parties agree that the law applicable to the present contract is that of the French Republic. Questions which are not settled either by an express clause of the present contract or by that law shall be resolved by the International Court of Justice which shall draw on the general principles of law found in the 6 member States of the Community.'

ANNEX

Secondary or Derived Sources

Are the three formal sources listed above the only sources of international law, or are other less important sources derived from them?

Let us repeat that the original source of present-day international law is custom, which is the basis of the binding force of treaties; one could imagine that custom or treaties might establish different formal procedures which lead to the creation of rules of law.

From a practical point of view we should examine four points: jurisprudence, unilateral acts, *actes règlementaires* and equity.

Case law is considered by some authors and in some systems as a source of law distinguishable from custom. Custom, they say, comes from the repetition of identical acts laid down by subjects of law; jurisprudential law, on the other hand, comes from the action of the judge himself. This conception of custom is rather different from that given here. In any case the claim that jurisprudence is a distinct source of law conflicts with the tendency to assign the judge a subordinate role in international law. Article 38(d) of the Statute of the ICJ lays down, very aptly: 'The court shall apply . . . subject to the provisions of Article 59, judicial decisions and the teachings of the most highly qualified publicists of the various nations, as subsidiary means for the determination of rules of law.' *Contra*, see G. Scelle, *Essai sur les sources formelles du droit international* (*Recueil d'études sur les sources du droit en l'honneur de François Gény*, t. III, pp. 400–431).

International law ascribes many effects to *unilateral acts*; written or customary rules make provision for all kinds of unilateral acts; notification, recognition, renunciation, denunciation, etc. Attempts have been made (principally by Italian jurists) to make a general theory of unilateral acts in international law, but it is not normally included in a study of the sources of law.

Actes règlementaires already figure in international law. Various institutions, principally international organisations, have power to make regulations and States have agreed to abide by their decisions. It is therefore a source derived from treaties, but it is nevertheless very important because it is the outline of genuine legislation. It will be studied in Part Three in connection with international organisations.

Equity sometimes appears in arbitration claims which make provision for verdicts based on equity. The Statutes of the PCIJ and the ICJ authorise the Court 'if the parties agree thereto' to decide a case *ex aequo et bono*. There is still much controversy about the notion of equity and its theoretical and practical scope, and its vocabulary does not even seem to be settled.

But it seems clear that following the practice of municipal law where the parties to a dispute can give a third party powers of informal arbitrator, States can give a court, or a body acting in that capacity, the power to settle a dispute in the light of extra legal considerations. In bilateral negotiations States generally settle their affairs by compromise, and nothing therefore prevents them asking a third party to propose a solution (which is then a form of mediation) or to impose one. In that case it appears to exercise genuine governmental or legislative power. It is understandable that States are not anxious to commit the settlement of certain types of disputes to this procedure, and that the proposals to this end in the General Act for the Pacific Settlement of International Disputes in 1928 failed.

Equity can in no way be regarded as a formal source of law.

PART TWO

THE STATES

CHAPTER ONE

The Constituent Elements

Three elements are needed to make a State: a territory, a population and a government capable of carrying out the internal and external functions of the State, above all of establishing an effective system of law and order.

Together these elements constitute a State. International law attributes to each element special powers. The most important are connected with territory, so territory, population and government will be dealt with in that order.

Changes are occurring which affect all these elements and throw out of balance the life of the States. Some of the most typical problems raised by these changes must be examined, particularly those connected with the emergence of new States and changes of government.

Section I

THE CONSTITUENT ELEMENTS

§ 1 TERRITORY

The relations which link a State and its territory are numerous and complex. As has been shown in the Introduction (p. 20), a monopoly of physical force is inconceivable if there is no defined area within which it is to be exercised. Since the functions of the State derive from or depend upon this monopoly of force, the territory may be defined as the physical framework within which a State exclusively exercises the full plenitude of its powers.

There is much abstract theorising about the territory of the State; the object is often to justify particular solutions relating either to the cession of territories and the succession of States, or to structural relations which are studied in Chapter Three.

(A) *Different parts of state territory*

The territory of the State consists mainly of land; the area must be very precisely defined, so that it is possible to enforce exclusive jurisdiction. This is the purpose of frontiers between territories. In addition to the land the territory of a State also comprises certain maritime areas and air space.

Modern land frontiers are lines either agreed to by treaty or decided by geography or scientific measurement. The actual frontier lines are drawn up by boundary commissions. Although their purpose is to separate the territories they also lead to intensive contacts between the neighbouring States.

In present-day international practice the territory of the State comprises the air space above it and a belt of sea along the coasts called *territorial waters*; the width of this belt varies with different countries, with a minimum of three sea miles. But, as has been seen (p. 98), this width is fixed in accordance with certain principles of international law, of which the International Court of Justice mentioned in its judgment of 18 December, 1951, in the Fisheries Case the following: territorial waters should closely correspond to the national mainland, and to certain geographical and geological features. States have claimed to incorporate into their territory the continental shelf which slopes away gently under the sea: this claim is very much to the fore today. The legal system of territorial waters (and also to a lesser extent of air space) must take special account of the needs of international communications, particularly freedom of innocent passage; there are therefore special features to their territoriality.

(B) *Incorporation into the State*

Relations between a State and a territory may vary considerably.

Sometimes this relation comes about when the State first comes into being; sometimes an existing State 'acquires' a new piece of territory. The difficulties which arise in the first case will be examined in Section II dealing with the birth of a State. But the circumstances of incorporation vary greatly: occupation of *terra nullius*, cession by treaty, annexation, the break up of a single State into several new States, etc.

Here are some general remarks on the way international law deals with these changes.

The main principle for creating a title to territory is that of *exercise of effective authority*. According to this principle any incorporation is legitimate if it is accompanied by the effective exercise of State authority.

This principle is generally applicable to *terra nullius*. Through the General Act of Berlin and several court and arbitral decisions, the idea has emerged that effective occupation is a condition of legitimate acquisition. This is a very empirical point of view: occupation is effective if the State exercises authority in that territory in accordance with its geographical position and its general nature. According to international jurisprudence it could be shown that there is effective occupation of Greenland, Clipperton Island, the Minquiers archipelago, in a way that is not true in the Gabon or South America.

This problem is acute only in the Arctic and Antarctic Circles; there has been an attempt to apportion sovereignty over the ice-cap by 'sectors', but there is no general agreement about this; there is still keen competition for the immense continent inside the Antarctic Circle (R. Dollot, *Le Droit international des espaces polaires*, RCADI 1949, II, 121).

A delicate situation arises when one State has a legitimate title to a territory but this conflicts with other States who lay claim to other titles or to effective occupation; in this case jurisprudence always tends to give preference to effective occupation. The incorporation into a State of territories already under the dominion of another State usually comes about through an international agreement which creates a legitimate title. Agreement is reached either directly with the consent of the States concerned or indirectly when the States ask a third party to adjudicate (arbitrator, judge, international organisation, international *de facto* government).

The problem is more complicated for territories conquered by force. This question has not arisen for a long time because international law recognised the legitimacy of the use of force and of the conquests resulting from it. Not only were partial conquests legitimate so long as they were accepted in a treaty by the State concerned, but also when all the territory of the State was conquered (*debellatio*), and it ceased to exist. These principles no longer hold good since international law no longer recognises situations based on the unlawful use of force. But the rule of effective occupation has not been entirely abandoned (cf. *infra*, p. 151).

(C) *The jurisdiction of a State within its own territory*

A State's jurisdiction inside its own territory is exclusive and all-embracing.

States exercise all functions within their territory and carry out all forms of legal and material activity; in particular they exercise the powers of compulsion and execution vested in a government. In international law *any authority a State exerts within its territory is presumed legitimate.* This full authority is limited by the full authority of other States inside their territories; a State cannot allow its territory to be used for acts contrary to the rights of other States. This is the principle of exclusive territorial jurisdiction.

Every State has exclusive jurisdiction within its own territory, but there are exceptions to this rule. International law recognises that certain other elements in the State have some powers, notably in regard to foreign nationals and public services. These have to be harmonised with those pertaining to the territory. A further distinction must be made regarding a State's action on foreign territory and how far it affects the legal system of that State, and how far the act is of a material or legal nature, etc. In short, the question is not at all simple.

Clearly the use of force is absolutely exclusive: State A cannot use force within the territory of State B. It has also been held that State A cannot set up courts to work within the territory of State B even if their jurisdiction is limited to its own nationals: legal activity involves compulsion.

In principle, however, State A can make laws applicable to its own nationals who are within the territory of State B; this does not violate the territory of State B because it does not contest its jurisdiction; this legislation can only be enforced within territory B with the consent and assistance of its authorities, in particular the courts. Has a State the right to make laws on matters which have nothing to do with its territory and do not concern its nationals? There is disagreement as to whether this is permissible except when that legislation is directed at matters affecting public order within the State (counterfeiting, for example).

It is important to know whether State A's jurisdiction within the territory of State B affects B's legal system. Heads of States travelling privately, army chiefs on official missions, members of governments staying in a foreign country for an international conference, have often taken legal decisions which in no way affected the legal system of the State within whose territory they happened to be (for examples

see Rousseau, *Droit international public*, p. 316). But we can imagine
cases which could be controversial—for example, whether nationals
of State A residing within the territory of State B may vote in an
election for one of the organs of State B; the significance of such an
operation could vary considerably. Even more delicate problems are
posed by the presence within the territory of State A of the centre of
intellectual activity of a movement which affects State B and threatens
to undermine established order.

§ 2 POPULATION AND NATIONALITY

Individuals are not only under the dominion of the State whose
territory they happen to be in at a given moment. They are also
attached to a specific State by a personal bond of nationality.
This has varied at different periods of history; there has been, and in
exceptional cases there still is, a bond of allegiance between a Prince
and his subjects. The International Court of Justice has defined
nationality in the following way (Nottebohm Case, Judgment 6 April,
1955, Reports, p. 23):

'According to the practice of States, to arbitral and judicial
decisions and to the opinions of writers, nationality is a legal bond
having as its basis a social fact of attachment, a genuine connection
of existence, interests and sentiments, together with the existence of
reciprocal rights and duties. It may be said to constitute the juridical
expression of the fact that the individual upon whom it is conferred,
either directly by the law or as the result of an act of the authorities,
is in fact more closely connected with the population of the State
conferring nationality than with that of any other State.'

The idea of nationality has been applied to entities like ships, aircraft and
corporations; it simply lays down, by analogy, the rules which bind situations,
even if by nature extra-territorial, to a legal order.

(A) *Establishing nationality*

International law authorises States within broad limits to determine
the conditions under which individuals can acquire their nationality,
States may take into account heredity or marriage (nationality *jure
sanguinis*), place of birth, or length of residence (nationality *jure
solis*). Are there any limits to this freedom in international law?

The problem may be stated in terms of prohibition; a State is
forbidden by international customary law to use entirely arbitrary
rules. Most authors agree on this.

On this point see Güggenheim, *Traité de droit international public*, t. I, p. 29, n.l, p. 314, and Charles de Visscher, *Théories et réalités*, p. 188.

States sometimes take into consideration elements other than those usually recognised in international law when they grant their nationality; thus, for some time Soviet Russia conferred Russian nationality on foreigners belonging to a certain social class and holding certain opinions (art. 20 of First Soviet Constitution, Ivo Lapenna, *Conceptions soviétiques de droit international public*, p. 175); the way Israeli nationality is granted in terms of the Law of Return should also be studied.

The position adopted by the International Court of Justice in the Nottebohm Case (p. 98) is that nationality conferred by one State can only be maintained against other States if its purpose is to confirm an individual's genuine connection with a national society.

International law leaves States enough freedom to create serious problems; many individuals find themselves, often against their will, with *double nationality*; some do not have one at all: they are known as stateless persons; their numbers have increased through racial and political persecutions. An effort has been made to solve these problems by a development in conventional law; there has been a great increase in international assistance to refugees, and an attempt made to give stateless persons a legal status (Convention relating to the Status of Stateless Persons, New York, 8 September, 1954).

One might imagine that nationality is a personal right of the individual; he would then have at all times the right to a nationality and the right to change it. This view is not supported by positive law, it simply reflects the still embryonic protection of human rights. On the basis of collective rather than individual choice, there are several theories maintaining the right of whole human societies to opt freely for a State of their own choosing. This was the purpose of the 'principle of nationalities' of the 'self-determination of peoples'.

International conventional law has given some weight to these ideas in individual territorial settlements. The fate of some territories has been decided on the basis of the wishes of the population consulted by *plebiscite*. To take account of individual preference, some territorial changes have allowed a *right of option*. Unfortunately in the present day nationality problems posed by transfers of territory have often been solved by the most barbarous method: the forced displacement of the population.

According to the French Constitution of 1946, article 27, §2: 'No cession, exchange or acquisition of territory is valid without the consent of the populations concerned.' This provision was waived in the case of Cochin China in favour of article 75 of the Constitution, which is open to criticism (law of 14 March, 1949);

it was not possible to apply the clause in the normal way to the trading posts in India except for Chandernagor. But article 27 was put into effect in carrying out, at Tende and Brigue, article 2 of the Treaty of Paris, 12 October, 1947, with Italy. It is the only case so far of a genuine plebiscite after the Second World War. S. Bastid, *Le rattachement de Tende et de Brigue* (RGDIP 1949, p. 321).

(B) *The effects of nationality*

A State's nationals have specific rights and duties which distinguish them from foreigners.

This is only fully appreciated taken in conjunction with the territorial framework within which the State may act.

(a) Outside its territory. In principle the State has no jurisdiction over foreigners, but it has jurisdiction over its own nationals. Through its consular service (p. 165) it administers them, renders them services and enforces obligations (military service). Its legislation covers its nationals in accordance with the rules of private international law: thus a person's legal capacity is generally assessed in foreign courts according to his own national law.

The State has the right to protect the rights and interests of its nationals abroad. It can do this, short of taking legal steps, by drawing the foreign State's attention to the matter; it can also, as has been shown (p. 89), 'endorse' its nationals' claims. International law is fairly strict about the conditions governing the right of diplomatic protection: a State can only endorse a claim of one of its nationals if he has retained its nationality continuously since the incident which caused him damage. In the case of dual nationality international jurisprudence tends to consider *de facto* nationality in deciding whether diplomatic action is permissible, that is the nationality which the plaintiff normally uses in his daily business.

(b) Within its territory. Apart from conventional rules for the protection of minorities or human rights, the State is free in principle to treat its nationals as it pleases, while its jurisdiction over foreigners is somewhat more limited. It is generally agreed that, in the absence of stipulations to the contrary, foreigners must enjoy minimum protection and guarantees of their rights and interests, their property, and of access to the normal internal courts.

This minimum protection has some sense in the case of badly organised States (which are rare nowadays) or in the event of serious political or social disturbances. On the other hand these rules are only operative when foreigners have continual access to a State's territory. There is today, however, no general rule which forbids

States to close their territory to foreigners. In fact there are increasing restrictions on the admission of foreigners depending on the length of their stay, whether or not it will be permanent, and above all whether or not they propose to work.

The main feature of the position of foreigners in most States today is indeed tacit exclusion from economic activity. They are also subject to secondary restrictions, in particular exclusion from political rights and duties (military service, access to public office, voting rights). Some modern States consider it such a favour to allow foreigners to work on their territory that they impose burdens like military service from which they were hitherto exempt. The position of foreigners is still precarious, they are subject to various measures of supervision and control, and are liable to be expelled.

In practice many States have made conventional provisions for improving the position of foreigners. These agreements, most of which are 'law-making treaties', guarantee specific rights for foreign nationals belonging to a specific State. They also contain general abstract clauses of which the best known are *'traitement national'* (treatment of foreigners as nationals in certain specific ways) and 'most-favoured nation' (all rights conferred on nationals of third States shall also be extended to the nationals of the most-favoured State for as long as they are enjoyed by the nationals of the other States).

§ 3 THE GOVERNMENT

(A) *General*

A people living in a territory does not make a State. There must also be a government, an organisation capable of assuming the functions of the State.

A government can be examined from three points of view: effectiveness, freedom of its political system and sovereignty.

(a) *Effectiveness.* A government must be genuinely able to discharge the internal and external functions of the State, that is to ensure law and order.

After a revolution or a war there may be no such authority. While this is so there is no State.

After the First World War Finland broke away from the Russian Empire; some States recognised it as a State, though in fact it was torn by civil war. The question of the future of the Aaland Islands belonging to Finland was raised in the League of Nations and some of the people of the Islands spontaneously demonstrated their desire to join Sweden. A Committee of Jurists was consulted on several points, in particular whether international law reserved the problems raised to the exclusive jurisdiction of States. The Committee decided that 'the dispute . . . does not refer to a definitive, established political situation, depending exclusively upon the territorial sovereignty of a State.'

(b) *Freedom in the choice of the State's political system.* International law is not concerned with the form of a State's political system. The government can therefore be monarchical, republican, parliamentary, democratic, etc. Nor is international law concerned with the political philosophy governing relations between individuals and the State or the State's powers of intervention.

But this principle of non-intervention ignores certain basic political realities: the influence of one country's way of life on other countries, and the influence State systems may have on international relations. This accounts for periodical attempts to introduce into international law the principle that a particular type of government alone is legitimate: legitimacy of monarchical régimes at the time of the Holy Alliance, of democratic governments today.

There has been some attempt to establish a connection between effective power and democratic government, on the grounds that effectiveness means stability, and stability must rest on popular support. Dr. Tobar, Foreign Minister of Ecuador, has suggested that no government should be recognised *before* it has been proved constitutionally legitimate by popular approval. This principle was embodied in two conventions, which have since been denounced, between 5 Central American Republics (Washington, 20 December, 1907 and 7 February, 1923); this has been, and sometimes still is, an underlying current of American policy.

If the idea of international legitimacy were introduced into international law, it would lead to States intervening in the domestic affairs of other States in order to guarantee this legitimacy; so far it has been avoided on the grounds that it is incompatible with the present conception of the international community. This is a further difference between the international community and federal government, in that the powers of the member States shall be respected on condition that the States obey certain over-riding principles (generally the republican form of government, and all the specifications deriving from the federal constitution).

Freedom to choose a political system means that internal revolutions are recognised in international law. But revolutions create complications since they involve changes in the organs charged with international relations (p. 157).

(c) *Sovereign powers.* As has already been shown (p. 96) State powers do not depend upon any organised power superior to their own. This springs from the nature of present-day international society. According to international practice the States together constitute an international community; the essence of State powers is that they are conferred directly by the international community which allocates State functions between the States.

This view is strongly supported by authors who hold that the State draws its authority *directly* from international *customary* law.

The question of the character of State powers has been the subject of several controversies. Some authors have denied both the validity and the expediency of the notion of sovereignty; others have said it is not a satisfactory criterion of the State. It has been proposed that other factors of a historical nature be taken into account. The situations which have caused hesitation and disagreement will be examined in the chapter on structural relations (p. 178): very small States are still States, even though they are not capable of discharging all the functions of a modern State; territories with a special international status and also those forming part of a federation cause many difficulties. The existence of international organisations does not alter the character of the member States so long as those organisations are not federal in character (and at the moment they are not).

(B) *Powers of governments*

All State functions are discharged by the government. This needs no comment; but if we try to define a State's right of jurisdiction, we find that some rights are connected with its territory, some with its nationals. Are any uniquely connected with its government? Let us take a case where State jurisdiction is connected neither with its own territory nor with its own nationals. There is one general example: military forces operating outside the national territory and exercising some jurisdiction over foreigners. This is the case of warships outside territorial waters or troops operating in or occupying foreign territory. This jurisdiction may conflict with the territorial or personal jurisdiction of other States.

A famous example is given in the decision of 22 May, 1909, of the Permanent Court of Arbitration in the case of the Deserters of Casablanca (RGDIP, 1909, Doc., p. 36); the Court distinguished between the jurisdiction of the French military authorities (powers of government) and the jurisdiction of the German and Moroccan consuls (personal jurisdiction) over German deserters from the Foreign Legion.

Diplomatic and consular services also enjoy certain immunities within the territory of foreign States where they discharge their functions. These immunities are, broadly speaking, restrictions placed on the territorial jurisdiction of one State in favour of the government authorities of the other State.

Section II

CHANGES IN A STATE AND THEIR RECOGNITION

§ 1 GENERAL PRINCIPLES

(A) *The elements of change*

The constituent elements of the State, as they have just been described, may be changed. Some changes have nothing to do with international law; others on the other hand affect international relations. We have already cited (p. 141) some of the problems which arise when parts of the State become the territory of another State. Here we shall keep to two particularly important instances: the appearance of new States and revolutionary changes of government.

Their importance is obvious. Although international law does not set a limit to the number of States which can legitimately exist, the emergence in the international community of a new subject of law is obviously of great importance. The rules of customary law are going to apply to that State, normal relations will have to be established, it must have a place in existing organisations. In the political field the interests of some groupings will be affected, and there will be a shift in the political balance of power. Nowadays the birth of a new State must be at the expense of existing States since there are no longer territories not under the rule of any State. It might seem that a revolutionary change of government would have fewer repercussions on international relations, since it is mainly a domestic affair. In fact this is not so. International relations are between the constituted authorities of different States, and these authorities are equally organs of international relations. States belonging to the international community must therefore decide with whom they will enter into regular contact.

In practice the two problems are inter-connected. A new State implies a new government, since the government is an essential element of a State.

The two principle criteria used in international law are the effectiveness of the authority exercised and the continuity of the State.

The principle of effective authority has already been studied (p. 146). At first sight its value seems slight, for it amounts to saying that *de facto* power justifies *de jure* power. But this is normal for a society where in the absence of bodies endowed with ultimate authority *de facto* situations play such a large part. One advantage it offers is that it leaves States masters of their own internal affairs. There are logically two possibilities:

— either effective authority is legitimate in international law because it is effective;
— or else the legitimacy of a new State or of changes of government is fixed by international rules sanctioned by an international organisation. In which case the international organisation must itself have effective authority, that is it must assume some of the properties of a State.

International practice favours the first alternative; nevertheless we can already see tentative and often misleading efforts to forestall changes that do not satisfy more exacting conditions; these efforts are mostly concerned with condemning the use of force, and with developing international organisation.

The principle of the continuity of the State is used to balance the legitimacy of changes in the nature of the government of a State. It asserts the permanent nature of obligations duly undertaken by a State regardless of subsequent transformations. The precise content of this principle is less well established than the principle of effective power. It means that when there is a change of government in a State the new government is expected to accept all the obligations contracted by its predecessors. It does not always do so after a civil war, especially when it has led to a general upheaval in the country. When a new State comes into being or even when the frontier between two States is changed, the question is more delicate: how far does the principle of the continuity of a State allow one State to transfer rights and duties to another State? This is part of the general subject of State succession which can not be dealt with in this book.

(B) *General application of the theory of recognition*

Problems relating to changes in States are made more complicated by difficulties over recognition. In fact the other problems often lie behind the problem of recognition.

Recognition of a new State or of a new government is a special formal institution in international law which has already been touched on (p. 97).

Recognition of a State or government is, like every other kind of re-cognition, conferred by each State individually according to its own judgment of a particular situation. But a third party, lawfully vested with the necessary jurisdiction, can also do so; an international arbitrator, an international judge, or an international organisation can be asked to decide whether a State exists, or whether a govern-ment exercises effective authority. Thus a State or a government may be legitimate in the eyes of some States, but not in the eyes of others; a classic instance of the relativity of international law.

Logically a State or government should either exist in the full sense of the word or not exist at all: we ought to be able to say that State B exists for State A, but not that it exists in certain respects only. Nothing of the kind. International practice is perfectly willing to admit degrees of existence. This is important to understand the recognition of a State or government and how it differs from other forms of recognition.

To recognise a State or government is not to recognise a juristic act, nor even a juridical rule, but to recognise a state of fact, which thus becomes a state of law, a permanent source of a whole series of acts and rules. For this reason States often prefer to settle diffi-culties over the existence of a State or a government by *ad hoc* decisions rather than to commit themselves definitively. Of course, this attitude is only possible up to a certain point; you cannot settle major difficulties with an unrecognised State or government if settling them would naturally imply total recognition of that State or government.

This tendency not to carry a *de facto* situation to its logical conclusion is reflected in the practice which varies from State to State of having degrees of recognition: this gives rise to the distinction between *de facto* and *de jure* recogni-tion.

States may hesitate to recognise new States or governments be-cause of uncertainty as to whether they exercise effective authority; it is not always easy to determine this nor to decide whether all the elements necessary to a State are present. Another factor enters into this: recognition is to the advantage of the State or government recognised; by withholding it a third State may hope for a *quid pro quo*. There are many examples of this and various possible motives. It may be self-interest, but it may also be to obtain perfectly legitimate guarantees for which, in the present state of international relations, States use whatever means of pressure they have. For example, if State A has certain rights over State B and State B changes its government, it is quite proper for State A not to recognise the new government until it has assurances that its rights will be observed. It is not clear that refusal to recognise is really an effective means of pressure, but that is another matter. The question arises in its most acute form in connection with recognition of a situation contrary to international law. As a sanction, refusal of recognition is only marginally effective; as an institution of international law its efficacy depends on an international order in which the effective exercise of power is no longer a criterion of legitimacy. This international order does not yet exist.

Mr. Stimson, American Secretary of State, informed China and Japan in a note of 7 January, 1932, that the United States government would not recognise any *de facto* situation, treaty or agreement brought about by means contrary to the covenant and obligations of the General Pact for the renunciation of war (the Treaty of Paris, 27 August, 1928, known as the Kellogg Pact). This principle is sometimes known as the Stimson Doctrine. The League of Nations, in a resolution to the Assembly, called upon its members to refuse to recognise any situation which was contrary to the League Covenant or to the Treaty of Paris (Manchuria case). The same principle was the subject of a resolution of the Assembly concerning the annexation of Ethiopia by Italy (4 July, 1936). It was also reasserted by the USSR, UK and France over the setting up of the German protectorate in Czechoslovakia (1939) and by the United States over the annexation of the Baltic States by the USSR. After being proclaimed in a number of cases on the American continent, it has been incorporated into several general acts as a fundamental principle of American international law. (Langer, R. *Seizure of territory, the Stimson doctrine and related principles in legal theory and diplomatic practice*, Princeton Univ. Press, 1947.)

In this elementary account of recognition we shall omit theoretical controversies as to the constitutive or declaratory character of recognition; they are only really appropriate in a theoretical treatise on international law.

The possible advantages to be gained by international institutions concerning themselves with recognition in the present state of international relations must not be exaggerated. They may recognise a State in the course of exercising their jurisdiction; thus a judge may declare that a State exists in order to settle a legal difficulty with which he is faced, but this declaration will not have the force of *res judicata* which is usually recognised in an international decision. If an international organisation admits a new State as a member it settles the question of its existence as far as its own jurisdiction is concerned; it does not oblige other States to recognise it; this, at least, is the United Nations rule (cf. memorandum of Secretary General of the United Nations, 6 March, 1950). But the opposite could easily be the case; it would simply have to be clearly stated in the constituent documents of the organisation or be implicit in the inter-State relations brought about by the organisation. In this case it would be quite clear which organ is empowered to grant recognition. With the United Nations Charter as it stands it would be possible for a State to be represented by one government in one organ of the United Nations and by a different one in another organ.

§ 2 RECOGNITION OF STATES

(A) *Conditions*

It is possible to recognise a State as soon as it has all the constituent elements. The only condition of recognition is therefore an effective organised government; it does not matter whether this government is organised in *terra nullius* or after the violent breakaway of provinces from an already existing State.

This raises two points about the position of States set up as a result of international agreements and the position of non-existent States.

(*a*) *States founded as a result of international agreements.* There are some international agreements whose purpose is to create a State: to unite separate States into one State by an international agreement to promote the drafting of a common constitution; to detach from a State certain parts of its territory in order to make them into separate States, either under municipal law or by an international convention with the newly created States; to create a new State by a collective treaty (common in peace treaties), etc. Whatever the international procedure employed, the recognition is equally valid in all these cases. It is never any sort of international agreement which brings a State into being, it is the fact of its having a population, a territory and an organised government. As soon as it has these a State in fact exists. This does not in the least detract from the rights and duties contained in agreements; recognition of a new State may take a particular form for the signatories, but this cannot change either its nature or its effect.

(*b*) *Position of a non-existent State.* A State can certainly recognise another State even if there is some doubt as to whether it exists; that is, that its foundations are not firmly established. Actually there is a broad measure of discretion in this domain. But is it permissible for a State to recognise a non-existent State? This is clearly a hypothetical case, for although there are frequent doubtful cases it is difficult to imagine recognition of a State which obviously did not exist. Such an act would not constitute 'recognition'; it might have juridical effects for the beneficiary if it were also a subject of international law; third States might also regard it as an illegal act; if an insurrection broke out in a State with the aim of making certain provinces into a separate State, premature recognition of the insurgents' organisation as a government might be very harmful to the original State; if the new government is really non-existent it may constitute an international offence.

In practice, rather than recognise a non-existent State, governments simply recognise certain competences attached to a particular body which may subsequently develop into the basis for a new State. The governments do not then commit themselves. During the First World War the Allies set up and recognised a 'Polish National Committee' and a 'Czech National Council' with very limited powers which were far removed from the powers of a State.

(B) *Forms and effects of recognising a State*

When one State recognises another State it certifies that the other State really exists and that it accepts all the implications of that fact.

We shall omit here the hypothesis where a judge or an international arbitrator declares that at a given time a State shall be considered as being in existence; this is generally a matter of discretion confined to the precise question at issue. One cannot say in general that *the* recognition of a given State was the work of a judge. But these judicial decisions are very often interesting because of the formulae they use. The mixed arbitral tribunals set up after the First World War made some famous awards (27 April, 1923, Loy and Makus *v.* Germany, *Recueil des Décisions des tribunaux arbitraux mixtes*, vol. III, p. 998; also 22 March, 1924, Poznanski *v.* Lenz, *eo. loc.*, vol. IX, p. 353). In some cases the arbitrator takes recognition by some States as proof that the State exists; up to a point it is a matter of presumption (case of Germany *v.* Reparations commission, 3 September, 1924, Reports of International Arbitral Awards, vol I, p. 524).

We must make the following three points about recognition:

(a) *Forms of recognition.* There is no procedure for obliging one State to recognise another (except under a treaty), but when it does so recognition is not in the least formalistic: it is not subject to any particular legal forms: recognition is made by the organs of State charged with international relations; it may be through diplomatic correspondence, a unilateral declaration, or a bilateral or multilateral agreement. It may be implicit. One thing is essential: that its action should leave no doubt about the intention to recognise.

(b) *Recognition and diplomatic relations.* As we shall see in the following chapter, normal relations between States involve diplomatic contacts through permanent and specialised services. States are under no circumstances obliged to establish these relations. It is unthinkable for a State to recognise another State without establishing diplomatic relations; on the other hand it is impossible to establish diplomatic relations without recognition. The most frequent case of implicit recognition is precisely the establishment of diplomatic relations. Naturally this means diplomatic relations in its precise technical sense. Even before recognition States may maintain technical relations or political contacts, but not through a duly accredited staff.

(c) *General and particular effects of recognition.* When a State has recognised the existence of another State it agrees not to question its existence, and concedes to that State the general rights recognised to foreign States in international law.

But for certain States recognition has special effects. Claims based on treaties before the new State was created are renounced, as when one State recognises another State even in the face of previous treaties and commitments; the simplest example of this is when a province is detached and made into an independent State. For this reason recognition is often written into complex international agreements.

In the last century the creation of the Belgian State gave rise to difficulties which serve to illustrate this. The treaty of 31 May, 1815, signed by Austria, the UK, Prussia, Russia and the Netherlands, together with the Final Act of Vienna which included France, defined the constituent part of the Kingdom of the Netherlands; these provisions were part of 'European public law'. Recognition of the new Belgian State therefore raised a number of difficulties. The Great Powers recognised Belgium at the same time as they imposed on her certain obligations by the Treaty of 15 November, 1831; recognition by the Netherlands, which involved grave consequences for that country, did not come until the treaties of 19 April, 1839.

(C) *Position of an unrecognised State*

A State whose existence is not recognised by another State has none the less some juridical relations with it.

But instead of issuing from a principle (the existence of the State) and developing on a simple pattern (diplomatic relations), intercourse with an unrecognised State is simply a series of isolated acts, each unconnected with the others, at the discretion of the interests involved, limited to indirect unofficial contacts and not touching matters which, by their very importance, would imply recognition.

There are many examples in international practice. Without recognising a State, other States delegate non-diplomatic representatives, under various titles, to make contact with its civil and military administrations; agreements are concluded, especially on technical

or so-called technical subjects; the States allow the consular agents
of an unrecognised State to perform their duties within their territory; their courts apply the laws of unrecognised States to conflicts
of law, or grant them jurisdictional immunity. An unrecognised State
can commit an international offence and incur international responsibility as a result.

One thing is evident from these cases: that the problems arising out
of the question of the existence of a new State do not have to be taken
together: States dispose of a number of individual practical difficulties before tackling the problem of their relations with each other.
Just as international organisations with extensive jurisdiction can
'objectively establish the fact that a State exists and from that
draw conclusions which apply to States which have not recognised
it'.

But the limited and restrictive relations of an unrecognised State
involve a good deal of inconvenience, and a State has a practical
interest in gaining recognition.

§ 3 RECOGNITION OF GOVERNMENTS

(A) *How it resembles recognition of States*

To recognise a State implies recognition of the government of that
State; in general, then, the principles for recognising a State apply
to recognising a government. It is simpler to apply the principle of
the continuity of a State, since it is not the identity of the State which
is at issue but simply the quality of certain persons to act in its
name. For this reason it is more common for an international institution to testify to the effective authority of a particular government. International courts have repeatedly ruled that a government
with effective power, whether recognised or not, is qualified to bind
the State by international agreements, and to engage the State's
international responsibility, etc.

If an effective but unrecognised government disappears and is subsequently
replaced by another effective government, the latter is bound by the undertakings
of its predecessor in the name of the continuity of the State (Tinoco Case, U.N.
Reports of arbitral awards, vol. I, p. 369, and Hopkins Case, *eo. loc.* vol. IV, p. 41).
But the recognition of a non-effective government would not suffice to make it
an organ of State; the debts which it contracted could not be claimed from its
successors (Cuculla Case, Moore, International Arbitration, vol. III, p. 2873).

In the Corfu Channel Case the International Court of Justice recognised a
conflict between the United Kingdom and Albania although the United Kingdom
had not recognised the Albanian government.

(B) *Special features*

A new State may come into existence without a conflict, and even if there is a conflict one side does not claim to represent the interests of the State from which it is trying to break away, but only those of the new community which is seeking to establish a separate State. In a revolutionary change of government, however, two organisations claim to represent the same State. The results of this fundamental difference vary with the stage and form of the conflict.

In the first instance the situation is often this: the legitimate recognised government no longer controls the whole country, part of which is in the hands of an insurrectional government. In international relations only the recognised government represents the State, the other has no international standing.

Nevertheless equity, and the principle of effective authority mean that its acts are not entirely disregarded. It has been agreed that taxes raised by the insurgents cannot be levied again by the recognised government (Guastini Case, Mixed Italo-Venezuelan Commission, 1903, Ralston, *The law and procedure of international tribunals*, no. 557; De Forge Case, Mixed Franco-US Commission, Moore, *International Arbitration*, vol. III, p. 2781). The courts of third States often cease to apply measures which the recognised government cannot enforce, and apply those which the insurrectionist government can.

If the conflict lasts for some time it inevitably involves the interests of neighbouring States (ideological, commercial, political). As long as a conflict is confined to the land it is strictly speaking internal, but as soon as it extends to the sea it may become international in character.

It is important to grasp the significance of this change. All the while the conflict remains internal the legal government can apply the laws of its own municipal penal code against the insurgents; it may not do so from fear of reprisals or from humanitarian reasons, but other States must not help the insurgents in any way and must consider them as offenders in common law. But as soon as the conflict threatens shipping, by the force of circumstances others become involved. Other States will often continue to interpret their rights and duties on the basis that it is a purely internal conflict and does not constitute a war, but difficulties inevitably arise.

If one of the sides blockades a port controlled by the other side, does this apply to the ships of other States, even though there is no state of war? This has sometimes been maintained on the basis of the strictly territorial character of such a blockade. In any case insurgents' warships are in a very irregular position in relation to the rules of international law on the open sea. American practice has devised a 'recognition as insurgency'; which would regularise the position of insurgent warships without giving them any specific rights over the ships of other States; but this has given rise to much controversy.

A domestic conflict becomes an international conflict by 'recognition of belligerency'. When a State has recognised the insurgents as belligerents its situation is similar to that of neutral States in an international war between two equal powers, the legitimate government and the insurgent government. Theoretically recognition of belligerency could come from the legitimate government, but in fact it always comes from third States. Such recognition has very important consequences. On the open sea 'belligerents' can exercise belligerent rights which are enforceable against neutrals (search for contraband goods, capture for breaking a blockade, aid to the enemy, etc.); broadly speaking third States are bound by the law of neutrality. In law recognition of belligerency is to the advantage of the insurgents who are henceforth on an equal footing with the legitimate government; in practice it is to the advantage of whichever side has supremacy on the sea.

Actually recognition of belligerency is always governed by political considerations. In the Spanish Civil War the States chiefly concerned devised, in a special convention, a statute of equal non-intervention for both sides; this was the only solution which prevented the conflict from spreading.

(C) *Case of the French government during the Second World War*

After the military defeat of France in 1940, a new Constitutional Law of 10 July, 1940, followed by 'constitutional acts' laid down the bases for what is today called the Vichy régime. The legitimacy of this French government is a problem of French constitutional law, but this problem will be left entirely on one side. Its position in respect of international law, on the other hand, is worth explaining; it is of historical interest and it is also a typical example of the technique of recognition, how the effects can vary with the situation, and how recognition can be dictated by political considerations.

In 1940 the Vichy government was the effective authority in France; no foreign State denied this, not even Great Britain who kept up diplomatic relations until 5 July, 1940, when they were broken off with all other countries on the side of the Axis. Moreover Great Britain maintained *unofficial* contacts with the Vichy government, as well as consular relations.

On 22 June, General de Gaulle formed the 'Committee of the Free French'; on 28 June, 1940, General de Gaulle was recognised

by the British government as head of all the Free French. Soon afterwards he was recognised by the same government as military head
of the Free French Forces, and administrative head of the overseas
territories which had rallied to him. The Committee for the Defence
of the Empire and later the French National Committee (CNF) were
the first bodies claiming governmental status. The latter was fused
with the French authorities in North Africa and became the French
Committee of National Liberation (CFLN). 'Recognition' for limited
and varied purposes was accorded to the CNF and the CFLN; their
competence was limited both geographically and materially. The
USSR recognised the CFLN as the *de facto* government; the UK
and in particular the US were very cautious about the 'effectiveness'
of the Free French authorities. The Free French Government, presided over by General de Gaulle, was only recognised unreservedly
as the Government of the French State by the United Kingdom and
the United States on 23 October, 1944. It was recognised by Spain and
Switzerland on 31 October, and by the Vatican on 9 December. The
Axis powers did not recognise the Free French Forces as belligerents.
In 1942 Germany declared that prisoners from the Free French
Forces would not be executed, but on purely humanitarian grounds.
Neutral States did not accord belligerent status to the Free French
Forces, but most of them (except Switzerland) agreed to unofficial
or semi-official contacts with Free French representatives. Some
international organisations like the International Red Cross refused
to admit the Free French Red Cross.

CHAPTER TWO

General Intercourse Between States

Intercourse between States may take various forms. Some permanently affect the structure of the State, and these will be dealt with in the following chapter; we shall give here first a general picture of intercourse between States when no conflict is involved (Section I); second their relations when involved in a conflict with each other. This can in turn be divided into two questions: conflicts which involve the use of force for their settlement and those to be settled by peaceful means (Sections II and III).

Section I

INTERCOURSE BETWEEN STATES WHEN NO CONFLICT IS INVOLVED

A typical feature of the international community at the present day is the continuous official contact between governments through specialised agents which States agree to keep in each other's territory. These agents form the *diplomatic services*; complementary work is done on the administrative level by the *consular services*.

But the diplomatic services, and *a fortiori* the consular services, are not autonomous; they are subordinate to the heads of State and the Foreign Ministers.

We must begin our general account of intercourse between States with a description of the organs through which international relations are conducted (§ 1). This will be followed by a brief account of the technical side to these relations (§ 2).

There is a theoretical question here which has already been broached in connection with treaties: are the rules for international relations governed by international law or municipal law? International law regulates international relations

160

as a whole, but as we have seen in the case of treaties (*supra*, p. 128) it refers back to municipal law to decide which agents are authorised to deal with international relations. In trying to describe their functions therefore, jurists have talked of such things as 'two-fold functions', 'organs vested with a double authority' and even 'personal union between organs of the law of nations and organs of the law of the State'. This description reflects a basic sociological fact: the needs of each epoch react simultaneously on both political and international institutions. We have already shown how this may give rise to discrepancies between the letter of written constitutions and their practice.

§ 1 ORGANS

The many survivals and the astonishing flexibility of modern relations show the extent of historical evolution. In the fifteenth century the political form of government nearly everywhere was monarchy. The monarch, supreme head of the State, had the right of universal representation (*jus repraesentationis omnimodae*), and he alone was regarded as responsible for the conduct of international relations. All acts were in his name and on his instructions. There are still deeply entrenched survivals of this conception in the treaty system and in the formalism of protocol in international relations. It was possible to have the simplest form of international relations between monarchs: direct or indirect contacts between some fifty heads of State.

But present-day practice no longer fits this conception. We have already pointed out the tendency for informal agreements to replace treaties. Relations through diplomatic and consular corps, regarded as direct representatives of the head of the State, can still be taken into account, but the increase in international relations and the importance of representative and democratic systems of government have increased the importance of the Foreign Minister. At the same time direct relations between various national administrations are increasing.

We shall now examine the position of the head of the State, the Foreign Minister, the diplomatic envoys, the consular agents and other agents or officials.

(A) *The head of the State*

States still conduct relations with each other through their heads of State. Diplomatic envoys are accredited by and to them. They represent their State at public ceremonies and when they travel abroad special measures are taken to protect their persons; outrages, abuse and other offences against them are punished with special severity.

F

Heads of State are wholly exempt from criminal proceedings before foreign courts.

But the head of State has lost much of his former importance. At the beginning of the nineteenth century treaties were signed in person by the heads of State, for example the treaty of 26 September, 1815, setting up the Holy Alliance. This practice has almost died out. The Treaty of Alliance between Austria, Great Britain, Prussia and Russia of 20 November, 1815, provided for a meeting of the allied sovereigns or their ministers if the alliance should be put to the test. But in the course of the nineteenth century the political role of the heads of State has varied a great deal. In constitutional monarchies they still have a symbolic role, important mainly at a time of crisis. Where there have been authoritarian régimes some sovereigns have played an important role, for example Napoleon III in France.

On the whole the role of the head of State in international relations accurately reflects his position in general constitutional practice; some constitutions have done away with the head of the State; others have retained the office in a reduced capacity.

In the 1946 French Constitution the role of the head of the State is not negligible, but it depends on the personal influence he can exert. The strength of his position lies in the fact that under Article 31 of the Constitution: 'The President of the Republic shall be kept informed of international negotiations', information he shares with the Foreign Minister to the exclusion of the other members of the cabinet.

It would be interesting to make a comparison with Swiss practice; according to Article 103 of the Federal Constitution the head of the State is a composite body (Güggenheim, *op. cit.*, p. 485).

(B) *The Foreign Minister*

In all States foreign affairs are in the hands of a separate ministry under a minister called the Minister of Foreign Affairs, or the Secretary of State for Foreign Affairs.

Under the Minister is all the staff of the Foreign Office and all personnel, diplomatic and consular, serving abroad. The Minister is reponsible for the administration and discipline of all his staff, for organisation and finance, and he issues instructions to agents serving abroad laying down policy towards foreign States. He can summon the representatives of foreign powers and he receives them at their request.

The Foreign Minister, then, conducts foreign policy. In a parliamentary system he takes political responsibility for the actions of the head of the State, and he also has some powers in his own right; some diplomatic agents of lower rank are accredited to him personally; he may in proper cases make declarations binding the State (even oral declarations, PCIJ, Case of the Legal Status of Eastern Greenland, Series A-B, No. 53, p. 71).

The growing practice of meetings of Foreign Ministers illustrates the political importance of the Foreign Minister. These meetings are of two kinds:

(i) There have been general meetings of Foreign Ministers since the nineteenth century, often accompanied by the heads of governments. All major questions of foreign policy have been discussed and often decided at meetings of the Foreign Ministers. They have come to sign the most important treaties (for example, the Atlantic Pact of 4 April, 1949; the treaty of 18 April, 1951, setting up the European Coal and Steel Community; the Paris Agreements of 23 October, 1954, ending the Occupation of Germany, etc).

(ii) In a narrower field most political international organisations have an organ composed of Foreign Ministers: annual meetings of Foreign Ministers are provided for under the Act of Chapultepec of 6 March, 1945, the Bogotá Charter (art. 39), and the Committee of Ministers of the Council of Europe (art. 13 and 14 of Statute of the Council of Europe), Northern Council of Scandinavian countries, etc.

A history of the internal organisation of the central services would be very interesting, and would bring out the growing importance of foreign affairs in all countries, the growing tendency to recruit more jurists and technicians, and in France at least a constant wavering between two major patterns of organisation: the one geographical by region or country, the other by subject (political affairs, administrative, economic, cultural, etc.).

(C) *Diplomatic agents*

States maintain permanent diplomatic delegations within other States. In principle the rank of the head of each delegation is fixed by the kind of post he holds. Reciprocity is the rule in diplomatic relations, so some States have embassies, others legations. The Ruling of Vienna of 19 March, 1815, and the Protocol of Aix La Chapelle of 21 November, 1818, made a distinction of great importance from the point of view of protocol between four classes of diplomatic agents: *ambassadors* and *nuncios* (the latter have precedence over all others in Catholic or predominantly Catholic States); *envoys, ministers plenipotentiary* and *internuncios*; *resident ministers*; *chargés d'affaires* who are accredited to the Foreign Minister and not to the head of the State (very often *chargés d'affaires* are only temporary or substitute heads of mission). These regulations have become less important since many more States have attained the rank which in the past allowed them to exchange ambassadors with other States.

Protocol accurately registers the growth in the number of sovereign States: in Asia it rose from 6 in 1939 to 20 in 1952. Apart from the great European powers the US, soon followed by Japan, exchanged ambassadors on a reciprocal basis after 1898. The US had 14 ambassadors in 1929, 55 in 1950 and 68 in 1954. The number of ambassadors accredited to France has risen from 15 in 1939 to 50-odd in 1955, as against about 20 legations. The development of international organisations has started more far-reaching changes; the official chiefs of protocol have noted this transformation (*Diplomatie, protocole et égalité des Etats*, E. de La Chauvinière, *Le Monde diplomatique*, July, 1954).

There is a traditional procedure by which diplomatic envoys take up their duties. First it is ascertained that no objection will be raised to their appointment by the State in which they will serve. They then receive letters of credence from the head of their own State and a copy of these is sent to the Foreign Minister of the country to which they are sent. They then present their letters of credence to the head of the State. The mission of the diplomatic envoy ends either with his recall by his own State or at the request of the State to which he is accredited (if his conduct calls for some sanction); alternatively he is handed his passport following a rupture of diplomatic relations between the two States.

The head of each diplomatic mission is assisted by a large and growing staff. Important embassies include all sorts of specialists: military, naval, air, financial, commercial, cultural, information, labour attachés, etc. They all enjoy diplomatic status, but these specialists are usually drawn from administrations other than the Ministry of Foreign Affairs and are only partially under that authority.

The role of diplomatic envoys varies a great deal: (1) They transmit and receive official communications between States; (2) they represent their State on all public occasions: ceremonial, negotiations; in fact official diplomacy has always been combined with other contacts; at one time princes used personal and secret envoys, today parliamentary or political negotiators work together side by side with non-diplomatic specialists; (3) they collect and transmit all information useful to the conduct of foreign relations; (4) they protect nationals abroad.

In order to exercise these functions diplomatic envoys are accorded privileges and immunities, in particular immunity from legal process in respect of acts done in the course of their official duties. This means that no civil or criminal action can be brought against a diplomatic envoy, his wife or his children, and that he is immune from enforcement of the local law. The premises, personal property and transport of a legation are inviolable. Diplomatic envoys have the right to use cipher for diplomatic correspondence, and to have diplomatic mail (diplomatic bag) carried by a member of the service exempt from police or customs inspection. With the authorisation of the State to which they are accredited embassies and legations may also use a radio transmitter. The premises used by the diplomatic services are inviolable; if a criminal seeks refuge in the building the head of mission must either hand him over to the State or authorise the police to come and arrest him. On the other hand, it has been maintained that a political refugee has a right of asylum. At present this right is contested except as between some Latin American States (cf. on this point two decisions of the ICJ of 20 November, 1950, and 13 June, 1951, in the Asylum Case).

In addition, diplomatic missions have fiscal immunity which includes direct and sometimes indirect taxes. It is not certain whether this particular immunity is allowed as a matter of customary law or by courtesy.

(D) *Consular agents*

Consuls are agents appointed by a State to serve in another State and help its nationals resident there.

They do not represent the State for which they act as do diplomatic envoys; they are in contact with foreign local authorities and not with those of higher rank. States are free to accept or refuse foreign consular agents, to fix their number and their place of residence.

While the status of diplomatic envoys is determined by international custom, the status of consuls is, apart from a few elementary rules, laid down in bilateral conventions and by national legislation. Much of the work of consuls does not concern the local territorial authorities, but only the country which appointed the consul.

Besides career consuls, some countries have consuls who are not officials but generally business men; they are not necessarily nationals of the State for which they act and may even be nationals of the State where they carry out their duties. Consuls are appointed by letters patent (commissions), either from the head of State or from the Foreign Minister, and they receive an *exequatur* from the same authorities of the State where they fulfil their duties. Their mission may be terminated under the same conditions as diplomatic envoys, but the rupture of consular relations does not necessarily entail a rupture of diplomatic relations.

Consuls perform the following tasks: (1) To assist nationals in their dealings with local authorities; (2) to collect general information, particularly on commercial matters; (3) to perform, with respect to nationals, general administrative tasks (passports, visas, military service formalities, payments to the State) and certain legal formalities (investigations, depositions for legal purposes, authentication of documents). They have especially important commercial, fiscal, administrative and civil functions, connected with merchant and naval shipping.

Consular immunities are more restricted than those of diplomatic envoys and more closely related to the exercise of their functions. Their personal acts are not protected by jurisdictional immunity, and they are only immune from the process of local law in so far as they are exempt from preventive arrest, except after due warning to the State concerned. Only archives and correspondence are inviolable, except where there are special provisions by consular convention. Fiscal immunity is usually limited to direct taxes.

(E) *Other agents and officials*

For a long time the head of the State, the Foreign Minister, diplomatic and consular agents were the only State organs for international relations.

Now the armed forces, land, sea and air, play an important part in international affairs. The international competence of the armed forces is not confined to material acts, but extends to juristic acts such as the conclusion of international agreements (armistices, capitulations, or even agreements within the framework of an alliance).

Direct international contacts have now become common between representatives or agents of many other government services.

First in importance are the direct contacts between members or governments other than the Foreign Ministers. There have been frequent international meetings between heads of governments or ministers of technical departments (national defence, economy, finance, health, etc.). In overseas territories local representatives of the central power make direct contact with the heads of neighbouring territories in the names of their respective States. Sometimes there are international meetings at the administrative level; the more international relations involve technical affairs the more this is true.

In some sectors and between certain States we notice a fusion of political and administrative representation. This is especially noticeable in international organisations (cf. p. 247).

One example is the Brussels Protocol of 17 October, 1953, which set up a 'conference' to be attended by 'Ministers in charge of internal transport in their own government'. Furthermore: 'Whenever the conclusion of a general or restricted international agreement seems necessary, each Minister of Transport concerned shall seek from his government full powers to enable him, or any person or persons specially appointed for the purpose, to conclude the international agreement in question' (art. 9 (b)).

We should examine in the light of what has just been said the jurisdictional privileges and immunities accorded to foreign States. It is agreed in present-day international practice that national courts shall not allow litigation against a foreign State to proceed, nor may a writ be executed against property belonging to a foreign country. However, in each country the courts interpret these immunities differently, especially since States have increased their intervention in the economic field and have often acted in many ways like private businesses. Immunities are justified on various theoretical grounds in different countries. In many countries, and in particular in France, they are based on the courts' refusal to intervene directly in international relations. The courts, more than any other branch of the State, have shown themselves most reserved and unwilling to interfere with the monopoly of external relations in the hands of special organs. For a similar attitude, see the decision of the United States Supreme Court of 7 March, 1955, National City Bank of New York v. Republic of China.

§2 CONDUCT OF FOREIGN RELATIONS

Intercourse between States is generally through what is known as the diplomatic channel; but this normal way may be modified or even replaced by some other method.

(A) *The diplomatic channel*

The Foreign Minister and his heads of department are in constant touch with all the diplomatic envoys abroad. The latter are in turn in contact with the Foreign Minister of the country to which they are accredited, and with his heads of department. Foreign Ministers and Ministries are then in contact with each other through diplomatic envoys; it takes the form of personal contacts and considerable correspondence; this constitutes the diplomatic channel, the normal means of intercourse between States.

It has certain general features. It is *comprehensive and continuous*; all matters, without exception, whether political, administrative, juridical or technical, in principle pass through this channel, and authorities are able to communicate at every level, depending on the nature of the case, through a diplomatic envoy of corresponding rank. The fact that envoys are in permanent residence makes possible continuous diplomatic relations. It is as if diplomatic envoys were simultaneously in the service of both States. To this extent relations may he said to be *direct*; the States are in immediate contact without need of an intermediary, whether third State, independent person, international organisation, etc. More than two States may seek an exchange of views through diplomatic channels, but it is not a convenient method for doing so once more than two States are involved, except for elementary discussions. A State is always free to maintain normal diplomatic relations but it has no legal obligation to do so. States are therefore free to reduce the status of their envoy (recall of ambassadors) or even to break off relations. Even then States can continue to have direct contacts, but only on a temporary *ad hoc* basis. In theory the maintenance or establishment of diplomatic relations is independent of recognition (*supra*, p. 155), but it is impossible to have diplomatic relations with an unrecognised State or government; indeed the very fact of establishing diplomatic relations is an implicit act of recognition. The breaking off of diplomatic relations is a sign of tension between two countries, but it does not alter the peaceful *status quo*, and does not in itself imply the use of force.

Diplomatic relations entail a great many discussions and a good deal of correspondence. It is not true that these proceedings are over-formalistic. Each State regulates correspondence between its diplomatic envoys and the Foreign Ministry as it thinks best. Relations between diplomatic envoys and the central ministries abroad are, by international practice, courteous and flexible, but without formalities. It is useless to give details of terminology since they vary from one country to another. The importance of diplomatic approaches and contacts is commensurate with the rank of the person engaged in them, and with the extent of the formal authentication accorded them. For instance, after some oral discussions an impersonal, unsigned written text is delivered summarising the conversation (*note verbale*); if the note is signed it indicates a further degree of authentication, etc.

(B) *Relations outside the diplomatic channel*

States can enter into relations in many ways other than diplomatic channels. It often depends, as in the past, on the temperament and attitude of the people in charge of foreign policy. There are still in some circumstances direct contacts or contacts through personal envoys, and these have been quite important at top level. We shall take a more frequent and routine example. To negotiate a bilateral agreement it is usual for States not to communicate through their diplomatic envoys, but instead specialist officials of the respective central ministries usually get in touch with each other directly, and in any case it is they who conduct the negotiations. The foreign service personnel pave the way for the negotiations, but the actual discussions are conducted by temporary delegations which meet in an agreed place.

There are two special cases which must be mentioned for their theoretical and practical importance.

When diplomatic relations are broken off, there are nationals and interests left undefended. International practice has tried to find a method whereby a State may still defend some of its basic interests in a State with whom it has broken off diplomatic relations. The solution is to ask a third State to undertake this task through its own representatives. This solution is widely used in the event of war. With the common consent of the two belligerent States, a neutral State is called upon to defend the interests of one of the States in the other country. This neutral State is known as the protecting power. Humanitarian conventions in time of war make extensive use of the intervention of protecting powers, for instance the Geneva Conventions of 27 July, 1929 and 12 August, 1949. If representation by third States became a general practice it would radically change certain international relations; but we must not attach too much importance to the intervention of third States in place of national diplomatic envoys; it cannot be regarded as representation in the strict sense of the word (cf. Chevreau Case, Permanent Court of Arbitration, 9 June, 1931, U.N. Reports of International Arbitral Awards, vol. II, p. 1141).

Relations between more than two States are often conducted through *international conferences*, which have now become an accepted method of intercourse between States. These conferences may properly be regarded, from the point of view of international agreements, as the arena for negotiating. Their frequency offsets their inherent lack of continuity and they are a step on the way to international organisations in the full sense of the word. Standard rules are emerging for international conferences, with their own procedure (we might almost say 'prescriptions') for calling international conferences (who calls them, which States are invited), for preparing the conferences (diplomatic soundings or preliminary conferences drawing up the programme of the conference or even preparing papers), and for organising the conferences (presidency, bureau, rules of procedure, commissions, drafting committee, right of amendment, minutes of proceedings, public relations). All this is very complicated and has been very carefully studied. The organisation of conferences varies and is often rudimentary, but the *direction* is unmistakable. All international conferences run into technical problems inherent in the work of large assemblies, whether international or not. On the other hand, because they are organised, international conferences are obliged to accept a certain inequality between the States (composition of commissions, majority rules for voting, general leadership in the work of the conferences, etc.). Sometimes, especially at political conferences, the advantage lies with the great powers; sometimes, by means of voting procedure, small and medium-sized powers can exercise pressure on the great powers. In any case the guiding principle of diplomatic relations, reciprocal equality of States, is not entirely observed. For this reason conferences are a transitional stage between diplomatic relations and international organisation.

Section II

PEACEFUL SETTLEMENT OF INTERNATIONAL DISPUTES

§ 1 GENERAL CONSIDERATIONS

There are tensions in international society as in any other society, and they are for the sociologist to examine; the terms employed in international practice and treaties suggest that there is no settled definition for describing states of tension: 'conflicts', 'disputes', 'situations which might lead to a breach of the peace', 'situations which might lead to international friction or give rise to a dispute', etc.

This vagueness is not peculiar to international relations; we are often only aware of disputes through the methods the parties choose for settling them.

While the dispute is limited to the States immediately concerned there is only one method of peaceful settlement: negotiation first using the diplomatic channel to conclude an international agreement. Diplomatic channels and negotiation are still the primary and basic machinery for easing tension between States. It has been suggested that, even where there is a treaty obligation to resort to other means of settlement, the diplomatic channel should be tried first. But success depends on the good will of the States and on their relative strength, which sometimes induces one of them to submit 'voluntarily'. If negotiations break down tension remains and is aggravated, and the only solution then is either the use of force or the intervention of a third party.

There are several methods in international practice of inviting the intervention of a third party. No State is ever obliged to accept it unless it has expressly undertaken to do so. The general conditions for such procedure have been elaborated in conventional law. The provisions so incorporated have had to contend with two difficulties.

The major difficulty concerns the definition of disputes. When States call in a third party they must state their claim and justify it. A claim may or may not be based on recognised legal rules. Those that are are generally called legal disputes, the others political disputes. But the very notion of a dispute not based on juridical rules is far from clear. International conventions have tried to find a definition in two directions:

(i) Disputes are political if they issue from a claim not based on a rule of law because no applicable rule exists in the law.

(ii) Disputes are political if their purpose is to change the existing law.

Both definitions agree on one point: not all disputes can be settled under the existing law. In the most difficult cases the third party discharges an extremely important function: to fill a lacuna in international law or to change an existing rule; in both cases his role is that of the legislator in a municipal system. Thus it follows that not every international dispute can be solved peacefully unless a third party is given the full powers of a legislator.

A second difficulty is to get States to agree to refer a question to a third party. Their consent is necessary and may be given in one of two ways: either in advance, once and for all, before a dispute arises, so that third party intervention is virtually automatic, or *ad hoc* for each dispute. The first solution is infinitely preferable for easing tension swiftly, but it can only be done if an appropriate body already exists. A major role of international organisations is, as we shall see later, to provide the machinery for the pacific settlement of international disputes.

§ 2 CLASSIFICATION

The methods by which third parties can intervene to settle international disputes peacefully can be classified according to the following criteria: whether the parties concerned choose the third party, the extent of their mission (can they enquire into the facts of the case or state the law, can they take account of extra-legal factors), the legal effects of their intervention (are the States bound by their findings). These are the differences underlying the various forms of good offices: mediation, enquiry, conciliation, arbitration and judicial settlement. These various methods are mentioned in several texts (First Hague Convention on the Pacific Settlement of International Disputes; United Nations Charter, article 33; Bogotá Charter, article 21).

(A) *Good Offices*

A State is said to use its 'good offices' when spontaneously or by invitation it tries to find the basis for an arrangement between two parties without going so far as to propose a precise solution to the dispute.

For instance France and Siam accepted the good offices of the United States in 1946 to settle their territorial disputes, and similarly in August, 1947, Holland and Indonesia ceased hostilities through the good offices of the United States.

(B) *Mediation*

A State is said to mediate when, spontaneously or by invitation, it proposes a solution to a dispute between two States. The parties are not bound to adopt this solution, nor is it necessarily based on legal considerations.

Since the middle of the nineteenth century obligations to settle disputes by mediation have been written into some treaties (article 8 of the Treaty of Paris, 30 March, 1856). In fact most mediation was usually voluntary. Thus Pope Leo XIII refused to act as arbitrator in the dispute between Spain and Germany over the Caroline Islands, but he agreed to act as mediator in the matter (22 October, 1885); France was mediator at the end of the Spanish-American war (Treaty of Paris, 10 December, 1898).

Since the end of the First World War certain international organisations have acted as mediators in international conflicts. Mediation may be through States, represented by their governments, international institutions, or even independent persons (Count Folke Bernadotte in the Palestine questions).

(C) *Enquiry*

The function of a Commission of Inquiry is simply to investigate the facts of a dispute without suggesting any conclusion to be drawn from them. This procedure was laid down by the Hague Conferences and used in maritime cases (Dogger Bank Dispute, Cases of the Hull Fishermen, the *Tavignano* and the *Tubantia*). It was modified by the treaties which provided for commissions to be set up before a dispute arose, to which all States were required to submit their disputes and not go to war until the commissions had concluded their inquiry (Bryan Treaties). In the great recent international organisations (League of Nations and United Nations) the enquiry is only one of many procedures used in the interests of peace.

(D) *Conciliation*

Conciliation commissions are composed of nationals of the disputing parties and nationals of third States. Their task is to make proposals for a settlement which is not binding nor necessarily based on law. They have more scope than a commission of inquiry; conciliation is not quite the same as mediation, being non-political and having some of the features of arbitration. Permanent conciliation commissions were set up after the First World War under several treaties, together with various other procedures for the peaceful settlement of disputes. In fact these commissions did not fulfil expectations.

Güggenheim (*op. cit.*, vol. II. p, 212), quotes 9 cases, the only important one being the Franco-Siamese Conciliation Commission of 1947. S. Bastid, *Etudes en l'Honneur de G. Scelle*, 1950, vol. I, p. 1. A practical account of the work of a commission is given by Rolin in connection with the Belgian-Danish Commission in the case of the Danish steamships *Gorm* and *Stava* (RGDIP 1953, p. 353). The Swiss government has referred several cases to conciliation commissions, particularly against France.

(E) *Arbitration and judicial settlement*

When States submit a dispute to arbitration they agree to accept the binding decision of a third party which shall in principle be based on law. Although this is the theory there have often been political considerations as well. If the parties agree the arbitrators may be given discretion to decide without reference to the existing law (amicable settlement, right to decide *ex aequo et bono*). Judicial settlement differs from arbitration in that the parties are not free to choose the judges.

Arbitral procedure has improved in two respects:

(i) in the composition of the jurisdictional bodies: at first they were either heads of States or commissions composed of representatives of the parties presided over by a neutral, later they were composed of professional jurisconsults;

(ii) in the procedure for referring matters to the jurisdictional body. Arbitration has become gradually independent of the good will of the interested parties. States undertake in advance, by arbitration clauses (*clauses compromissoires*), to refer certain kinds of disputes to arbitration. But even then they had to agree to draft a compromise and appoint arbitrators. To get round this formality and allow a State to refer a dispute to arbitration unilaterally, a preconstituted court had to exist. In 1899 the Hague Conference did not get this far; the Permanent Court of Arbitration was no more than a list of possible arbitrators from which the parties could choose. The first proposals for a Court of Justice at the Hague Conference of 1907 fell through because no agreement was reached about the appointment of judges. The Covenant of the League of Nations provided for a permanent court, the Permanent Court of International Justice set up in 1920, which has been succeeded under the United Nations Charter by the International Court of Justice. Other international jurisdictions have been set up either by separate treaties or by regional international organisations: Central American Court of Justice, Court of Justice of the European Coal and Steel Community, etc.

Section III

SETTLEMENT OF INTERNATIONAL DISPUTES BY FORCE

Force, in this context, is not necessarily destructive physical force, but any open, undisguised means of constraint.

A few rudimentary notions on retorsion, reprisals and the development of the rules of warfare are needed to complete this general picture of intercourse between States.

(A) *Retorsion*

Measures of *retorsion* are the mildest form of constraint. They do not interfere with any legal obligation and generally their purpose is to reduce the facilities granted to a State or its nationals in international trade. The devolopment of international law and of treaty obligations limits the scope of retorsion since both States' freedom of action is reduced at the same time.

(B) *Reprisals*

Reprisals is the term used when a State takes coercive action which constitutes a violation of the rule of law, but which is based on a previous violation of the law by the State against which it is directed. The law is broken twice: first by the action which provoked reprisals, and second by the reprisals themselves. Reprisals may take various forms: from the non-application of a trade agreement or a law-making treaty, to specific acts of violence. The latter are the most open to question. In the nineteenth century reprisals took the form of: the occupation of part of the territory of a State, bombardment by a naval squadron, temporary seizure of merchant ships (embargo), the prohibition of communication with ports by means of a naval force (pacific blockade).

Contemporary writers give other striking examples (Franz von Liszt, *Le Droit International*, p. 297). A State may commit two kinds of coercive act against another State; either singly as reprisals, or as a consequence of a state of war. Sometimes States only want to coerce up to a certain point; by using the terms 'reprisals', 'pacific blockade', 'embargo', etc., the States indicate that they intend to keep within limits, and also (but not always) to avoid involving other States.

These coercive measures are mainly used against militarily weak States.

In the nineteenth century war was not simply the use of force but there was a 'state of war' which only existed after a declaration of the intention of the States.

Certain military operations on behalf of third States which did not entail a declaration of war bear this out. For instance, by a Convention with Belgium of 22 October, 1832, France and the United Kingdom undertook to use force against the Netherlands if the latter did not withdraw her troops from Belgian territory. Without declaring war the British fleet partially blockaded Dutch ports and French troops took up positions outside Antwerp.

(C) *War*

War has been defined as 'an armed struggle between two or more States, implying the possible use of all weapons not forbidden by international law and imposing on other States the rights and duties of neutrals'. War profoundly affects the position of all other States, particularly concerning maritime trade. In this sense we can talk of a *state* of war, which can only exist after a general declaration of intentions.

Since the middle of the nineteenth century there have been attempts to define the rules of warfare (*jus in bello*), and to insist that all military operations should be preceeded by a formal declaration of war. This was one of the aims of the Hague Conferences and the London Naval Declaration in 1909. There has been a general movement to regulate and humanise the conduct of wars.

Are countries free to resort to war or not as they wish? Leaving aside questions of morality and confining discussion to the strict letter of the law it is clear that in the nineteenth century States considered they had a discretionary competence to go to war. There were no rules forbidding it.

However, some treaties of alliance distinguished between offensive and defensive wars. States justified going to war not only in defence of their interests but also their rights. The best example is the use of force for the recovery of contract debts. The 2nd Hague Convention (Porter Convention) forbade the use of force for this purpose without first offering to go to arbitration; a State may use force only if the debtor State refuses to submit to arbitration or having agreed to do so has failed to carry out the award. The institution of permanent neutrality also gives rise to individual cases of lawful and unlawful war.

If we imagine a case of permanent neutrality not only recognised but guaranteed by third States, we wonder whether there would not be collective security in an international society where the neutrality of all States was guaranteed by the rest?

Some authors consider that to maintain that States have a discretionary competence to go to war shows an utter disregard of what is meant by an international juridical order since this in itself means that force is used only as a sanction (cf. Güggenheim, vol. II, p. 94, taking up points made by Kelsen).

Since the League of Nations there has been a tendency to forbid the discretionary use of force. The Covenant of the League of Nations defined lawful and unlawful wars, but still allowed lawful wars. On the other hand the Covenant did not sufficiently condemn the use of force short of war. Even a conflict on the scale of the Sino-Japanese conflict in 1931 was not considered by the States concerned to constitute a state of war.

A series of additional agreements, both regional and universal, have sought to lay down rules and definitions about all operations involving the use of force.

Particular mention must be made of the General Pact for the Renunciation of War, known as the Kellogg Pact of 27 August, 1928, which had been signed by 63 States by 1939. The signatory States renounced war as an instrument of national policy in their relations with one another. Henceforward the only lawful wars would be wars for self-defence or wars undertaken as a legitimate collective sanction decided by an international organisation. The Kellogg Pact did not prevent the Second World War but its violation was one of the grounds for the judgment against the major war criminals.

But it is not easy to put into effect the terms of the Pact governing the use of force. A previous legal right does not in itself justify the use of force; it depends how that title was acquired and how it can be established. When force is used each side will claim to have a legitimate motive, usually self-defence. The main problem is to decide who is the aggressor.

The only satisfactory settlement would be if there was an international body with a proper procedure for settling disputes, and empowered to declare whether and by whom the use of force was justified in every individual case.

If there is to be international peace, every State with a just cause must be strong enough to win, and this means it must have the support of the other States. This poses the problem of collective security.

Many things are needed to enforce the law. The force itself must be organised and the law must be universally recognised. The use of force as a means of settling disputes should be subordinate to the development of pacific methods of settlement. There must be an international legislator as well as a judge or a secular arm to declare that force must only be used as a purely legal sanction. The solution (still very incomplete) to all these closely connected problems lies in international organisations.

CHAPTER THREE

Structural Relations Between States

Section I

GENERAL CONSIDERATIONS

The lands and peoples of the world are not neatly parcelled out under the sole jurisdiction of a single State. Some are the concern of several States, others are administered and governed by other States without becoming part of them.

This is due to the fact that States are often structurally inter-related, in addition to the normal intercourse described in the preceding chapter. If the territory, population and government constitute the structure of the State, structural relations are *those relations which permanently modify the structure of a State in relation to one or several other States*.

Structural relations vary. In the Introduction (p. 28) several elementary points were made about structural relations between groups. In Section II one of the most interesting types of structural relations will be described; in Section III some factual examples will be given. As a preliminary we shall give a brief general outline and discuss the legal framework.

§ 1 DESCRIPTION

Structural relations in the world today have very different historical origins. We can classify them either by the period when they came into being, or by the great social movements which inspired them. Structural changes are often retained long after the circumstances which justifed them have disappeared. The purely descriptive account which follows will be modified and systematised later in the chapter.

(A) *From feudalism and monarchy*

Apart from the *vassal* status of certain Christian princedoms under the Ottoman Empire which later became the Balkan States, there are still several survivals of the feudal system.

The *Valleys of Andorra* have two co-princes, the head of the French State and the Spanish Bishop of Urgel, by virtue of treaties going back to the thirteenth century. These valleys do not constitute a State, but have a system which combines local autonomy with certain French and Spanish public services; the resulting structural relations are quite exceptional.

The *Principalities of Lichtenstein, Monaco and San Marino* are States, but because of their tiny size they have to enter into special relations with the neighbouring States of Switzerland, France and Italy respectively.

Until fairly recently there were examples of *personal union*. Personal union occurs when the same person, through an accident of succession, becomes the head of two different States. Personal union has disappeared. The last well-known examples were the unions of England and Hanover (1714–1837), of the Netherlands and Luxembourg (1815–1890), of Belgium and the independent State of the Congo (1885–1908).

As in private law, feudal law is still invoked in some international disputes; cf. the case presented by France and UK in the case of the Ecrehos and Minquiers, (ICJ, 17 November, 1953, p. 53).

(B) *From colonisation*

Colonisation gave rise to many new structural relations in international law.

In a *protectorate* one State assumes responsibility for the external relations of another State and also directs or controls part of its internal administration. French protectorates in Tunisia and Morocco were classic examples of official protectorates.

International leases are when a State surrenders its jurisdiction over a part of its territory (usually a small part) for a fairly long period (usually 20–50 years).

The old forms of colonialism have given place to the new formulae of *mandate* or *trusteeship*. Under this system territories are not States, but they are destined to be in the future. The administering power exercises State jurisdiction in the territory until such time as its own organs have developed.

As we have already seen colonialism tends to lead to federal structures. Territories are re-grouped along with extensive measures of decentralisation. A form of association is organised between the old colonial powers and the new States, often along federal lines, but generally adopting procedures closer to international practice. The three present-day examples are the Commonwealth, the French Union, and the Dutch-Indonesian Union; the first is the most interesting and will be examined separately in Section III.

(C) *From federalism*

For a long time neighbouring States, or States with a common culture and common interests, or sometimes a personal union, have conferred jurisdiction in certain matters, particularly economic and foreign affairs, on common organs. In modern times there have been the Swedish-Norwegian union (1815–1905), the Austro-Hungarian (1867–1918), the Danish-Icelandic (1918–1944). These were all based on a monarchy and only involved two States each.

Elsewhere (in Switzerland, United States, Germany, and later South Africa, Australia, Canada, New Zealand, and various South American Republics), there has been a different kind of union. Each union involved a large number of States, and the common services were set up within the framework of representative institutions. This is the origin of the 'composite States', *confederations*, *federations* and *united states*. The best-known instances (Switzerland, United States of America, Germany) seem to show a tendency for the common organs to expand in scope and importance. The member States of the association begin by having the quality of States, but by the end it is the association which is the State in the full sense of the word and the original member States only retain the nominal title. This trend is very important for international law. The international relations of these associations of States give rise to special problems (international personality of the confederation, federation and member States, and the capacity of member States to conclude international agreements). Moreover these structural relations, which grew out of exceptionally favourable circumstances, are 'models' for the future development of societies which are not yet so advanced. The internal affairs of present-day federations are not directly relevant to international relations; but the history of federations is important for understanding other possible forms of development. The whole of Section II will therefore deal with confederations and federations.

(D) *From partitions of territory*

However frontiers are drawn they will fail to take account of some problem or other.

To settle these outstanding problems States have for a long time entered into undertakings which in principle are as permanent as the frontier. The primary consideration has always been political: to ensure a better balance of power or compromise between rival ambitions, a State's jurisdiction over a part of its territory is reduced. The simplest instance is to forbid fortifications. But the arrangements are often more complex, based on a joint administration of certain parts of the territory. There are many international conventions for the purpose of improving facilities for international communications despite an awkward frontier-line; and sometimes ports which serve several States have been internationalised. A further and more humanitarian consideration has been the wish to protect minorities cut off by a national frontier. The traditional formula for the protection of minorities, which was introduced after the First World War, was that States agreed to limit their normal jurisdiction over their nationals. There are further examples in the agreements of 5 September, 1946 between Austria and Italy and 5 October, 1954 between Italy and Jugoslavia.

The means of dealing with these problems are very varied. Besides the cases where a State agrees to limit the exercise of its jurisdiction, there are cases in which a genuine international administration is set up, whose jurisdiction is intimately connected with territorial settlements.

Here are a few brief examples.

Sometimes the territory concerned continues to belong to one State but a special autonomous régime guarantees the interests of another State which has some jurisdiction there. The *Memel Territory* was in this position under the Convention of 8 May, 1924. So was *Tangiers*, 'Moroccan city administered internationally' (Rousseau, *Droit international public*, p. 175). Tangiers continued to belong to Morocco and to come under the sovereign jurisdiction of the Sultan, but as a result of certain agreements (particularly the Convention of 18 December, 1923, the Final Act of Paris of 31 August, 1945, and the Convention and Protocol of 10 November, 1952), the zone of Tangiers was placed under several international bodies whose composition was determined by certain foreign States. Or the internationalised territory may be detached from the territory of the State concerned, for instance the *Free Territory of Trieste*, created by article I of the Italian Peace Treaty. The Protocol Agreement of

London drew a new demarcation line between the part of the territory under Italian jurisdiction and the part under Jugoslav jurisdiction. The *Free City of Danzig* was similarly detached from the German Reich, internationalised, and complicated provisions concerning its port functions were made in favour of Poland; these stressed the role of Danzig as a port. This is a classic example of 'functional internationalisation'. The proposals drafted by the Security Council of the United Nations in 1950 concerning the *Holy Places*, are on the same lines; the territory is internationalised so that different religions may have better access to their holy places.

§ 2 LEGAL ANALYSIS

(A) *General*

In the foregoing account we have used the terms 'protectorate', 'federation', 'international lease', etc. Do these expressions denote general legal categories on the basis of which one could solve a problem of law, or are they politico-sociological notions?

We can say at once that these notions have no general legal significance. All structural relations are based on treaties or agreements; problems relating to them must be solved by interpreting those treaties; in this field no two situations are alike. There is no general international system of protectorates, but a number of individual protectorates; the same is true of federations. In international law we must be careful not to misuse legal categories. These are only abstractions based on insufficient concrete examples. There is such variety in practice that it is impossible to analyse an abstract notion strictly. We can arrange the various examples in 'series', according to a particular criterion, but we should not overestimate the differences or the similarities; this would inevitably happen if we tried to set up legal categories.

All structural relations amount to changes in State jurisdictions. Sometimes a single State's jurisdiction is limited and no more: a State gives up its freedom to act in a particular way. But it is often more complicated than this; the competence a State has been exercising does not just cease to exist, it is instead exercised by another State or by an international body, sometimes in the name of the State which has ceased to exercise it, sometimes in the name of the State or the body which exercises it in its place. There is thus a *substitution* or *transfer* of competence. Then all kinds of problems arise, in particular the problem of *representation*.

It is also important to enquire whether the relations are based on common interests and defined and defended in law; in this case we must examine how these interests are technically defined and how the institutions responsible for defending them have been set up. The legal machinery set up for this purpose is always complex and reveals structural relations of a higher order. The delimitation of common interests and the setting up of bodies to defend them raises the most interesting problems.

(B) *Delimitation of common interests*

To define common interests is to define the underlying reasons for the introduction of structural changes. Precise and clear definition is always difficult in these matters; but an additional difficulty is the intimate connection between the various branches of State activity. For example is it possible to make a clear and valid distinction between 'defence questions', 'economic affairs' and 'foreign affairs'? Examination shows that each of them calls for an entirely different approach; for example, postal and radio communications is a subject which can be defined in terms of a precise concrete objective. But 'defence questions' is not only concerned with a concrete sector, the Armed Forces, but also with any other subject likely to affect the *end in view*, national defence; and 'foreign affairs' are defined neither in terms of a precise concrete objective nor an end in view, but solely in terms of the persons who conduct them (States and international organisations), or even the territorial framework of such relations; all questions come under the heading of foreign affairs the moment they are of an 'external' character.

We are therefore faced with a *formal* difficulty of legal definition and the *practical* difficulty that in the modern world it is not easy to disentangle 'questions', 'interests' and 'subjects'.

(C) *Organs responsible for common interests*

There are two possible alternatives: either the local collectivities concerned set up the organs to further common interests, or this is done from outside.

Gierke made a similar distinction in his theory of moral persons, later widely accepted. Gierke distinguished in organisations between the *interest* served and the *will* expressed for this purpose. When the will which called the organisation into being belongs to those whose interests are affected we have a *corporation* (society, association); when, on the other hand, the will and the interests differ in origin we have a *foundation*.

An illustration will show how this works. The Act of Algeciras of 1906 involved Morocco and several other powers. It laid down a number of interests common to those powers. Those interests were also interests of the Moroccan State: public order, public health, major public works, public finance, etc. However, the same Act might have recognised that the Shereefian State had interests in the affairs of the other States parties to the Act, for example in their customs system, but it did not do so. It defined common interests unilaterally and in a limited sense. To manage these common interests in Morocco it set up several bodies in which all the powers participated: Diplomatic Body of Tangiers (art. 61, 63, 64, 65), Permanent Committee of Customs (art. 97), Committee on Customs Valuations (art. 96), State Bank, etc. A careful study of the way these bodies worked shows that in many cases their intervention in common affairs amounted to an abrogation of the powers of the Shereefian authorities. So although this is a very interesting system, apparently organised on federal lines, the way common interests were defined and managed made it more like a protectorate vested in a group of States.

Thus a close analysis brings out the legal consequences of the underlying notion of equality and inequality of States (cf. p. 29). When States concurrently define the interests which they have in common and set up special organs to deal with them, a federation or a confederation is formed.

Section II

CONFEDERATION AND FEDERATION

These unions of States are the most intimate form of structural relations possible between States. Their relations are so close as to threaten individual personality (§ 1). We can also say that the common organs are most highly developed (§ 2), and that they presuppose a complex system of checks and balances (§ 3).

§ 1 INTERNATIONAL PERSONALITY IN CONFEDERATIONS AND FEDERATIONS

(A) *Difference between confederation and federation*
There is a classic distinction between confederation and federation.
In a confederation relations between the States are laid down by

international treaty; the confederation may have extensive jurisdiction over common interests, but the member States remain States. The confederation may be empowered by the terms of the original treaty to represent the member States in international relations and to conclude international engagements, but the member States generally retain their international competence in all cases not expressly covered by the treaty.

In a federation the relations between the States are laid down in a constitution; the States lose their international personality and are no longer States in the proper sense of the word, since external relations are entirely in the hands of the federation.

This distinction is broadly valid, but there are variations, and one has to consider them as two tendencies rather than two clearly defined categories. A rigorous distinction of this kind between federation and confederation does not correspond to reality. Broadly speaking, most confederations are based on a treaty, and most federations are based on a constitution. But historically an original treaty may undergo changes and become a constitution, and moreover some of those subsequent changes may be adopted without the consent of all the original parties. Some unitary States were founded by treaties; why should not a federal State? Moreover, international practice offers an extraordinary variety of solutions. The 1871 Constitution of the German Empire gave the member countries the right to conduct international relations. Article 18a of the Soviet Constitution of 1936 allows the Soviet Republics, members of the USSR, to retain full international personality. The only practical application of this rule has been the admission of two extra Soviet representatives to the United Nations in the name of the Ukraine and Dyelorussia. The Swiss cantons also have a certain degree of international competence, although there is disagreement on this point about the interpretation of the Swiss Constitution (Güggenheim, *op. cit.*, vol. I, p. 306).

> The question of whether relations between member States (for example frontier conflicts) should be settled according to international law or simply by analogy with international law, seems from the purely customary character of the rules applied to be a purely theoretical matter. Compare L. Oppenheim, *International law*, vol. I, p. 167, and Güggenheim, vol. I, p. 306.

(B) *Relative indivisibility of external relations*

So far international practice has shown that jurisdiction over foreign affairs is not shared *equally* between the States of the union and the union government. There are strictly practical reasons for this; the allocation of functions has to be relatively simple since it would be impossible for third States to observe a very complicated set of rules for the allocation of international functions in a foreign system. There is also the point already mentioned about the general competence to conclude treaties. Yet the process by which a confederation becomes progressively more integrated until it becomes a federation is not always steady and continuous. There is a big step forward each time a question arises which it is impossible or very difficult to divide (cf. *infra*, Section III, § 3, example of the United States).

If the federation and not the member States has almost exclusive competence for international relations, this gives rise to the further problem whether the federation can also conclude treaties on matters reserved to the member States. If it cannot, then a federal State is unable to enter into undertakings on any of those matters; and its international competence is limited by its internal structure. If the federation can conclude such treaties and does so very frequently it will encroach on the jurisdiction of the member States. The federation will therefore be able to achieve through international relations what it is forbidden to do by internal procedures. *International relations are therefore an instrument of centralisation in composite structures.* In a federal State which belongs to an international society with intensive international relations, we can distinguish three levels of social relations and legal institutions: international, federal and local. It is very difficult to build up such complex political structures. The machinery of the federal State is itself fairly complicated. The additional complication of international affairs naturally makes it necessary to centralise matters inside the State as far as possible. Political structures must always remain relatively simple.

Federal States have solved this problem in various ways. In some (United States, Switzerland) the federation can conclude treaties on matters reserved to the member States; in others it cannot do so.

The difference between the international capacity of federal and unitary States has already raised serious difficulties in the working of machinery like the International Labour Conventions. Max Sørensen, *Federal States and the international protection of human rights*, AJ 1952, p. 195.

There are two broad tendencies in all federal States; one clearly dominant at the present day towards increasingly unitary structures, and the other to preserve the rights of the member States from any encroachment by the federation,

§ 2 THE EVOLUTION OF COMMON ORGANS

Common organs develop on simple lines. First the functions of a confederation or federation are differentiated, as they are in all groups, between legislative, executive and judicial organs.

Second, federalism has a special problem: *to associate the member States with the formation of the common will.*

There are three stages of development (which we shall return to in connection with international organisations, p. 209).

(1) The common organs first appear in the form of meetings of representatives of the member States. Once these are started, the conditions must be determined under which decisions of these common organs are made. This poses a fundamental political problem of the respective influence of the small, medium and large States. A compromise has to be found which guarantees the influence of each of them, either by fixing the number of representatives of each State, or the number of votes each State is allowed, or the sort of majority required to pass resolutions (simple majority, virtual unanimity, or special rights like *veto* for the representatives of certain States). There are all sorts of possible combinations. If no satisfactory solution is found it is always possible to create two organs composed of representatives of the member States, each with slightly different membership and powers. The best historical example of this is the Diet of the German Confederation set up by the Acts of Vienna of 8 June, 1815, and of 15 May, 1820.

As we have remarked in the Introduction (p. 26) the practical arrangements depend on the number and importance of the States concerned. The greater the number of States the easier it is to find a satisfactory arrangement. If there are only two States either one is completely subjected to the will of the other, or they are put on an absolutely equal footing and this parity principle is very difficult to put into effect in practice.

In this case it is truer to say that the two States are acting on parallel lines rather than that they have a common will, and it was precisely the existence of two States which used to be the distinction between a real union and a confederal or federal State (for this see Rousseau, p. 99) (cf. CPJI, B/8, p. 42). For the same reasons the federal system set up in Ethiopia and Eritrea following on Resolution 309v of 2 December, 1950, of the United Nations General Assembly, proved very difficult to apply. Report of a group of jurists (A/AC.4 4SCI/RI), *La cronique de Colliard, Revue Jur. et Pol. de l'Union Française*, 1952, p. 266, and report of the United Nations Commissioner in Eritrea (General Assembly, 7th Spec. sess. 15 (A (2188)), 1952.

(2) Besides the common organs composed of representatives of the States there are the organs composed of officials of the federation. These officials constitute the nucleus of a common administration. The existence of such an administration makes the task of the organ composed of representatives of the States much simpler. But the latter is still handicapped politically in that it represents the confederation or federation *collectively*, while there is no one person to represent it directly and *individually*.

A typical example of this situation was when the States which emerged from the revolt of the former English colonies in America were united under the *Articles of the Confederation* (1781). During this period a Congress composed of one representative from each government proved quite inadequate to administer common affairs (foreign affairs, currency, loans, army and navy).

(3) *Representative government* brought a profound change, as fundamental for federalism as the monarchy was for personal union. If it is thought that the population of the States is sufficiently homogeneous to appoint its *own* representatives it becomes easy to increase the number of union organs. This produces the classical type of federal bicameralism. A clearly differentiated executive can be established and a Court of Justice responsible for maintaining the complex legal machinery of this type of structure.

3 FEDERAL CHECKS AND BALANCES

In its complete form federalism is based on a balance between local societies and the federal society.

This equilibrium is only possible through the operation of an elaborate system of checks and balances.

(1) The creation of two distinct superimposed legal systems, each with separate rules and separate organs to legislate and to execute them.

(2) The allocation of functions between the local and central legal systems in such a way that local interests are safeguarded by the local legal system and general interests by the central legal system. In certain circumstances questions of both local and common interest come under the jurisdiction of both local and central authorities. These are concurrent powers, but the central authority takes precedence over the local if called upon.

(3) Participation of local organs in some central organs in order to ensure a proper political balance. This conception has already been

explained in § 2; the classic example is the United States Senate which is composed of two representatives from each local State and together with the House of Representatives forms the Congress of the United States. It ensures that local interests are defended in federal policy through its special role in the ratification of treaties (authorisation to ratify requiring a two thirds majority) and in the nomination of certain high officers of State.

(4) Collaboration between local and central agents and between the local agents of the different States. A drawback to the multiplication of legal systems is the increase in the number of agents and services each specialising in a particular field. Constant collaboration between the representatives of the various systems and between their agents should make it possible to overcome these difficulties. There is nothing to stop an official of one system working for another system. Moreover the local States and the federation are free to conclude agreements to eliminate the worst distortions and discrepancies. For this reason local States in many federal systems have sought to unify as far as possible the local legislation within their jurisdiction.

Section III

APPLICATIONS

§ 1 THE STATE OF THE VATICAN CITY

(A) *Position of the Holy See and the Catholic Church before the Lateran Treaties*

Until 1870 the Supreme Pontiff combined in his person two quite distinct functions, Head of the Catholic Church and Head of the Papal States. His diplomatic agents, the nuncios, represented him in this dual capacity and representatives of foreign States were accredited to him in his dual capacity. The Holy See, however, distinguished between two kinds of international agreement: treaties concerning the Papal States and concordats concerning the position of the Catholic faith in foreign countries.

From 1870 onwards, of the Supreme Pontiff's two titles, that of Head of the Catholic Church was the most important; concordats were already more important in the life of the Catholic Church than treaties relating to the Papal States. This is still basically true today.

A foreign head of State, acting with full territorial sovereignty, can in law refuse to recognise the bond between his Catholic nationals and the Supreme Pontiff; equally, Catholics and the Supreme Pontiff hold that these bonds and the development of the life of the Church are quite independent of the temporal power. But it is clearly not in the interest of either the Church or the State (when it has a strong Catholic element) to refuse to come to terms and lay down certain rights and duties on both sides. This is the origin of concordats, which grant the Church certain rights and withhold others. For a long time each claimed to regard them as unilateral concessions made on his sole authority so as to safeguard his own rights more effectively. Today it is generally recognised that they have the same force as international agreements (this is agreed even by 'positivists' such as Anzilotti). Concordats are proof that the Catholic Church is the only international organisation powerful enough to be treated by States as an equal.

Settlements by concordat have tended to be unsatisfactory and short-lived, chiefly owing to frequent conflicts between States and the Holy See. In particular States claim the right to forbid contacts between the nuncio and the local clergy, although this contact is the simplest expression of the international character of the Church. In a reply to a question by M. Deixonne, deputy, the French Foreign Minister said (11 February, 1954): 'There is no rule in international law covering the canonical powers of the nuncios, some countries apply canon 267 and others are against it.' Many countries only have relations with the Holy See in order to oppose these contacts. Some international institutions have considered concordats as treaties; thus a number of them were registered with the League of Nations (for example, Treaty Series, vol. XVII, p. 365; vol. LXXIX, p. 157).

The conquest of the City of Rome by Italian troops in 1871 put an end to the Papal States. In his relations with States the Supreme Pontiff lost those rights attached to his temporal sovereignty. In practice the Holy See's passive and active right of legation was exercised as in the past and concordats were concluded. The Italian government sought to give the Holy See an international status. Just after the occupation of Rome it sent many assurances to foreign chancelleries and even offered to enter into synallagmatic undertakings. Foreign States took note of the Italian declarations. The Italian law of 13 May, 1871, known as the Law of Guarantees, made provision in Italian municipal law for guarantees for the Supreme Pontiff: (1) A personal status as in the past; (2) Total freedom in international relations with foreign States. The Italian government simply recognised the Head of the Catholic Church as an international person (Anzilotti, *Cours de Droit International*, vol. I, p. 152).

Italian authors have always admitted that the Law of Guarantees could be modified by the Italian government, provided that it did not affect the general object of the Law, which amounted to an international obligation.

The legal nature of an agreement concluded by the Holy See on these lines might have been contested and it might have had an uneasy passage. Everyone was well aware of the spiritual character of the Church, but this itself was a difficulty in some ways. States like to deal only with their equals and to acknowledge that a purely spiritual power had an international personality was perhaps more difficult for some of them to accept than if that power had, at least in appearance, some temporal power.

Out of all this came the Lateran Treaties in 1929, which ended the rupture between Italy and the Holy See.

(B) *Position of the Holy See after the Lateran Treaties of* 11 *February,* 1929

The Lateran Treaties are several acts linked together, a treaty, a concordat and a financial convention. The treaty created the *State of the Vatican City*. Thereafter the Supreme Pontiff united in his person the two functions of Head of the State and Head of the Catholic Church. In the latter capacity his rights were again recognised in article 2 of the treaty which acknowledges 'the sovereignty of the Holy See in international matters as inherent in its nature, and in conformity with its tradition and the requirements of its mission in the world.'

The treaty granted the Holy See material advantages which would allow it freely to exercise its rights; to support these material advantages juridically a State was created. There was no more argument about the nature of the acts binding Italy and the Holy See; the latter has an objective position which can be recognised by third States. Diplomatic contacts were facilitated between the Holy See and the States who had no special reason for recognising the Church as a legal person.

It has often been said that the State of the Vatican City is a fictitious State by reason of:

(1) The tiny size of its scattered territory;

(2) The functional character of Vatican nationality; the treaty provides for a Vatican nationality 'in conformity with the rules of international law', but Vatican nationality usually goes with the exercise of certain functions and is therefore only temporary.

(3) The absence of really autonomous public services.

As against this it is agreed that the State of the Vatican City has a territory, a population (there are examples of non-functional nationality) and a government.

To judge this question we must refer to definitions of a State. If we take a sociological-political definition of the State it presupposes some degree of physical force; then we can argue that the Vatican City is not a State. But in law the fact that the Vatican City is recognised as a State by other States is enough for it to be considered as such. It is certainly recognised by Italy and it seems to have been recognised by several other States, particularly after the military operations in Italy in the course of the Second World War.

The nature of the State of the Vatican City has led to very special structural relations between it and the Italian State. The State of the Vatican City can only live through a measure of symbiosis with the Italian State. It has its own political organisation, an autonomous government and its own legislation; on the other hand it has renounced certain State competences and has delegated the exercise of some of them to the Italian State.

The Vatican City will in all circumstances be considered as neutral and inviolable territory (art. 24 of the Lateran Treaty); the Holy See declares that it does not desire to take part in temporal rivalries between other States, nor in international conferences which these rivalries provoke unless the conflicting parties unanimously appeal to it to do so. This provision confines the State of the Vatican City to politically 'disinterested' international activities.

In 1930 the intervention of the Holy See in the form of mediation put an end to the dispute between Haiti and San Domingo. On 25 July, 1951, the Holy See signed the Final Act of the Conference on the status of refugees or stateless persons and also the convention of 28 September, 1954, regarding the status of stateless persons. The Food and Agriculture Organisation allows 'permanent observers' and the State of the Vatican City has been admitted in this capacity and contributes $1,000 a year; it also attended the Atomic Energy Conference in 1955.

The Vatican City can and has created civil and criminal courts within its territory (basic law of 7 June, 1929, art. 9–17), but it has the right to ask Italy to punish offences committed within its territory and it uses this right. Nearly all communication services are undertaken by the Italian authorities on behalf of the City in virtue of individual conventions. The economic resources on which the City lives, from currency to all kinds of provisions, are provided by Italy and in agreement with her.

The main points about the Holy See may be summed up as follows:

(1) The Catholic Church is a non-governmental international organisation, recognised as an international person by a number of States who have diplomatic relations with her for particular matters;

(2) A State, the Vatican City, is in personal union with the Catholic Church and this is recognised by Italy and other States. Through this State, the Church has at its disposal relations and material facilities which enable it to fulfil its functions satisfactorily;

(3) There are intimate and complex structural relations between Italy and the Vatican City.

It has been said (Fr. Le Roy, *La personnalité juridique du Saint-Siège et de l'Eglise Catholique en droit international, Année canonique*, vol. II, 1953, p. 125), that the Lateran Treaty was nothing more than an *accord de siège* (headquarters agreement) between an international organisation and the State where it has its seat. The explanation is ingenious, but it is not in accordance with the clearly expressed intention of the parties. Moreover the creation of the State seems to have furnished a more solid basis for defending the interests of the Holy See during the world war.

§ 2 THE COMMONWEALTH

(A) *General practice*

The Commonwealth is a political system which at present unites the United Kingdom, Canada, Australia, New Zealand, the Union of South Africa, India, Pakistan, Ceylon, Ghana, Malaya and their dependent territories.

Even those most attached to classification recognise the singular character of this union. The Commonwealth has world-wide importance; in addition its interest may be summarised as follows:

(1) It is the only important and successful example of a political system being decentralised to such a point without losing its influence;

(2) It is the only system which has managed to unite such diverse elements. The position of each constituent element must be defined and examined separately;

(3) It has developed gradually, starting from a unitary State. British possessions overseas were first granted local representative assemblies (representative government), then the right to be governed

G

by authorities responsible to those assemblies (responsible government). The Durham Report, in 1839, marked the general adoption of this conception. The international personality of the 'Dominions', already outlined, was evident at the conclusion of peace in 1919; since then evolution has continued, embodied in general acts such as the Balfour Report of 1926 and the Statute of Westminster in 1931. A distinction emerges between laws and conventions: laws have sometimes been passed over in favour of conventions and this has always facilitated transition during the various stages of evolution.

Today the Commonwealth comprises: (1) Independent States, the Dominions, the most recent being India, Pakistan, Ceylon, Ghana, and Malaya, all of non-British stock; (2) Colonies which are in turn going through the stages already passed by the Dominions; they are being regrouped to strengthen their political balance, as in Central Africa, East Africa, the West Indies.

Outside the Commonwealth, but linked to the United Kingdom, are States like Iraq and Burma. Ireland considers herself outside the Commonwealth but is not looked upon by the Commonwealth as a completely foreign State.

(B) *Present position*

In terms of the relations between the United Kingdom and the Dominions, the Commonwealth is a union of States whose real strength lies in their solidarity of interests—(this is not to deny the force of symbolism)—and which will only agree to methods of unification based on co-operation.

(a) *Solidarity of interests.* The United Kingdom and the Dominions are united by ties of various kinds. The most important has been race: the British Dominions have been peopled with British stock and the home country has been a necessary demographic reservoir (less than 25 million white inhabitants for the 4 British Dominions).

This solidarity is reflected in a common citizenship, since each member of the Commonwealth is free to decide not only its own citizenship but the extent and effects of this double citizenship.

Even after the entry of India there are still close linguistic and cultural ties between India, Pakistan and Ceylon and the United Kingdom and other Dominions. Her sea and air power ensure the United Kingdom a decisive influence in world communications and in wartime a not insignificant role in common defence. The United

Kingdom's efforts in the nuclear and electronic fields have strengthened her position. The Commonwealth is still a real force; in trade, finance and economics; organisation and control of the world's most important raw material markets, trade facilities through tariff preferences, the sterling area, a common pool of strong currencies and the creation of privileged currency transfers (particularly after the Second World War when the UK was in debt to the Dominions).

(b) *Symbolic force*. For a long time the symbol of the Commonwealth has been the Crown, which was regarded as indivisible and embodied the fact that the King of England was head of State for all the Dominions. The final secession of Ireland followed from her rejection of the Crown. But it has been different in the case of India. The Congress of India refused allegiance to the Crown and set up a republican régime. A simple communiqué published on 28 April, 1949, after a conference of Commonwealth Prime Ministers changed the symbol and perhaps its significance. For the British Dominions the Crown and allegiance to the Crown are elements of the Commonwealth, but for India there is only a 'King as the symbol of the free association of its independent member nations and as such the head of the Commonwealth'. For India, at least, the King is only the symbol of the fact that the Dominions 'remain united as free and equal members of the Commonwealth of Nations freely co-operating in the pursuit of peace, liberty and progress'. This is why Queen Elizabeth bears the title of Head of the Commonwealth.

Equality of status is the very basis of the Commonwealth. According to the famous Balfour Report: 'Great Britain and the Dominions . . . are Communities within the British Empire, equal in status, in no way subordinate one to another in any respect of their domestic or external affairs.' But in 1926 this same report was still thinking in terms of 'functional' equality; by which it was understood that in military as in foreign affairs 'the major responsibility rests now, and must for some time continue to rest, with His Majesty's Government in Great Britain.'

Since that time this *de facto* inequality has disappeared. A number of legal survivals of the old inequality have been eliminated or are in process of being so. The Dominions have acquired the right to amend their constitutions freely. The Statute of Westminster conferred on the Dominions freedom to pass their own legislation and this right has been used in all the Dominions. The Judicial Committee of the Privy Council as a supreme court of appeal only survives in a few exceptional cases for Australia and New Zealand.

Each of the Dominions freely exercises its right to conduct international relations in peace and war. During the war of 1939 the Dominions entered the war voluntarily beside the United Kingdom, whereas the United Kingdom's entry into the First World War virtually compelled them to become belligerents. Since 1945 the members of the Commonwealth have acted perfectly freely in foreign affairs, often acting on personal initiative. Not only do the Dominions have diplomatic representation in most States, but also in Great Britain and the other Dominions through High Commissioners.

The King of England signs (but does not countersign) the letters of credence of the Dominions which recognise him as Head of the State; this is why the title of High Commissioner was created, since the King of England could not accredit his own representatives to himself. Since 1948 the High Commissioners have ranked as Ambassadors.

(c) *Co-operation*. The machinery for co-operation is very simple: it is based on meetings of the political representatives, officials or agents of similar status of the Commonwealth States seeking a common approach without encroaching on each member's self-determination. There is no legal 'obligation' involved in all this; it is entirely a matter of the community of interests on which the Commonwealth is based and which it always accurately reflects. This definition of co-operation is very important, because, as will be seen later, it is valid not only for relations inside the Commonwealth, but for world organisations based on the Commonwealth model or dominated by it.

While the machinery for this co-operation and the channels of communication are very important in practice, they are chiefly remarkable for their variety and flexibility. For a time, formal conferences of Prime Ministers were the official expression of co-operation in the Commonwealth (imperial conferences); the last one was in 1937. Since the war there have been frequent but less formal meetings of Prime Ministers or of ministers concerned with particular problems: defence, economics, etc. These meetings take place in one of the capitals. Important decisions have been taken at some of them; for instance the meeting of Foreign Ministers at Colombo in January, 1950, decided to set up a consultative committee and in September to create in London a Council for Technical Co-operation to promote the economic development of the Commonwealth countries in Asia comprising, with 570 million inhabitants, a quarter of the world's population. The plan for economic development made up of the combined proposals of each State is known as the Colombo Plan.

There have been proposals for new work in all fields and several bodies have been created with varying degrees of permanence.

The heart of Commonwealth relations is the Commonwealth Relations Office in London, which is the centre for mutual contacts essential for co-operation.

This is an outline of the Commonwealth. Apart from its theoretical importance and the practical interest attached to a form of organisation covering more than a quarter of all international relations, there is one final important fact about the political structure of the Commonwealth. The scope and intensity of mutual relations between the members of the Commonwealth and the United Kingdom is greater than their relations with any other part of the world. *This then is the maximum concession of sovereignty which the Commonwealth States are prepared to make for any international organisation.*

§ 3 FEDERALISM AND ECONOMIC UNIFICATION

(A) *In general*

The development of federalism depends on the methods and extent of the economic unification which is one of the reasons for its creation.

The benefits anticipated from economic unification are at the root of many federal movements. The acts which lay down the relations between the confederation or federation on the one hand and the member States on the other, attempt to define for this purpose the respective rights of the member States and the confederation. How is this problem posed and how solved? What happens later?

(*a*) *Original position.* The historical context is important. The great examples of federalism were all probably influenced by economic liberalism, from the United States (1787), Switzerland (1848), the German Federalism of the *Zollverein*, to the British Dominions and the Latin American States. *Federalism is intimately connected with economic liberalism; both were challenged at the same time, both were modified simultaneously.*

Apart from some sophisticated conceptions, this liberalism was based on simple, well-known ideas: liberty is good in itself because it ensures the best conditions for economic development; it is, moreover, a natural state; to bring it about the government must simply refrain from interfering. Liberalism was hostile to State powers.

Obviously this favoured a federal structure. Since all State intervention was condemned there was no serious difficulty about sharing competences between the federation and the member States. Federal pacts had a purely negative purpose: to get rid of obstacles to liberty.

Those who drafted international and constitutional acts and those who put them into effect seem to have had in mind a twofold distinction.

First between the circulation and the production of wealth, and second between local society and federal society.

The most obvious obstacles to economic unification were seen at frontiers: customs duties, port duties, shipping dues, etc. The unions therefore abolished these between the member States. Federalism is essentially concerned with the circulation of goods. The rules it lays down must make for free transit. In its historical context this was sufficient for liberalism; States were generally interested in the transit of goods but not in production. This was the position at the beginning of the nineteenth century. Federal acts contained provisions on the movement of goods but they said nothing about conditions of production.

This is partly because the State hardly interfered at all in production, and partly because of the distinction between local and federal society. As has been shown in the Introduction, a society is defined in terms of the intensity of social intercourse and the appearance of common interests. At the beginning of the nineteenth century, in the countries under consideration, there was hardly any contact between local economies and a federal economy. Most trade was still localised, and this only changed with the prodigious expansion of transport following on the development of railways. Economic groups, principally private firms, only worked for a local market; only a few products with fairly limited uses were traded over long distances. There was therefore a fairly simple distinction between local and federal production. By passing over problems of production in the first place, the unions of States avoided a disturbing element.

Economic unification, then, can be begun without conferring extensive powers on the federation, simply by eliminating all obstacles the member States might put in the way of free movement of wealth within the federation.

(b) *Changes brought about by State intervention.* This initial position became increasingly complicated, and in about a hundred years the system collapsed and destroyed the balance of the political institutions as well.

It became obvious that the tenets of liberalism did not satisfy the hopes and needs of those people concerned. The cult of liberalism was preserved but its legal framework was modified. Economic freedom is not a natural phenomenon. The exercise of liberty destroys that fluidity and flexibility in the market which are the technical expression of free enterprise. The government tries then to ensure a free market by legal rules and intervenes in the name of liberty. Such powers, in the nature of things, are exercised at the highest level, that is at the federal level. But the change goes deeper. Those concerned turn their back on economic freedom; this is reflected in the importance attached to so-called 'social' conditions; labour conditions all over the world are settled by State intervention.

The intervention of the State increased in many ways. Sometimes it was based on a concerted plan, more often for financial purposes, or in response to the social pressure of combined interests.

Every fresh intervention revealed the federal dilemma. If the member States reserve the right to decide when, where and how to intervene, the economic unity built up under cover of official liberalism dissolves in a multitude of contradictory local systems of legislation; if the federation reserves the right to intervene, its jurisdiction gradually extends to all branches of production.

During the same period economic conditions have made the old state frontiers meaningless. They still mark the frontiers of the States' jurisdiction, but they no longer delimit a society economically distinct and separate from the federal society. The change is often most noticeable in particularly advanced sectors. Thus the question of transport, which played an important role in the development of many federations, has been the source of many State-federation conflicts. The same was true of all services essential to trade such as banking and insurance.

An impartial observer who examined the present state of federalism in countries where it has traditionally been strong would conclude that local prerogatives are losing ground to the central powers. Economic development and modern forms of State intervention have destroyed the old equilibrium.

The conception of a balance of power is not necessarily out of date. Certainly even in a country the size of the United States there is not much future in a territorial redistribution of powers. But another question is a form of decentralisation which is not territorial but by sectors of economic activity, to prevent the State assuming complete control over the whole of business. However that may be, the future of international economic relations has different horizons.

It is natural today in small or medium-sized States for governments or public opinion to seek economic unification. They follow the successful example of the United States. But reflection, based on a better knowledge of historical facts, indicates that obstacles to any kind of unification between States are far more formidable in the middle of the twentieth century than at the beginning of the nineteenth century. The old federal techniques are no longer valid. New methods must be found, based in part on the experience of the past, but they will not have an easy success.

(B) *The example of the United States*

The insurrection of the English colonies in America was intimately connected with trade problems and economic legislation. It was the exclusive and authoritarian system known as the 'Colonial Pact' which led to the colonies breaking away from the home country. But the new States which came into being were not at first reconciled to the idea of a unified economic system. When the Confederation was first established the States which enjoyed the advantage of having ports open to foreign trade taxed the States who traded through their territory and even levied harsher tolls on goods from neighbouring States than on goods from Great Britain.

The Constitution of 1787 forbade States to obstruct inter-State commerce. Article one, section 8, of the Constitution says: 'Congress shall have the power to regulate commerce with foreign nations, and among the several States and with the Indian tribes.'

This principle made illegal all measures taken by the States which constituted an obstruction to inter-State commerce, since the power to regulate was with Congress alone.

But the States did not submit to federal supremacy without a struggle. The Constitution contained other articles which, taken in conjunction with article one, could give rise to various interpretations. The tenth amendment laid down: 'The powers not delegated to the United States by the Constitution nor prohibited by it to the States, are reserved to the States respectively or to the people.' All kinds of political and economic influences entered into the double conflict between the supporters of State rights and supporters of the federation, and between the defenders and opponents of liberalism.

At the beginning of the century Chief Justice Marshall, in a number of famous cases, laid down the principles which allowed for the constructive development of federal powers. In Gibbons v. Ogden (9 Wheaton I, 1824) he upheld federal rights in coastal trade; the federation had the right to 'prescribe the rules governing trade'.

This power was 'complete in itself, may be exercised to the full and knows no limits other than those prescribed by the Constitution'. In Maculloch v. Maryland (4 Wheaton, 316) he recognised the validity of a federal bank and so sterilised the tenth amendment by developing the famous theory of implied powers (cf. p. 229).

It is not always simple to distinguish between inter- and intra-State commerce. The courts have tried, by careful phrasing, to allow for the possibility of some concurrent jurisdiction between States and federation, as in the case of Cooley v. Board of Wardens of Philadelphia (12 Howard, 229).

The conflict of interests between North and South which divided the federation for a long time was at first tempered by the moderating influence of the West; when the West ranged itself with the North conflict became inevitable. As a result of the War of Secession the powers of the federation were strengthened by the fourteenth amendment. Nevertheless the movement was not so marked as has been supposed. The West, with its unsettled lands, was important in promoting the unity of the American nation by fusing together different peoples; and so social difficulties did not become acute until 1890. When they were forced on the government's attention both the federation and the States were faced with constitutional provisions which indirectly compelled them to conform to some degree of liberalism. The courts' attitude was sharply criticised and the judges were accused of pursuing class interests under the pretext of observing the Constitution. This interpretation of United States jurisprudence is not necessarily correct, because there is a fundamental contradiction between federalism and State intervention. The end of the nineteenth century saw extensive federal intervention in coordinating transport, and in the struggle against monopolistic practices (Sherman Anti-Trust Law, 1890).

The last great test of American federalism was the world economic crisis of 1929. President Roosevelt set in motion remedial legislative measures, the whole constituting the policy known as the 'New Deal'. In a succession of famous judgments: Hammer v. Dagenhart, Railroad Retirement Board v. The Alton Railway, Schechter Poultry Co. v. US, Carter v. Carter Coal Co., the Supreme Court blocked interventionist legislation by a strict interpretation of article one, and, as it had already done several times before, it made a distinction between commerce and production, and between measures affecting inter-State commerce directly and indirectly. But when the elections confirmed the popular support for presidential policy the Supreme Court gave in. Since that time a war economy has unified the

American economy still more. In a series of cases: National Labor Relations Board v. Jones and Laughlin Steel Corporation, US v. Wrightwood Dairy Co, US v. Derby, Jam v. US, the courts have drawn the logical conclusions from the decline of regional economies and the appearance of business on a national scale. Henceforth no domain is out of reach of federal intervention. The structure of the United States is certainly federal in appearance, but that federalism is no longer based on a balance between dual legislative systems. This federalism is now a legal form which barely disguises a unitary nation and economy.

PART THREE

INTERNATIONAL ORGANISATIONS

CHAPTER ONE

The Notion of International Organisation

Section I

ITS ORIGIN

International organisations are formed as soon as international societies have their own organs and through them become groups.

This definition rests on the sociological ideas in the Introduction; it stresses one fundamental point: the emergence of separate organs, independent of the States. But this notion only gradually emerged in international practice, after great obstacles and setbacks. We must therefore examine the salient points in its historical development in more detail than in Chapter One.

§ 1 PRINCIPAL HISTORICAL FACTORS

These are determined by the needs to be met and the methods which can be used.

(A) *The needs*

Since international organisations began to develop in the nineteenth century two separate needs have been met: first a general desire for peace and the growth of peaceful relations; and second a series of precise and limited objectives to meet specific cases.

The first requires *one* international organisation, in principle universal in scope and object; the second can be met through several different organisations.

This meant that efforts were directed along two lines; while earlier efforts did not try to be universal, they were a source of useful experience, and were always subordinate to any universal organisation.

(B) *The methods*

They were empirical. International organisation only gradually emerged as a power distinct from the States. It derived from the classical institution in international law, the international conference.

International organisations began as an extension of the international conferences called to conclude treaties. The multiplication of treaties, frequency of conferences, and international organisations all reflected the same need.

The episodic international conference gave place to periodic meetings, and then, with a secretariat, gained some degree of permanence. The secretariat was organised by the organising State's own administration and was only concerned with the mechanical organisation of the conference. The 'conference' dealt only with common interests. In accordance with diplomatic practice its decisions were unanimous. Can we really speak of a 'decision'? The common interests dealt with at these conferences were regarded as a collection rather than a community of interests. The conferences tried to formulate a common approach and not to exercise real power. They sought to obtain parallel action by the States rather than impose an authority of their own.

Only later did international organisations gradually acquire an identity independent of the States: independent secretariat, decisions taken by majority voting, organs and powers definitively withdrawn from the competence of the States.

There is no straightforward, absolute change. States always retain the most important powers. Every time a new international organisation is contemplated, the old restrictive conceptions are raised again, although they have long been abandoned in lesser organisations.

It would be a mistake to think that there has been uniform progress in the notion of international organisation. Some organisations have not progressed from their point of departure, and in general they have developed along very varied lines.

§ 2 STAGES OF EVOLUTION

(A) *Before* 1919

At the beginning of this book we suggested that during this period there was an evident desire for an organisation with the general aim of maintaining world peace, but in terms of world organisation they got no further than the vague promise of regular Hague Conferences, and at a regional level the modest 'bureau' which was the basis of the Pan American Union. These first attempts were specialised technical organisations. We must see how far this movement extended and how it was interpreted at the time.

(*a*) *Extent of the movement.* There seem to be three groups of organisations.

First the International River Commissions set up by the Treaty of Paris, 30 May, 1814 (art. 5), and the Treaty of Vienna, 1815 (art. 108–116 of the Final Act). These acts recognised freedom of navigation on international rivers, that is rivers which separate or traverse two or more States. Individual agreements were made for each river based on the principles laid down in the Act of Vienna. Some formed commissions; one of them still exists today and is the *doyen* of international organisations: the Central Commission of the Navigation of the Rhine. These commissions passed unanimous resolutions and only proposed measures for each State to incorporate into its national law. Some of their functions seem to belong to a past era, such as the judicial role of the Rhine Commission. The role of these commissions must not be overestimated. Some of those provided for in treaties have never been set up; for instance, those for the Congo and the Niger. One of them has benefited for a long time from favourable circumstances: the European Danube Commission, set up in 1856 to regulate navigation on the lower Danube; it had greater powers than its predecessors to control navigation and execute public works essential to navigability, but these powers were only justified by the semi-colonial character of the territories which should have carried out this work; in this respect the Danube Commission resembles the second group of organisations.

This second group of international organisations in this period is clearly connected with temporary situations of a colonial type. In the Middle East, in the countries formerly under Turkish domination, and in the Far East, the diplomatic, financial or military representatives of the European States jointly administered or controlled services unsatisfactorily performed by the local authorities. The fact that the European powers acted jointly in this field compelled them to form international organisations of sorts, though they were often precarious. They covered all kinds of subjects: public health (Commissions of Bucharest, Constantinople, Tangiers), finance (Ottoman, Egyptian, Greek, Moroccan, Chinese public debts), military (intervention in Crete and China), administration (Act of Algeciras in Morocco, cf. *supra*, p. 184), etc. Theoretically these are interesting examples of organisations; but the special conditions under which they were created prevented them from lasting very long.

The third group comprised what for a long time were called 'administrative unions'. Their purpose was the adequate protection of common interests resulting from the expansion of trade and international contacts. Some covered communications and transport; the first was the Universal Telegraphic Union created by the Paris Convention 17 May, 1865, and later absorbed in the movement which resulted in the present Telecommunication Union. Other unions have been kept up in more or less the same form to the present day; for instance a Central Office for International Transport by Rail to supervise railway goods transport, was formed to put into effect the Berne Agreements, 14 October, 1890; this, together with other international organisations concerned with railways, still exists.

The International Postal Commission was created in 1863, followed by the conference at Berne of 15 September, 1874, which created the General Postal Union, and this in turn became the Universal Postal Union in 1878.

Other Unions covered *economic* interests: the International Union for the Publication of Customs Tariffs (Brussels, 5 July, 1890, still in force), the organisation set up for the sugar industry by the Treaty of Brussels, 5 March, 1902, the International Agricultural Institute (Convention of 7 June, 1905). And others *administrative, scientific and social* affairs: Union for the Protection of Industrial Property and Union for the Protection of Works of Art and Literature (Conventions of 20 March, 1883 and 9 September, 1886, still in force), International Bureau of Weights and Measures created by the International Convention for the Unification and Improvement of the Metric System (Paris, 20 May, 1875, still in force), the *Bureau International d'Hygiène* (Conventions of 3 December, 1905, and 9 December, 1907), etc.

These various unions were only rudimentary international organisations. The transition from international conference to organisation was barely perceptible. Most of these unions worked on very simple lines; the organs of the union were: (1) periodic meetings of representatives of the member States where decisions were usually unanimous; (2) a permanent secretariat called a 'bureau' for administration (various notices, distribution of documents and information, etc.). It comprised a limited official staff and it was legally incorporated according to the municipal law of the State in which the organisation had its seat. Sometimes the agents and finances of the organisation were part of the administration of this State, which rendered account of its management to the other members of the union.

The jurisdiction of this kind of organisation was very limited and predominantly administrative. Most of its duties were administrative, but there were exceptions. The European Danube Commission, whose special features have already been mentioned, exercised original regulating and executive powers. The Central Commission of the Navigation of the Rhine had a jurisdictional competence (disputes between individuals) and the Universal Postal Union arbitral powers for certain disputes between its members. A permanent commission of the Sugar Union of 1902 could establish infractions committed by member States but only a meeting of the representatives of all the States could decide what action to take.

(b) *Interpretation.* The movement as a whole could not pass unnoticed. Some sought from the start to minimise its importance, and see it simply as an effort to co-ordinate State activity, a new development in the classic theory of treaties; some regarded international organisations as purely 'collective' organs of the will of States; others wanted to provide such organisations with special characteristics and field of action. Although effective universal political organisation was incompatible with the existence of States, this was not so for universal administrative organisations. And so international organisations were a basis for what was, not particularly accurately, called 'international administrative law'. Finally there were people who studied these limited experiments for general political problems common to all international organisations. International organisations were an open challenge to State sovereignty and the equality of States once their organs could take decisions other than unanimously despite the presence of State representatives. This then was the key to the development of the organisations. State equality was threatened by the way various kinds of influence were distributed within the organisation, especially through representation and voting. The Great Powers were reluctant to grant small powers the right of veto and the small powers would not give way to their easy coalitions. Neither unanimous nor simple majority voting were satisfactory solutions, and as soon as the international organisation tried to do bigger things it had to devise more complex arrangements. Nevertheless, the success of administrative organisations proved to many people that a universal organisation was possible. The task of transforming limited secondary organisations into increasingly powerful political organisations was the work of the writers and movements which tried to give the international community organic shape after the First World War.

Pitmann B. Potter (*Origin of the term international organisation*, AJ 1945, p. 804) suggests that a communication by Lorimer of 18 May, 1867 to the Edinburgh Academy, 'on the application of the principle of proportional or relative equality to international organisations', is the first use of the expression 'international organisation'; it rapidly became general. Constantin Franz, considered after a long eclipse as one of the pioneers on the subject, used it in 1879 in the title of his work *Föderalismus als . . . Prinzip für . . . Internationale Organisation* (re-edited Koblenz, Historisch-politischer Verlag, 1947).

From an early date authors tried to find an adjective other than 'international' to denote an organisation which does more than co-ordinate States, and actually subordinates them. H. Wehberg, in his work on the proposals for an International Prize Court (open to individuals) provided for by the XIIth Hague Convention, used the expression *überstaatlich*; L. S. Woolf, after his work *International Government* (1916), published a 'Project by a Fabian Committee for a supernational authority which will prevent war'; 'supranational' also appears in Sack, *Les effets des transformations des Etats sur leurs dettes publiques et autres obligations financières* (Sirey, 1927, pp. 40, 88), quoted by N. Politis in his preface (p. iv); but the expression 'supranational' is only generally used in connection with proposals for European integration (cf., however, in connection with the United Nations, Brierly, *infra*, p. 269).

(B) *From 1919 to 1945*

This period is dominated by one universal political organisation, the League of Nations. It went far beyond other political organisations of the same period. The gradual process by which Commonwealth relations became international relations was a specifically British phenomenon and did not give rise to any clearly formulated principles (*supra*, p. 193). The Pan American Union was based on mere resolutions of conferences and only became efficient at the prospect of the Second World War. As for the other political organisations of the time like the Little Entente (16 February, 1933), the Balkan Entente (12 September, 1934), and the Baltic Union (12 September, 1934), they were only of local significance and without lasting effects; their principal organ was a periodic meeting of Foreign Ministers (*supra*, p. 163).

It soon became clear that the League of Nations fell short of the highest and most popular aspiration: namely to prevent the use of force, or at least to make force the instrument of law. The reason is simple: a universal organisation of international society had no social basis distinct from that of the States. It was therefore merely a framework for State policy, a platform from which to expound it and justify intervention. The only reason for the final failure of the League of Nations was that the policies of the Great Powers were out of line with it.

And so the soil in which international organisation would develop was the first universal organisation devoted to maintaining peace. It embodied the idea of organisation and it could also develop solutions suggested by the experience of earlier individual organisations. The League broke new ground in one direction: it tried to solve the problem of State representation on federal lines by setting up two organs with largely parallel jurisdiction, the Council and the Assembly, so that the Great Powers would have privileged representation. But individual organisations continued to do useful work; it was they who tried out new methods for freeing the organisations further from the will of the States.

People other than State representatives began to hold office in international organisations. The Permanent Court of Justice had a legal personality of its own independent of the States, though there was direct State representation. There were other examples of great political significance: the most important was the participation of representatives of workers' and employers' organisations in organs of the International Labour Organisation. Further advances could be made once international organisations were not made up entirely of governments acting as such.

The administrative and financial problems of international organisations were no longer theoretical. Organisations had to be endowed with important administrative and financial machinery which made them quite independent of the States in which they had their headquarters. There were problems of international officials, international budgets, headquarters agreements, etc.

The multiplicity of these administrative organisations gave rise to serious problems of co-existence. As there were more organs, each independent of the rest, so there were more agents, services, expenditure, and this was strongly criticised. But each organisation was founded in law on the will of the founder States and adhering States embodied in a treaty. The same States were not all members of the same organisations. And so, despite considerations of administrative expediency, legal considerations put an absolute limit to the extent to which international organisations could be unified. The League Covenant provided (article 24) that international bureaux previously set up by collective treaties should be placed, with the consent of the parties, 'under the direction of the League'; this should also be done for any new organisations. These principles were rarely carried out for the old organisations. New ones were however incorporated into the League, even the ILO whose budget was always voted by the League Assembly. The institutions known as Organisation for Communications and Transit, Health Organisation, Economic and Financial Organisation, etc., were never administratively and financially part of the League of Nations, but always made use of its secretariat and received financial aid. Nevertheless the general problems of the unity of international administration, decentralisation, and control within a central organisation had been posed.

Problems of international organisation were studied in political and academic circles. It was necessary to view them in a federal perspective. Some writers like Scelle used a general theory of federalism for analysis; others examined the problem historically, comparing for example the League of Nations with the German Confederation created by the Act of 8 June, 1815 (art. 53–63 of the Final Act of the Congress of Vienna) and the Act of 15 May, 1820. The practical problems were discussed in general terms under the title 'international administrative law', or in individual monographs.

(C) *Since 1945*

The Second World War weighed even more heavily than the First in determining the direction taken by international society once the fighting was over. The war was ideological; the United Nations Declaration of 1 January, 1942 made this plain. From the time of the Conferences at Moscow (October 1943) and Teheran (December 1943), the powers which signed this Declaration or subsequently adhered to it had to make clear their ideas on the term international organisation. With, between them, a mass of forces unequalled in history the Great Powers, and in particular the US and the USSR, looked at international organisation in the light of political considerations. The most important seems to have been: international organisation can do everything if the Great Powers agree and nothing without them. The war threw up a great many international organisations of yet another kind: interallied wartime organisations comprising teams of technicians all ready, as soon as the war was over, to turn themselves into a world-wide international organisation.

There is no doubt that Allied Wartime Organisations were in some way international organisations; their generally military structure should not disguise this fact. They should be studied in this light but so far they have never been studied as a whole. For the 1914–18 War see, as an example, J. A. Salter, *Allied Shipping Control*, Part V, *International administration* (OUP, 1921); cf. the study by A. Armengaud, *La coordination de l'économie americaine en temps de guerre*, in *l'Organisation économique internationale* (*Collection 'Droit Social'*, No. XXXIII).

The United Nations Organisation was the essential political force in postwar international society, and was based on the supremacy of the Great Powers. Its political role was entirely dependent on a satisfactory understanding between the US and the USSR; from this point of view it has had no chance to show what it could do.

It also became the focal point for other political and administrative international organisations, whose complete autonomy could never now be accepted.

While the war was still in progress certain organisations, mainly concerned with economic affairs, were set up. Some were based on agreements reached before the San Francisco Charter which set up the United Nations, for example the International Bank for Reconstruction and Development and the International Monetary Fund (IMF), but they all made part of the overall plan of the United Nations, parallel to the United Nations Organisation and bound to it as 'specialised agencies' by individual agreements. Apart from the two already mentioned, there are now the International Labour Organisation (ILO), the World Health Organisation (WHO), the Food and Agriculture Organisation (FAO) (which took over some of the functions of the International Agriculture Institute), the International Civil Aviation Organisation (ICAO), the United Nations Educational, Scientific and Cultural Organisation (UNESCO), the World Meteorological Organisation (WMO), the Universal Postal Union (UPU), the Intergovernmental Maritime Consultative Organisation (whose creation is still awaiting ratification); the International Refugee Organisation (IRO) has disappeared and various other organisations are still attached to the United Nations.

In fact this list is very far from giving a complete picture of all international organisations. On the economic plane mistakes were made from the start. Chronologically monetary problems were the first to give rise to an international organisation; next exchange questions were considered, and after the failure of the International Trade Organisation (ITO) (Havana Convention, 1948) they were tackled in a limited way by the General Agreement on Tariffs and Trade (GATT). In fact after the Second World War the dominant problems were reconstruction and international assistance, but public opinion in the countries concerned, and particularly American opinion, was not yet ready to accept this and its corollary: free aid. It was only later that international organisations grew up for administering unattached disinterested aid.

Even if there had been a fair measure of understanding between the Great Powers, the United Nations would still have had room for regional organisations and would have had to decentralise the work of organisations attached to it, as has in fact been done. But these activities would have appeared less ostentatious. International tension reinforced the autonomy of organisations attached to the Organisation of American States, which was the final stage in the efforts to organise the American continent after the Bogotá Charter. The development of European organisation, too, might have taken a rather different turn. Europe's limited place in world affairs, the absence of States like Germany and Italy from the United Nations, and all kinds of common difficulties would have led to a more extensive European organisation; but several European organisations have assumed a military or political character as a result of the division of the world into two blocks. Moreover, compared with other attempts at regional organisation, some European ideas are clearly federal or pre-federal; they are sometimes called efforts at 'integration'.

They have clearly posed juridical problems, which were less obvious in previous organisations.

After the war international organisations were in the forefront of all international relations, both from the political and from the legal point of view.

Section II

DEFINITION

We shall try to establish and analyse a definition of international organisation in terms of political science. There is nothing wrong with this so long as we do not try to draw juridical conclusions from it. Internal rules in various States mention 'international organisations'; there may also be conventional or customary rules about certain aspects of specialised organisations. If we examine each one of these rules we might then have some idea of the full meaning of the term international organisation.

With this reservation we might say a few words about the two words 'international organisation'.

As an *organisation* there must be a group which can permanently express a juristic will distinct from that of its individual members.

As an *international* organisation this group is normally, but not exclusively, composed of States.

(A) '*Organisation*'
It implies permanence and an individual will.

(*a*) *Permanence*. There is no organisation which is not *permanent*. This does not mean that all the organs of an organisation are *in fact* always in a position to exercise their functions, but it implies that they are so arranged as to be constantly active within the organisation's sphere of jurisdiction. The real sociological justification for international organisations lies in common interests (*supra*, p. 25); these interests are constant and the organisation responsible for them must be so too. In another sense the permanent nature of the organisation is a measure of its independence; if it is not permanent it can only act in accordance with the will of the member States; if it is permanent it can stand up to the States.

(*b*) *Individual will*. The distinctive feature of an international organisation is that it has in law its own will distinct from the will of the member States. It is this which distinguishes an organisation from a conference. A conference can only lead to international agreements, and the binding force of these agreements comes from the will of the States, subject to their consent and the terms under which it is given. An organisation has its own will, is responsible for how it is used within the limits allowed by the rules. The existence of will implies that the organisation has a defined and definite sphere of jurisdiction.

In this analysis the political and legal points of view do not necessarily coincide. From the political point of view all the while the deliberative organ of the organisation is composed of State representatives taking unanimous decisions, the organisation amounts to a conference; politically, the organisation's will is not apparently independent of the States. But it is different in law; if the organisation has jurisdiction then its decisions, even when taken unanimously by the member States, have the immediate force of law and bind the States as decisions and not as agreements subject to national conditions of constitutional validity. This would only *not* be so if the organisation was authorised not to take decisions but simply to draft treaty proposals, or projects for each State to take up as the basis for municipal legislation on whatever lines it saw fit to adopt. This is the position in some organisations.

An organisation could still have an individual will even if its only task was to collect and transmit information. Modern organisations certainly exert an individual will in all acts concerning their administrative and financial arrangements.

Many organisations occur spontaneously from treaties, which establish them *de facto* rather than *de jure*, deliberately avoiding the usual formulae. One of the best examples is the North Atlantic Treaty, whose members agreed to 'self help and mutual aid' (art. 3), and a Council, assisted by a Defence Committee (art. 9). On this basis, by means of resolutions and conventions, a North Atlantic Treaty Organisation (NATO) has grown up. The same thing is happening on a reduced scale in South-East Asia, where, at the Bangkok Conference, a Council of Ministers, a Permanent Council and a Secretariat were set up (final communiqué of 26 February, 1955), to give effect to the Manila Pact. This last agreement explicitly stated that it should not involve the creation of an international organisation (cf. vague wording of article 5 of the Treaty of 2 September, 1954).

Sometimes the member States deliberately keep the organisation as rudimentary as possible, on the grounds that to give the appearance of creating an organisation would only raise political and legal difficulties which would delay its coming into force (cf. *infra*, p. 233). Examples of this procedure are:

1. The Brussels Protocol of 17 October, 1953, set up a 'European Conference of Ministers of Transport', which could not make international rules (art. 9) and which relied on OEEC for its secretariat; several other aspects of this so-called Conference are open to question.

2. The General Agreement on Tariffs and Trade (GATT). So as not to create an organisation the members of the Agreement have resorted to drafting subtleties art. XXV, §§1 and 4: 'Representatives of the contracting parties shall meet from time to time for the purpose of giving effect to those provisions of this Agreement which involve joint action and, generally, with a view to facilitating the operation and furthering the objectives of this Agreement. Wherever reference is made in this Agreement to the contracting parties acting jointly they are designated as the CONTRACTING PARTIES. . . . Except as otherwise provided for in this Agreement, decisions of the CONTRACTING PARTIES shall be taken by a majority of the votes cast.'

On the other hand, according to the rules of procedure of the sessions of the contracting parties (*Basic Instruments and Selected Documents*, vol. I, p. 97), rule 15: 'The usual duties of a secretariat shall, by agreement with the Interim Commission for the International Trade Organisation, be performed by the Executive Secretary of the Interim Commission on a reimbursable basis.' But the International Trade Organisation has never seen the light of day, and the Interim Commission is based entirely on a fiction.

(B) '*International*'

The members of international organisations are generally States represented by members of the government or their representatives. The United Nations term 'inter-governmental organisations' is therefore justifiable. According to the Economic and Social Council, Resolution 288 (x) of 27 February, 1950 (3rd year, 10th session): 'Every international organisation which is not created by means of inter-governmental agreements shall be considered as a non-governmental international organisation'. This point of vocabulary enables us to clear up the following:

(a) *Certain organisations whose members are not States are recognised as having some international personality*; in particular the right to conclude agreements with a State independently of the national law of a State. This has long been true for the Catholic Church; but it might well be true of another Church, or of any interest group powerful enough for States to wish to come to terms with it yet unable to subject it to their own law.

We might perhaps quote in this context the agreement on missions to the Holy Land signed between Israel and the World Lutheran Federation (Friedenswarte, 1951, p. 172). For interest groups cf. the types quoted by Lauterpacht, *Rapports sur le droit des traités*, A/CN 4/63; Lena Goldfield case (*Annual Digest*, 1929–30, no. 1), and Chiekh and the Petroleum Development Company (*International and Comparative Law Quarterly*, 4th Series, I, 1952, p. 251), also the judgments of the Permanent Court of Arbitration of 13 April, 1935 between China and an American company (cf. *supra*, p. 54).

Apart from these exceptions, organisations which are not inter-governmental but under the national law of one or more States collaborate increasingly with existing international organisations, either by participating directly as will be explained later, or more generally by working through international organisations in collecting information or some other task. Article 25 of the Covenant of the League of Nations already envisaged this collaboration with national Red Cross societies. Under article 71 of the United Nations Charter these relations are arranged systematically under the Economic and Social Council: 'The Economic and Social Council may make all suitable arrangements for consultation with non-governmental organisations which are concerned with matters within its competence. Such arrangements may be made with international organisations and where appropriate national organisations after consultation with the member of the United Nations concerned.' Some specialised agencies have gone a long way to encourage these relations, for example, ICAO with airline companies and UNESCO with academic bodies and research centres.

(b) *Some inter-governmental organisations admit as members with reduced rights certain non-State territorial units:* territories, provinces, overseas territories, etc. This is perfectly understandable when technical organisations wish to give individual representation to territories with special problems, different from those of the parent

State. Thus the International Telecommunication Union, the Universal Postal Union, the World Meteorological Organisation, admit as members dependent territories, if they are in any real sense administered autonomously. There are cases where individual representation is essential: an economic organisation based on separate representation for producer and consumer countries of a particular product, must allow for separate representation of territories with a special interest in order to safeguard the general balance of the organisation (art. 3 of the International Tin Agreement, 25 June, 1954).

There are cases in which States admit territorial representation from areas which are not States, or which for diplomatic reasons cannot be recognised as such: for instance the Territory of Trieste was a member of OEEC, and the Council of Europe accepted member 'countries' as well as member States, so as to accommodate the Saar.

(c) *International organisations are not run entirely by State representatives*. Since States are the members of international organisations, the latter are generally run by an organ composed of State representatives, or more exactly government representatives. This is becoming less true; the organs of organisations are not composed solely of State representatives, but include other groups of people. These persons may still be connected with a State, but they are often politicians chosen by an assembly rather than official Foreign Office nominations.

This tendency will be studied later on from a technical point of view (p. 246), but it has been strongly and successfully resisted in the commissions attached to the Economic and Social Council (A. Loveday, An unfortunate decision, *International Organisation*, vol. I, p. 279) and in the UNESCO Council.

All this confirms a tendency already discernible in other institutions, particularly as regards treaties: international relations are conducted more and more at the different levels of State institutions, informal agreements are not always made by the organs responsible for external affairs, and members of all institutions are brought together in international organisations. There is a marked tendency for international organisations to move towards federal forms, from which they only differ in degree and not in kind.

Section III

CLASSIFICATION

To classify international organisations would strictly mean considering all the ways in which they can differ; but despite their growing numbers from the descriptive point of view we need only examine three questions: the purpose, powers and extent of these organisations.

§ 1 PURPOSE

We can distinguish between *general* organisations and *special* organisations.

General organisations are those whose defined purpose includes all peaceful relations and the solution of all international conflicts. In fact all questions would fall within the jurisdiction of an organisation defined in this way.

The principle general organisations are the League of Nations and the United Nations, and to a lesser degree the Organisation of American States.

Special organisations have limited purposes. They might be roughly classified under the following headings:

—*economic* organisations: relating either to products (wheat, sugar, tin, coal, steel), or to a specific economic technique: customs (customs unions, customs valuations, tariffs), banks of all kinds (Bank for International Settlements, International Bank for Reconstruction and Development), currency (monetary unions, IMF), or even more general purposes such as economic unification, economic recovery, or the development of trade (e.g. the proposed International Trade Organisation, Benelux, OEEC).

—*technical* organisations: either concerned with a particular legal or administrative problem, for example organisations for the protection of works of art or science; or scientific problems, for example, ITU, WMO. International organisations concerned with transport (railways, air and sea navigation, postal services) come into both this category and the preceding one.

—*social and humanitarian* organisations: all organisations for the protection of health (WHO, Permanent Central Opium Board), the weak (children, women, backward peoples), workers in general (ILO) or human rights.

—*military* organisations: these aim to set up a common system of defence, either within the framework of old-fashioned alliances or by modern treaties of mutual aid, for example the North Atlantic Treaty Organisation (NATO) or Western European Union.

—finally *political* organisations in the strict sense; that is, those not concerned with the international community but with fostering a common approach to third States through establishing a balance of power between States.

This analysis is purely descriptive; but it is frequently used for personal ends by politicians. For instance, economic organisations are generally welcomed: it is easy to hope for benefits without sacrifices, in particular in terms of sovereignty; hence a probable distortion of vocabulary. In the same way to call an organisation social rather than economic affects its outlook.

§2 POWERS

The powers of international organisations vary enormously from one organisation to another.

In a brief analysis, but one sufficient for political generalisations, we can distinguish between those organisations with strong powers and those with weak powers. The first can bind States in important matters, and their methods may involve the higher functions of the State (legislation, enforcement, justice). The second do not impinge upon State sovereignty and only make recommendations and proposals. They seek to co-ordinate State activities, but do not interfere with State sovereignty. In modern terms this is often referred to as 'co-operation', copying the Anglo-Saxon example (*supra*, about the Commonwealth, p. 196).

There is no doubt that the great majority of international organisations come into the second category. As soon as an international organisation has broad powers over States it begins to resemble a federation or confederation; in the present world situation this is exceptional.

We can carry these distinctions further.

(a) We can distinguish between the purely *material* functions and the *juridical* functions of organisations. Many organisations are

competent, some of them exclusively so, to perform acts which have
no legal consequences: collecting material, preparing and publishing
studies, disseminating information, etc. The activity of some organisations on the other hand can bind member States. This is not a rigorous
distinction. Even the most modest organisation has jurisdiction over
its own internal administration; it has a budget which has to be met
by the member States. The fact that certain functions have no legal
consequences does not mean that they are not defined in law. To make
studies and publish them is a function precisely laid down in the
constituent documents; it is therefore defined and enforceable in
law. We should also realise that the *political* and legal importance of
any competence may not be the same. International organisations
are at one and the same time political platforms and meetings of
experts. A discussion in an international assembly about the attitude
adopted by a State has more serious political consequences than the
adoption of a regulation for air distress signals. A reasoned opinion
of a team of international experts on the inadequate level of wages
in a State is more to be feared than the duty to notify all exports of a
particular drug.

(b) Limitation of powers can be distinguished from *transfer* of
powers. Limited powers continue to belong to the organs of the
State, but they undertake to exercise them in a certain manner.
Treaties usually lay down rules limiting the free exercise of powers.
A transfer of powers implies a body to which powers can be transferred, and which can exercise them in its own name; an international
organisation can do this.

The expression 'transfer of powers' has only been used recently,
since States do not willingly transfer powers; when they do so they
are not always conscious of it or try to disguise it. We have said
several times that there are still international organisations to which
States have only granted the simple right to make proposals; the
States reserve the right to give these proposals what legal consequences they please. But all international organisations involve
some transfer of powers. Thus in most States public expenditure is
authorised by the deliberative assemblies and given when the budget
is passed; nevertheless organisations of which the States are members
spend money without the authorisation of the national budgetary
authorities. It is as if the national assemblies had delegated a part of
their powers to the international organisation.

All the same we must be careful how we use this notion of transfer.
It has its place in a firmly established structure, but to apply it too

soon in some organisations is to risk creating difficulties and going beyond the intentions of the founders. The very word 'transfer' poses the question of whether the national authorities have granted the organisation *exclusive* jurisdiction and have renounced the exercise of national jurisdiction. The answer depends on the interpretation of the original documents. They rarely go so far. There is also some doubt as to how far powers transferred may constitutionally be *delegated*. It is understandable therefore that these questions have hardly ever been raised except in connection with treaties and proposals for so-called European integration.

The distinction between limited powers and transferred powers clarifies the role of international organisations. When an international convention limits competences it sometimes creates an international organisation to see that the States carry out the obligations they have undertaken. We can therefore distinguish between cases in which an organisation has powers of *inspection*, of *supervision* or even of *indirect administration*, and the very much rarer cases in which it has powers of *direct administration*.

There are additional difficulties of terminology. The corresponding expressions in French and English are not equivalent (for instance, control and *contrôle*). A general theory of *contrôle* by international organisations has been worked out (Kopelmanns, *Le contrôle international*, RCADI 1950, pp. 59, 77); there is always some attempt to limit the action of international organisation; but there is still no possibility of establishing effective inspection (*contrôle* in the French sense of the word). This was obvious when plans were being discussed to create an international foreign trade monopoly in opium, and also when an attempt was made to set up an atomic agency for the production of fissionable material, with powers of inspection to ensure observance of the rules for the pacific use of atomic energy.

(c) Finally a distinction can be made according to the *quality of the powers conferred* on the international organisation. The constitutional law of most States contains the classic separation of powers between judiciary, legislature and executive. Is it possible to classify the powers of an international organisation in these terms?

It seems reasonable to try, provided it is done cautiously and allowing for the peculiarities of each national system. By definition the more highly organised a group is the more rigorously are the functions and powers analysed and defined. Contemporary international organisations differ markedly from States, especially those organisations with very general powers. Judicial functions are not always clearly defined from legislative or executive functions; and judicial functions are those which develop most easily as theoretically they are purely supervisory. There is then a move to give executive or legislative functions to the judge because these functions are not generally developed separately. There is no simple way of subjecting States to the will of an organisation, and this is why there are legal forms in international law unknown to municipal law (except in commercial or industrial law); obedience is requested rather than required by the use of terms such as 'recommendations', 'reports', 'proposals', 'invitations', etc. Political pressure is one of the most widespread forms of constraint in international relations, and does not need to be formulated in legal forms. This is very clear if one looks at the powers of the major international organisations.

§ 3 EXTENT

The number of States making up an international organisation varies, according to the scope of the organisation and the procedure for obtaining membership.

(a) *The scope of the organisation.* The main question is whether or not an organisation is *universal* in scope. A universal organisation is, by definition, more complete than a non-universal organisation; two non-universal organisations can, if they are in the same field, be in competition with each other; their existence therefore implies that there is an unsolved conflict in the international community. Politically the two types of organisation are clearly different in kind. On the other hand a universal organisation, as an instrument of an unconsolidated society, will have a looser structure and fewer powers.

Non-universal organisations are sometimes described as 'regional' organisations. But it would be a mistake to think that this is a purely geographical term. It is sometimes, but often the underlying unity in a regional organisation is such that it cannot by definition be universal, for example race or political interests. Since there are non-universal societies it is inevitable that there should be non-universal international organisations.

The role and influence of 'regional' organisations depends on their origin.

When the regional organisation is geographic, it may be a form of *decentralisation* for a universal organisation with the same purpose. Decentralisation is an acute problem in nearly all international organisations. It can be solved either by the universal organisation deconcentrating its services and offices or by decentralising authority to regional organisations.

Most important universal organisations have had to decentralise work by setting up regional agencies or by suggesting that member States should conclude agreements on a regional basis. Thus the United Nations has set up Regional Economic Commissions and all organisations concerned with international transport have had to adapt their methods to different regions. The whole structure of the World Meteorological Organisation is on a regional basis. To give a concrete example, the World Health Organisation has set up several regional offices : New Delhi for South-East Asia, Alexandria for the Eastern Mediterranean, Manila for the Western Pacific, Geneva for Europe, Brazzaville for Africa; the Pan American Sanitary Bureau in Washington acts as the regional office of WHO. It must be added that regional committees admit 'associate members' (without international personality) to WHO.

On the other hand an organisation may be on a different basis and contiguity may be less important. A State may be surrounded by States which are members of an organisation and yet may not itself belong (for example, Israel and the Arab League), or again geographically distant States may be linked together (as in NATO). There is always the question as to whether regional politico-military organisations are compatible with a universal organisation.

Article 21 of the Covenant of the League of Nations provided that: 'Nothing in this Covenant shall be deemed to affect the validity of international engagements, such as treaties of arbitration or regional understandings like the Monroe doctrine, for securing the maintenance of peace.' The whole of Chapter VIII of the United Nations Charter is devoted to 'regional arrangements'. Its provisions subject all regional organisations which might interfere in any way in the settlement of 'local' disputes to the Security Council. These provisions, to be effective, must assume that the Security Council is not paralysed (cf. *infra*, p. 275). The question of regional understandings within the framework of the Charter has given rise to a good deal of controversy connected with opposition between the two liberty W. H. Woolcott, *The North Atlantic Treaty, the Brussels Treaty and the UNO Charter* (Stevens, London 1950); Hanna Saba, *Les accords régionaux dans le cadre de l'ONU*, RCADI 1952, pp. 80, 635

(b) *Entry procedure.* A universal organisation does not necessarily include all States, nor even all the States which would like to belong. The difficulty of joining international organisations varies.

(1) There is automatic entry to some organisations. Some treaties allow this: when a State wishes to enter the organisation it does no more than signify its adhesion to the original treaty. Automatic entry was the rule for the Universal Postal Union until 1947; it is still the rule for the specialised agencies for the member States of the United Nations.

(2) Entry to some organisations may be subject to certain conditions. Membership is then only open to States which fulfil these conditions,

and whether they do so or not allows some margin for discretion. Thus the conditions of entry to the League of Nations (art. 1. § 2) included: 'to be self-governing, to give effective guarantees of its sincere intention to observe its international obligations and accept such regulations as may be prescribed by the League in regard to its armed forces.' The first two conditions imply some degree of discretion which means that admission is not entirely automatic.

(3) Some organisations admit new members only if they fulfil certain conditions and if it is expedient to accept them. This is most likely when admission depends on an invitation from the organisation (art. 4 of the Statute of the Council of Europe, art. 10 of the North Atlantic Treaty).

To decide the conditions for entry in any concrete case one must refer to the original documents. But they are not always clear. The question was raised in the United Nations. The USSR only agreed to the entry of certain States to the United Nations on condition that certain other States were admitted at the same time. The Court was asked for an advisory opinion on the general conditions of admission. In an advisory opinion of 28 May, 1948, the Court decided that no conditions could be imposed in addition to those required by article 4 of the Charter, but this opinion has given rise to much discussion.

As a general rule international practice accepts expediency as a test for membership:

—of organisations engaged in political activity,
—of organisations with a complex internal structure. It is here not just a question of admitting a new member but of finding a place for him: number of representatives, voting rights, majority rules, etc.

There has been a movement to make access to international organisations as free as possible. Thus Recommendation 23 of the Council of Europe, of 11 December, 1951, has a Chapter VII entitled 'specialised authorities': article 38 (c) provides: 'There shall be no restriction on a member's right subsequently to belong to such a specialised authority of which it is not an original member.' Such attempts are quite in vain. In the present state of international society the universality of international organisations is in inverse proportion to the degree of integration they achieve.

To conclude, here is an empirical classification which takes into account more or less all international organisations.

1. Organisations comprising a large number of States, whose purpose is not specialised and whose powers are limited: e.g. the United Nations;

H

2. Organisations comprising a limited number of States, whose purpose is not specialised and whose powers are relatively important; they necessarily come near to the confederal or even federal type: e.g. the European political community for which the plan was drawn up in 1953 by the *ad hoc* Assembly;

3. Organisations with a specialised purpose and limited powers; they are sometimes universal, sometimes regional: e.g. the specialised agencies;

4. Organisations with a specialised purpose, important powers, comprising a limited number of States. They are rather exceptional because it is difficult to exercise important powers in a relatively narrow field; experience proves that in this case pressure is exerted to broaden the purpose of the organisation: e.g. the European Coal and Steel Community.

CHAPTER TWO

Some Major Juridical Problems of International Organisations

Chancelleries, political and legal circles are continually occupied with problems which arise from the creation and the administrative and financial operation of international organisations.

International organisations have been responsible for many cases brought before the PCIJ and the ICJ for an advisory opinion.

For the ICJ we shall note the following advisory opinions: Advisory opinion on the conditions of admission of a State to membership of the United Nations under article 4, § i (28 May, 1948, Reports, 1948, p. 65); advisory opinion on the competence of the General Assembly for the admission of a State to the United Nations (3 March, 1950, Reports, 1950, p. 4); advisory opinion on the interpretation of peace treaties with Bulgaria, Hungary and Rumania (30 March, 1950, Reports, 1950, p. 65 and 18 July, 1950, Reports, p. 221); advisory opinion on the reservations to the Genocide Convention (28 May, 1951, Reports, 1951, p. 21); advisory opinion on the International Status of South-West Africa (11 July, 1950, Reports, 1950, p. 128); and especially advisory opinion on Reparation for injuries suffered in the service of the United Nations (11 April, 1949, Reports, 1949, p. 177); and advisory opinion on the effect of awards of compensation by the United Nations Administrative Tribunal (13 July, 1954, Reports, 1954, p. 47). These last two advisory opinions are of major theoretical importance and were delivered in circumstances which make them extremely important precedents.

We shall give a brief account here of a few fundamental problems not dealt with in the preceding chapter.

They all show, more clearly and decisively than a purely historical account the conflicts and tensions attendant on the growth of international organisations in international society, and the efforts States make to escape their grasp or use them for their own ends.

Section I

DECIDING THE
JURISDICTION OF ORGANISATIONS

Organisations are in principle based on an international agreement; their functions and powers are laid down in the text of the agreement and the difficulties arise from the way it is interpreted. This comment needs expanding. The actual working of an international organisation throws up problems which the draftsmen of the constitution had not foreseen, and for which no provision was made. To meet these difficulties certain theories have been put forward (§ 1). On the other hand certain limits have been set to the extension of an organisation's jurisdiction (§ 2). Finally we shall describe a few of the most notable general powers possessed by organisations (§ 3).

§ 1 THE BROAD INTERPRETATION OF JURISDICTION

Until 1945, authors held that international agreements which set up international organisations should be interpreted restrictively because they derogated from State sovereignty. Since then however restrictive interpretation (which might equally have applied to all provisions binding States) has ceased to be the general principle.

An example is the judgment of the PCIJ in the case of the territorial jurisdiction of the International Commission of the River Oder, particularly page 26: 'the solution should be adopted which imposes the least restriction on the freedom of States. This argument, though sound in itself, must be employed only with the greatest caution. To rely upon it, it is not sufficient that the purely grammatical analysis of the text should not lead to definite results; there are many other methods of interpretation, in particular reference is properly had to the principles underlying the matter to which the text refers; it will be only when, in spite of all pertinent considerations, the intention of the Parties still remains doubtful, that that interpretation should be adopted which is most favourable to the freedom of States.'

Moreover, restrictive interpretation is not justified when extension of jurisdiction does not trespass on the liberty of States. Modern jurisprudence has formulated three interconnected notions which allow a more rational interpretation of the jurisdiction of international organisations. These are to be found in the jurisprudence of the International Court of Justice concerning the United Nations

Organisation; they are equally valid for other organisations allowing for differences between a universal organisation with general jurisdiction and other types of organisation.

(A) *Implied Powers*

The constituent documents of international organisations often begin by stating the purposes and principles of the organisation. The introductory articles of treaties setting up economic organisations happily string together lists of their purposes—which are not infrequently self-contradictory. The legal significance of these articles is difficult to determine. To define jurisdiction in terms of the objects to be pursued by the organisation goes beyond what is reasonable; but to say that these articles have no legal significance is also going too far. It is an old problem well known to federal systems. International judicial decisions try to determine from the text the common intention of the parties, and admit that part of an organisation's jurisdiction may be implied.

The tenth amendment of the United States' Constitution, designed to prevent the extension of federal powers, was neutralised by the judicial decisions of the Supreme Court inspired by Chief Justice Marshall. It built up a theory of implied powers based on the following reasoning: 'Let the end be legitimate, let it be within the scope of the Constitution, and all means which are appropriate, which are plainly adapted to that end, which are not prohibited but consist with the letter and spirit of the Constitution, are constitutional.' (MacCulloch *v.* Maryland, 4 Wheaton 316). The ICJ has been more restrictive.

The International Court of Justice stated its theory of implied powers for international organisations in its advisory opinion on reparation for injuries suffered in the service of the United Nations:

'It must be acknowledged that its members, by entrusting certain functions to it, with the attendant duties and responsibilities, have clothed it with the competence required to enable those functions to be effectively discharged. . . .

'The rights and duties of an entity such as the Organisation must depend upon its purposes and functions as specified or implied in its constituent documents and developed in practice . . .

'Under international law, the Organisation must be deemed to have those powers which, though not expressly provided in the Charter, are conferred upon it by necessary implication as being essential to the performance of its duties . . .'

The Court referred to the PCIJ's advisory opinion no. 13 of 23 July, 1926, on the work of master bakers, which had clearly used similar arguments. In the South West Africa Case it considered that article 80 implied international control. In considering the effect of awards of compensation by the United Nations Administrative Tribunal it argued that: 'The power to establish a tribunal . . . was essential to ensure the efficient working of the Secretariat . . . capacity to do this arose by necessary intendment out of the Charter.' (Reports, 1954, p. 57.)

(B) *Theory of functional competence*

If there are individual powers, then they must be intimately connected with the functions of the Organisation. The status and work of international organisations depends on their 'functions'. It is therefore clear that international organisations have no right to use their powers arbitrarily in relation to their functions. If the terms 'power', 'sovereignty' and so on imply a right to act without any need to justify the purpose, they cannot be used in connection with international organisations. We must instead speak of 'functional competence'. This notion is familiar in public law, that organs must use their powers in conformity with the general purpose of the organisation.

An international organisation's capacity to expand, and the limits set to its freedom are both determined by its functions. The Court has recognised that an organisation can extend functional protection to its agents, comparable with the diplomatic protection of States on behalf of their nationals, and can demand reparation for damages suffered by them in the performance of their duties. But in no case can an organ of an international organisation exercise 'sovereign' power. The whole theory of the immunities of international organisations is dominated and limited by the idea of functional protection. States are not liable, within the territory of another State, to the jurisdiction of its courts, nor can a writ be issued against their property within that territory (*supra*, p. 148). Organisations are in a more difficult position because all their activities are conducted in the territory of other States. They have therefore had to be given special immunities to exclude them from the authority and jurisdiction of those States. We shall not describe all these systems here (they are usually laid down in treaties). The guiding principle is this: organisations are protected in all they do within the scope of their functions, but not beyond that. This doctrine is the central point in determining the limits of immunity, in particular when immunity is likely to be raised. Finally, international organisations are not free to decide whether or not to carry out their functions: they have a legal obligation to do so. That is the general

principle. It must be taken in conjunction with provisions in constituent documents. In all its decisions the International Court of
Justice has firmly insisted on this as far as its own jurisdiction is
concerned, particularly as regards its duty to give advisory opinions.
Despite the fairly broad terms of article 65 of its Statute, the Court
has always insisted on its duty to give advisory opinions whenever it
was asked for them. It is equally impossible for an international
organisation to give up any of its functions or to delegate them except
by internal arrangements.

In some national systems of law such as the French there is a theory of the
specific function of corporate persons, principally in connection with public
corporations. The purpose of this theory is to restrict corporate bodies to the
terms of their statutes. People have wondered whether there is not a comparable
notion in international law. This may be so, in that when we define the jurisdiction
of an organisation in terms of its function, we not only make the function the
source of the jurisdiction but also set limits to it.

(C) *Theory of international personality*

According to the definition in the preceding chapter an international
organisation is based on the permanent expression of a juristic will
distinct from that of its members (*supra*, p. 215). In more abstract
terms we can say that organisations, *so defined*, have international
personality.

We have already seen (*supra*, p. 85) the necessary consequences of
the notion of international personality in present day international
law. The International Court of Justice defined international
personality in connection with the United Nations, emphasising the
importance of a will distinct from that of the States.

In the advisory opinion on reparation for injuries suffered in the service of the
United Nations, the Court declared (Reports, 1949, p. 178): 'The Charter has
not been content to make the Organisation created by it merely a centre "for har-
monising the actions of nations in the attainment of those ends". It has equipped
that centre with organs and has given it special tasks. It has defined the position
of the Members in relation to the Organisation...' And later, even more energetic-
ally, that the Organisation has 'a position in certain respects in detachment from
its members'.

The theory of the corporate personality of organisations should
not be too abstract. It means essentially 'to have the legal capacity to
be endowed with international rights and duties'. It has further
consequences in so far as the purposes and functions of the organisation are concerned.

Opinion quoted above of the ICJ: 'Whereas the State possesses the totality of international rights and duties recognised by international law, the rights and duties of an entity such as the Organisation must depend upon its purposes and functions as specified or implied in its constituent documents and developed in practice.'

At present the fact that international organisations have international personality has these results:

(1) International organisations help to formulate the rules of international law, in particular by recognising the existence of customary rules (*supra*, p. 117); they can perform certain juristic acts either by exercising their regulating powers or by making international agreements (cf. *infra*, p. 240).

(2) They have the right to 'bring international claims when necessitated by the discharge of their functions'; they exercise a 'functional protection' on behalf of their agents against other organisations or States.

(3) They have the right to accede to jurisdictions which are not expressly reserved to States and more generally to enter into official relations with States and other organisations.

(4) They have the right to claim under the national law of member States all the privileges necessary for the discharge of their functions; apart from the immunities which protect them from the jurisdiction of member States they have the right to obtain from the national law of each State the legal status appropriate to the proper exercise of their functions inside each country (cf. *supra*, p. 130).

Rights are laid down in the constituent documents of an organisation, but in the theory of international personality the silence of the texts does not necessarily deprive organisations of more general attributes; each concrete case is decided by international practice and in some cases by the national law of the States.

§ 2 LIMITS TO THE EXTENSION OF JURISDICTION

Just as States have reacted against treaties in general, so, after having accepted the development of organisations, States seek to limit their scope. The reaction takes three forms: opposition from municipal law, attempts to maintain State independence, methods of appeal against the activities of the organisations.

(A) *Opposition from municipal law*

This is noticeable in the increasing complexity of constitutional law with regard to treaties. For a long time the modest proportions of international organisations allowed them to escape the attention of constitutional law. Some constitutions, for instance the French Constitution of 1946, required that treaties 'relating to international organisation' should not be ratified without the authorisation of parliament (art. 27), but in practice this provision has been interpreted fairly loosely and negotiations (*supra*, p. 112) have managed to avoid giving the appearance of creating new organisations. But the creation of organisations for European integration met lively opposition, mainly on the grounds that it would be unconstitutional to 'delegate powers'. There is no doubt of the reaction of national constitutional law to the development of international organisations. As with treaties in general (*supra*, p. 130) some constitutions formally accept 'delegations of power' or 'transfers of sovereignty' to 'supranational' institutions, but the conditions laid down make them difficult to put into practice.

> In the Netherlands a two thirds majority is required in parliament; in Denmark a five sixths majority or a referendum. On the whole question see principally the parliamentary debates on EDC or the European Coal and Steel Community in the six countries concerned; also the proceedings of the Constitutional Court of the Federal German Republic. For France compare the divergent legal opinions expressed in the newspaper *Le Monde* by French professors (2 and 15 June, 1954 and 11 August, 1954).

Municipal courts find it difficult to adapt themselves to changes brought about by international organisations. We have seen (*supra*, p. 112) that municipal courts in many countries restrict their jurisdiction when a case involves relations between States. International organisations increase the number of such cases and create new variants. Municipal courts are faced with cases outside their usual competence. They have already had to decide the question of the authority of *res judicata* of an arbitral award, and of a judgment of an international court. Can they also enforce a decision of an international organisation? Opposition to this is fairly deeply entrenched. It is perfectly reasonable for municipal courts to refuse to take account of acts of which they have no official cognizance. But some States refuse to admit that publication of international acts makes them enforceable inside the country; many national courts hesitate to enforce them when errors and contradictions in interpretation cannot be rectified by appeal to an international court acting as a court of appeal for all States.

(B) *Attempts to maintain State independence*

Despite the growth in the jurisdiction of international organisations, States have several means of defending their freedom of action. The acts of international organisations often have only limited effects because they do not legally bind States. The rule of unanimity and its alternatives such as the right of veto permit States, or the most important of them, to safeguard their freedom of action within organisations by paralysing attempts to exercise jurisdiction. Furthermore, an organisation's jurisdiction is rarely exclusive; States have concurrent jurisdiction shared with the organisation; the jurisdictions of different organisations overlap, and States can use this for their own purposes by pitting one organisation against another.

This problem is connected with the problem of contradictory treaties; there are often practical difficulties concerning economic organisations, and no general principles for solving them.

States have another possible means of defence against organisations: the method used in treaties of adhering subject to reservations. According to the advisory opinion of the ICJ on reservations to the Genocide Convention, reservations must be compatible with the purpose of the treaty; some authors consider therefore that it is not possible to make reservations to a treaty setting up an organisation.

States can reserve their freedom of action within an organisation in three ways: by dissociating themselves from a decision, by insisting on reserved fields of activity, and by assessing the competence of the organisation.

(a) Dissociation from decisions. The very notion of international organisation implies that the member States are directly concerned with all the organisation's activities. If a State could, of its own free will, dissociate itself from a decision of the organisation, this would be reverting to the old technique of international conferences. The statutes of some organisations accept this. Thus the Convention of 16 April, 1948, art. 14, for the Organisation for European Economic Co-operation, adopted for the benefit of Switzerland the following rule: 'The abstention of any members declaring themselves not to be interested in the subject under discussion shall not invalidate decisions, which shall be binding for the other members.'

There are identical provisions in the Statutes of the Council of Europe (Resolution adopted by the Committee of Ministers in August, 1951, on partial agreements and in the Convention for setting up a European organisation for nuclear research (art. VII, 2)).

(*b*) *Reserved field.* The statutes of some international organisations refer to 'matters which are essentially within the domestic jurisdiction of any State' to keep them outside the jurisdiction of the organisation (Covenant of the League of Nations, art. 15, § 8; United Nations Charter, art. 2, § 7). Leaving aside the many controversial theories about these two provisions, it is obvious that this reserved field was mentioned in order to diminish the jurisdiction of the organisation. It is also clear that so far in United Nations practice this clause has not seriously prevented it from dealing with questions in these fields up to a certain point.

The *Institut de Droit International* clearly stated its views on this subject: 'The field reserved to the State is those activities where it is not bound by international law.' The extension of international law gradually restricts the field reserved to States. If the jurisdiction of organisations was precisely defined and delimited the allocation of functions would be settled as it is in federal systems. But jurisdiction is usually defined in terms of purposes, and this is liable to give organisations excessive scope (cf. p. 183). A compromise is to allow them to deal with questions in the reserved field but only in an abstract and general way (prepare conventions or address recommendations to all the member States). Since these organisations have so far no powers of decision, the point at issue is the lawful character of the political debates in which a State is arraigned for matters which it regards as within its sole jurisdiction. On this question see the report of Ch. Rousseau to the *Institut de Droit International* and the discussions, *Annuaire de l'Institut de Droit International*, 1950, p. 5; 1952, I, 137; and 1954, II, 108.

(*c*) *Assessing the competence of an organisation.* Who is competent to determine the jurisdiction of an international organisation? This raises several difficulties, and it seems that a State can contest the jurisdiction of an organisation and so obstruct it.

There is no doubt that every international organisation, or more accurately each organ of an organisation, determines its own jurisdiction every time the question arises. Without this elementary rule every time its jurisdiction was contested an international organisation would be obliged to suspend its decision. From the beginnings of international arbitration it has been recognised that the courts and arbitrators have complete authority to determine their own jurisdiction; it is the same for organs of international organisations. But State influence remains strong in international organisations. States can, for example, contest the way an international organisation interprets the documents which lay down its jurisdiction. No court can give an authentic interpretation of constituent texts. For instance the International Court of Justice can only interpret the United Nations Charter when asked for an advisory opinion.

On the other hand the various organs of an organisation can interpret documents in various ways, and involve the organisation in contradictory positions. The tendency in international practice is to accept the interpretation which trespasses least on State sovereignty, and this is sure to be given by assemblies composed of government delegates.

This at least is what happens in the political organisations. They are generally reluctant to have political texts interpreted by a judge, and therefore the organ which represents the greatest political force, that of the States, tends to prevail. The jurisdiction of political organisations is still mainly interpreted by the collective expression of State independence. But this solution may equally have disadvantages, and international organisations whose activities are virtually non-political or whose jurisdiction is amenable to rigorous definition opt when they can for disputes concerning their jurisdiction to be dealt with by judicial process.

This raises in an acute form the question of appeals.

(C) *The system of appeals*

If States must give way in every case in which they challenge the regularity of an organisation's act, they are at the mercy of any arbitrary action and will hesitate to enter into undertakings which leave them defenceless. At the other extreme, if the mere fact that a State contests the regularity of an act of an organisation is enough to release it from its engagement altogether, the organisation will be rendered completely ineffectual. International customary law has arrived at an intermediate position to deal with objections to awards in arbitration cases. It depends on the gravity of the alleged fault; when the fault is serious, particularly *ultra vires*, the State is not considered bound by the award (theory of *excès de pouvoir*). When the fault is trivial the State remains bound by the award. Whatever the merits of this system it is not in itself enough to eliminate disputes: this would need new arbitration, one is tempted to say 'superarbitration', to deal with the contested arbitral award.

It is the same for international organisations. Disputes between an organisation and a State can only be resolved harmoniously by expanding the organisation to include superimposed bodies to deal with disputes. In practice, if decisions of this kind are to be handled by judges, a proper system of appeals to quash irregular decisions has to be set up. This kind of appeal is already possible against acts of certain organisations, usually on grounds of *ultra vires*.

Even in 'non-political' organisations the intervention of a judge always raises all kinds of difficulties; it is particularly difficult to give a judge the power to assess an economic situation and override the assessment made by an organisation.

§ 3 GENERAL FORMS OF JURISDICTION

The jurisdiction common to all organisations cannot issue from their purpose, which varies in each particular case, but from the problems inherent in international political and administrative structures. This aspect of international organisation is not politically very important, but it reveals the process by which organisations develop, and some general conceptions mentioned in § 1 can be applied in practice. When we talk about 'common' jurisdiction we must bear in mind that the basis of an international organisation's jurisdiction is its constituent documents. Not all international organisations have the extensive jurisdiction we shall now discuss. We can say that their analogous structure and the fact that they work in the same social context leads to fairly uniform practical results. This is a sociological conclusion. A juristic conclusion can only be suggested after a study of each individual case.

We shall distinguish jurisdiction affecting the organisation itself from jurisdiction affecting its external relations.

(A) *The jurisdiction of an organisation*

Every international organisation makes for itself some of the rules for its own structure and operations. This corresponds to certain remarks in the Introduction (*supra*, p. 23). The need for such authority is obvious. The original documents founding an organisation cannot foresee every eventuality; they are compelled, then, whether openly or not, to leave a margin of general authority to the organisation itself, to elaborate details where necessary, or rather to make provision for effective execution. Thus, despite the apparent generality, this jurisdiction is dependent on the constituent documents.

Technically this jurisdiction is of two kinds: a regulating power and a power to set up subsidiary organs. They are often phrased in constituent documents in modest terms.

Thus the Interallied Reparation Agency 'discharges all other functions compatible with the provisions of the present act' (art. 5 of the agreement); the council set up by the International Sugar Agreement in 1953 'has such legal capacity as may be necessary in discharging its functions under this Agreement'.

(*a*) *The regulating power.* Arbitrators and international courts have traditionally exercised a regulating power in the form of rules of procedure. Assemblies and councils also possess this right.

The practical importance of rules of procedure may be seen in, e.g., the Year-book of the ICJ, 1953–54, which enumerates the times the various articles of the Court's rules of procedure have been applied. The rules of the assemblies are even more comprehensive than those of national parliaments, as they fix the rights of the representatives of States, whether recognised or not; e.g. the relations between the United Nations Assembly and the representatives of the Chinese Peoples' Republic.

This same problem arises in connection with administrative and financial questions: the status of officials, budgetary rules, etc. Generally speaking one can say that every article of the constituent documents can give rise to a ruling on their application. Thus the United Nations Charter explicitly gave the Assembly this power for financial questions (art. 17) and in administrative matters (art. 101); the Assembly, on its own authority, drew up on 14 December, 1946, a regulation under article 102 concerning the registration of treaties.

(*b*) *Subsidiary organs.* Nearly all international organisations have been authorised to create new organs to assist in carrying out the tasks assigned to them. These organs are generally known as 'subsidiary organs'. This is a bold step, since in some cases it involves a genuine delegation of powers; sometimes indeed delegation is expressly allowed, in others it is open to question. The Convention setting up OEEC (16 April, 1948) gave its Council the right ' to set up such technical committees or other bodies as may be required for the performance of the functions of the Organisation'. The United Nations Charter grants the power to set up subsidiary organs to the General Assembly (art. 22) and the Security Council (art. 29). Similarly the Atlantic Pact (art. 9), and the Convention setting up the European Organisation of Nuclear Research (art. 5, 10), etc. The power to create subsidiary organs has been important both for the number of additional organs created and for the functions assigned them.

In its advisory opinion on the effect of awards by the United Nations Administrative Tribunal, the ICJ recognised that the Assembly was legitimately empowered to set up the administrative tribunal as a subsidiary organ, but it defined this power solely in terms of the theory of functional competence. It appears, from the interesting communication the Secretary General's representative made to the Court on this occasion (Pleadings, p. 295) that since 1946 about a hundred subsidiary organs have been set up by the Assembly. Some are permanent, others set up for an indefinite period, others temporary or for a limited purpose. Some are composed of States, others of experts sitting in a personal capacity; some comprise only one person (the mediator in Palestine); the General Assembly elected or designated the members or had them chosen by other organs. These subsidiary organs have been given extremely varied tasks: study committees; interim committee known as the 'little assembly'; political and other commissions in Palestine, Libya, Eritrea, Korea, etc.; advisory committee on administrative and budgetary questions; International Children's Fund; and operational agencies (cf. *infra*, p. 261).

Another quite common example of a 'subsidiary organ' are the 'interim committees' which, between the signing of statutes and their entry into force, discharge the functions of organisations which sometimes never see the light of day, for example the International Trade Organisation. International practice recognises this procedure, and municipal courts sometimes allow such bodies a legal status.

(B) *External jurisdiction*

Organisations generally have full authority to take part in international relations consonant with their functions. The relations between organisations and member States are not sufficient evidence for this—they are simply proof of a State's *participation* in that organisation. The problem only appears when the organisation acts in an individual capacity distinct from the action of the member States, or when its own complex structure promotes organs comprising people who are not representatives of member States. But the problem is always present in the organisation's relations with third States or with other organisations.

The jurisdiction of international organisations takes all forms known to international relations: temporary or permanent representation, conferences, agreements or conventions, arbitration and even participation in another organisation.

International organisations do not generally keep permanent representatives in States, but there is nothing against States accrediting representatives to international organisations. International organisations are generally represented in all important sectors of international life by temporary representatives whose powers and position vary with each individual case. Organisations not only take part in international conferences, generally through observers, but they can call them.

This is current practice in the United Nations. Some conferences may be called by several organisations acting jointly. In 1953 the ILO and the European Coal and Steel Community called an inter-governmental conference on the social security of foreign workers, on the authority of a letter circulated by the executive directors of the two organisations.

The agreements concluded by organisations are by far the most interesting aspects of the question. We shall not discuss here whether these agreements should be considered as international agreements concluded by States (controversial question discussed at the International Law Commission, Reports of Brierly A/CN 4/23, 1950 and Lauterpacht A/CN 4/63, 1953). Their great variety is obvious. Some are made between international organisations; most seek to achieve some measure of co-operation. Some agreements, for example between the United Nations and Specialised Agencies (art. 63 of the Charter), establish formal liaison, others amount to absorption. Some agreements are made between an organisation and a State; notable amongst these are headquarters agreements to formalise arrangements between the organisation and the country in which it has its seat. They are similar to agreements concerning the privileges of organisations, for example the Convention of 13 February, 1946, concerning the United Nations, and of 21 November, 1947, for the specialised agencies, prepared and negotiated by special procedures. Other agreements attempt to lay down under what conditions member States shall provide the organisation with the money or services provided for in the constituent documents (art. 43 of the Charter; art. 70 and 71 of the Statutes of ICAO); alternatively the conditions under which the organisation or organisations shall provide services, as well as complex agreements over technical assistance.

There is a special type of agreement of 'association' as it is called in connection with treaties or treaty-proposals for European integration. The purpose of these agreements is to establish organic links between a State not party to the treaty of integration and the organisation and member States. This was mainly a question of associating the UK with European organisations such as the European Coal and Steel Community. There are very interesting legal aspects to agreements of association; for instance, the London Agreement of 21 December, 1954, on relations between the European Coal and Steel Community and the UK (*Notes et Etudes documentaires*, No. 1975); it does not go beyond mere co-operation.

Sometimes constituent documents state which authorities are empowered to conclude agreements and what those agreements may deal with. But often this is not so. One then has to work from basic principles. Some writers maintain that the proper organ to make agreements is the one which best represents the sovereign States which founded the organisation. Practice is not so rigid as this and the general tendency is to accept the model of States and allow the executive of the organisations to negotiate and sign agreements. But of course the internal constitution of the organisation must be observed, and every organ whose consent is required must approve the agreement.

For the United Nations the question has been studied by Parry, *Treaty-making power in the United Nations* (BYBIL, 1949, p. 108). For practical application see the constituent documents of each organisation. It would be interesting to compare the procedures used for the agreements between the United Nations and the specialised agencies (*cf.* the studies by Sharp in the review *International Organisation*, 1947, p. 460, and 1948, p. 247); for agreements concerning OEEC (art 15a and 20 of the Convention, and Annex IV), or the Council of Europe (Amendments adopted by the Committee of Ministers at their 8th and 9th Sessions, October, 1951), see the agreement of 23 November, 1951, between the Council of Europe and ILO; for the European Coal and Steel Community the advisory opinion of the Committee of Jurists (Council of Europe, Consultative Assembly, 4th ordinary session, S G (52)10); also the agreement on collaboration between ILO and the European Coal and Steel Community and the agreement of 21 December, 1954, on relations between the European Coal and Steel Community and the UK.

Section II

THE STRUCTURE OF ORGANISATIONS

With the development of international organisations there has been a great increase both in numbers and types of people concerned in their operation (§ 1); these people form the organs whose number and structure are designed to ensure the balanced and efficient operation of the organisation (§ 2).

§ 1 PERSONNEL OF INTERNATIONAL ORGANISATIONS

(A) *General remarks*

In the very first organisations (*supra*, p. 206) two categories of personnel could be distinguished: the representatives of the States and agents who may be described as international agents because they were not bound to any individual member State.

This is still roughly true today, but it is now more complicated. Everyone who participates in the work of an international organisation seems to fall into one of these two categories, but if we look at them more closely we can see an increasing variety of possible combinations; for instance, we have to take account of the diversity of their tasks or the influence of politics.

We shall consider this from three points of view : the accountability, independence, and the career structure of international personnel.

(a) *Accountability*. This is at the heart of the matter, and is closely connected with the very notion of international organisation (*supra*, p. 215). It is vital to know to whom an agent is accountable, to the organisation or to a State. In the first case he is an international agent, in the second a national agent. In theory this distinction is quite clear, but in practice often less so.

National agents representing member States in the organs of an international organisation sometimes act within the framework of that organisation, voting for example in a council or an assembly. In law their acts result in a collective decision of the organisation. But sometimes they act individually within the framework of the organisation, but not in its name : in this case, according to the usual rules of international relations, they only engage the legal responsibility of their national State. Sometimes the constituent documents of an organisation provide that member States (and not the organisation) shall take certain measures connected with the general work of the organisation; this was the case within the League of Nations for sanctions applied under article 16 of the Covenant. But doubtful situations can arise—and inevitably do so in a period of transition. For instance the status of military contingents placed at the disposal of an international organisation for enforcement action under the control of that organisation is very open to question.

(b) *The independence of international personnel*. We can assess this only after considering separately the system of appointment and the conditions under which functions are discharged.

A person is always in some measure dependent on those responsible for his appointment; but there is not necessarily any parallel between appointment and representation. The member governments of an organisation often appoint international agents who are in no sense their representatives. Any solution becomes confused if the right to propose, to nominate and to appoint are all run together.

Functions may be discharged under three sets of conditions. First, a person or group of persons may discharge their functions free of all influence and with no responsibility for the results of their acts; this is the position of an arbitrator or generally of any person invested with a judicial function; it is also the position of those independent persons frequently called into international organisations to exercise quasi-judicial functions. Second, some persons are subject to the hierarchic authority of superiors who may give them instructions; persons in the hierarchy take personal responsibility for performing their duties correctly; this, broadly speaking, is the position of officials. Third, some persons take their decisions independently but are subject to *a posteriori* control and have some personal responsibility at least on the political level; this responsibility is analogous to the responsibility of the executive in parliamentary systems, and is just beginning to grow up in international organisation.

(*c*) *Career structure.* Each national system of law lays down rules governing its agents. Each international organisation does the same. Nevertheless we can distinguish three broad groups of agents.

The first group hold permanent posts to the exclusion of any other professional activity. They are in the position of civil servants.

The second hold temporary posts, full time, to the exclusion of any other professional activity. Unlike the first group they are not on the permanent staff of the organisation.

The last group are employed part-time and they continue to exercise another profession.

We shall now examine the position of international agents and other persons who take part in the work of organisations.

(B) *International agents*

In its advisory opinion on reparation for injuries suffered in the service of the United Nations, the International Court of Justice defined an international agent as:

'Any person who, whether a paid official or not, and whether permanently employed or not, has been charged by an organ of the Organisation with carrying out or helping to carry out one of its functions. In short, any person through whom it acts.'

All international agents are subject to a few general rules: in the performance of their duties they must show complete independence of any 'other authority external to the organisation' (art. 100 of the Charter); on the other hand they enjoy the functional protection of the organisation in the event of injuries suffered in its service.

The conditions of service of international agents vary with their rank and with the precautions necessary to ensure their independence and responsibility.

(a) *From the career point of view.* As international administration has developed it has become more like a modern State administration. It is made up of international officials, temporary agents and part-time assistants. The last are usually called in for a particular assignment: expert advice, arbitral or technical functions, etc.; they have few or no financial rights but on the other hand they retain considerable freedom outside their particular functions. Temporary agents are found at the two extremes of the hierarchy; at one extreme in the lowest grades temporarily employed on contract, sometimes governed by the local law; at the other extreme persons at the very top in temporary posts, sometimes specially arranged for them by the highest organs of the organisation; such is the case of persons who are invested according to the Charter with the functions of a subsidiary organ (cf. *supra*, p. 238); as was Count Bernadotte, United Nations mediator in Palestine.

But most of the staff are permanent officials. In addition to being permanent and fulltime there are other aspects which give rise to very interesting legal problems. Since 1925 a theory of international public office has gradually grown up; it is based partly on the constituent documents of organisations, partly on the regulations made by their organs as part of their normal jurisdiction (*supra*, p. 237), and partly on the decisions of the international administrative courts set up to settle claims. Theories on this subject can only be built on a compromise between two political forces; the official trying to establish his personal rights based on doctrines of contract, and the public service which attempts to assert the priority of its own interests through a doctrine of prerogative power.

A legal approach to problems relating to international public service really began with the Monroe Case in 1925. On that occasion the Council of the League of Nations asked a committee of three persons for an advisory opinion (League of Nations, Official Journal, 6th Year, No. 10, p. 1441). Later a committee of five jurists examined the question of whether the Assembly had the right to reduce the salary of its officials (Official Journal, special supp. No. 107, p. 206). Individual administrative tribunals were set up and relations became normal, although crises were not avoided; e.g., when the Assembly of the League of Nations refused, when the League was wound up, to carry out a decision of its administrative tribunal (1946). There were serious difficulties some years ago as a result of certain measures taken by international organisations against their agents who had lost the confidence of their State for having refused to submit to investigation of their political opinions. These officials were awarded indemnities by the administrative tribunals of their organisation; the ICJ was consulted on the legal value of these decisions. Since every international organisation has a tendency to set up its own administrative tribunal the problem of how to simplify them and provide additional guarantees has become acute.

It is difficult to give precise figures for the number of international officials in international organisations. The following figures give a rough idea: United Nations, about 4,000; UPU, about 30; WMO about 50; UNESCO and WHO about 700 each; OEEC and NATO 600 each; ITU 200; European Coal and Steel Community 750; etc.

(b) *Independence and responsibility.* Most international agents are part of a hierarchy in which they are subject to the orders of their superior; this classic situation does not call for any particular comment.

On the other hand, two special posts must be mentioned: independent persons and agents with political responsibility.

Apart from judicial functions more tasks are being conferred on independent persons. Some functions are predominantly technical and non-political. It may then sometimes be advisable to take a person who is not an official, since officials are always involved in the political action of their superiors. But there is more to it than that. There is no one 'denationalised' in the social context, but some people can reach a level of the highest impartiality, less through social pressure than through their personal merits and the quality of their experience. In other words, at present an international mentality is more an individual phenomenon than a collective one, since it is a reaction to a given social environment. It may be a good thing to make use of these independent persons, especially if a personal appointment is not too great a burden on the organisation.

Apart from persons invited to sit on judicial bodies or commissions like the United Nations International Law Commission, other examples are the Permanent Opium Board (art. 19 of the Convention of 19 February, 1925); the International Office for the Registration of Frequencies, set up by art. 6 of the Atlantic City Convention and art. 10 and 11 of the Rules on Radiocommunications, chap. IV; the Interim Co-ordinating Committee for International Commodity Arrangements (Resolution of the Economic and Social Council of 28 March, 1947); on the other hand although the Executive Council of UNESCO was made up of 18 independent persons elected by the General Conference, it was agreed in 1954 that from then on those persons should represent their governments.

When an international agent is responsible to an organ whose functions and status are of a different kind from his own, we have a relationship which inevitably has political overtones. Excluding for a moment responsibilities exercised within a hierarchy, certain agents are under the political control of the deliberative organs of an international organisation, and in this position they are forced to accept responsibility which in certain respects is like that of a government. This was Bernadotte's position as defined by Resolution

of the United Nations General Assembly, 15 May, 1948; he
was not independent in quite the same way as an agent of a government would be since he was acting on the instructions of the
Assembly, but he was clearly undertaking a mission of a political
character.

More generally speaking this raises the whole question of the top
administrators in international organisations, in particular the
secretaries general. Some organisations formally provide that the
secretary or director general is only an official like the rest and that
his functions are purely executive. But the whole history of political
institutions in every country goes to show that administrative heads
become involved in political affairs and this must frequently happen
in international organisations.

(C) Persons other than international agents

These are chiefly representatives of States, but there are two other
tendencies: to appoint persons with other qualifications to organisations, and to modify the status of State representatives.

(a) Non-State representatives. Some persons, although they are
appointed more or less freely by the governments of member States,
do not represent the State but certain private interests. Thus, the
workers' and employers' delegates to the ILO do not represent their
national governments, although it appoints them; nor are they
representatives of the organisations to which they belong, if by a
representative we mean being bound by a mandate; if anything they
resemble elected members of a representative assembly. The same is
true of the Governing Body of the ILO which the delegates elect. The
members of the Consultative Committee set up by the European Coal
and Steel Community are in a similar position.

The assemblies of some European organisations are composed of
'delegates' chosen by their parliaments: they cannot be considered
representatives of their governments.

This is the case of the Consultative Assembly of the Council of Europe (compare
in this respect the original draft of art. 25 of the statutes with the amendment of May
1951); the evolution is even more marked in the Common Assembly of the
European Coal and Steel Community (art. 20 and 21 of the Treaty, 8 April, 1951).
The legal position of the members of the Common Assembly raises several
difficulties (for example the decree of 29 March, 1954). These assemblies are moving towards a pre-federal system.

(b) Change in the status of State representatives. At first State
representatives in an international organisation were automatically

the resident diplomatic or consular representatives of their country at the seat of the organisation.

Examples: the European Danube Commission; International Agricultural Institute of 7 June, 1905; Administrative Council of the Permanent Court of Arbitration (art. 49 of the First Hague Convention); Commercial Bureau, embryo of the future Pan American Union, created in 1890 at Washington and in 1898 placed under the supervision of an executive committee.

Subsequently States appointed special representatives, either career diplomats or politicians according to individual national practice. These representatives, known sometimes as 'para-diplomats', gradually achieved a special status: conditions have had to be laid down for their appointment, their special immunities, the methods of establishing their credentials, etc. Generally it has been the organisations rather than the States which have settled these questions. Sometimes the constituent documents contain general provisions on the subject.

On the other hand the State's freedom of choice is increasingly limited, at least in respect of technical organisations: State representatives must hold certain posts in the national administration or even in the government, or satisfy increasingly exacting qualifications.

Some cases have already been mentioned where State representatives have to be members of the government (*supra* p. 163); State representatives to WHO and WMO must be high-ranking national officials in the appropriate field.

Thus the status of State representatives is increasingly determined by the organisation concerned.

There are several other cases in which international organisations dominate the representatives of the States. In complex international organisations it often happens that the representatives of the same State in different organs of the organisation take up opposing positions, and this indicates some measure of independence. When organisations verify the powers of representatives they exercise a wide measure of discretion when representatives of more than one government contest the right to sit as representatives of a particular State. If no organ of the organisation can constitutionally impose its view on the rest, then each must decide the question for itself; hence the procedure for verification is part of the rules of procedure of each organ. In general the representative first admitted continues to sit until a decision is taken by the organ concerned; the question was hotly contested in the United Nations over China in 1950.

§ 2 THE ORGANS

(A) *General principles of organisation*

The various organs of an organisation have to be arranged in the light of general working efficiency and political equilibrium.

(a) Political equilibrium. Equilibrium must be obtained in three fields, the first of which is quite essential:

—balance between those member States actively concerned with the business of the organisation and those who are less so. The more political an organisation is the more this affects relations between the Great Powers and the powers with limited interests; the special purpose of technical organisations must be taken into account;

—balance between States and international agents; the latter are not yet a separate political force, but their influence begins to be felt;

—balance between governmental and non-governmental influence; as we have seen this problem only arises in the ILO, the Council of Europe and the European Coal and Steel Community.

(b) Efficiency. The elementary principles of a rational division of labour must be observed. Every organisation contains at least one organ composed of representatives of all the States. This organ is often large and generally has greater powers than the others. It is therefore necessary not only to have an international secretariat as a permanent bureaucracy, but also a second organ to duplicate the first: this will be one of the following types:

(1) Each State may have a representative in the second organ of a lower rank than in the first, which means it can be more permanent. The powers of the second organ are either delegated to it or loosely defined with reference to the principal organ. This system operates in NATO;

(2) The principal organ may appoint the members of the second organ. It is a smaller body in which not all the States are represented, and it is generally a permanent body or meets very frequently; this is the system for the executive committee of OEEC; the Economic and Social Council of the United Nations is also based on this principle;

(3) The principal organ may appoint the members of the second organ who sit in a personal capacity, for example the Board of Directors of the International Monetary Fund (art. 12 of the Statutes).

(B) *Procedure for maintaining political equilibrium*

(a) *Unequal representation in the different organs.* This is a method which has always been used in federal systems. In organisations with general jurisdiction such as the League of Nations or the United Nations there are, in addition to an organ in which States are equally represented, one or more other organs in which the Great Powers have special representation; for example the Council and the Assembly of the League of Nations; the Security Council, and to a lesser degree the Trusteeship Council, have a similar position *vis-à-vis* the General Assembly of the United Nations.

In specialised international organisations privileged representation is allowed to States most immediately concerned with its work; for instance, the Charter of ICAO provides (art. 50) that its Assembly should elect a Council of 21 members with special representation for 3 groups of States: those who have the largest air transport services, those who provide special facilities for international air communications, and lastly those whose presence on the Council will ensure equitable geographical representation for all parts of the world.

We can only really understand the political equilibrium between States inside an organ if we know the division of jurisdiction between those organs. If their jurisdiction is different an equilibrium will only be obtained if the powers of the two organs are broadly comparable. If they have concurrent jurisdiction there will be competition between the two organs and the balance between the States will vary. The Council and the Assembly of the League of Nations had concurrent jurisdiction. This has advantages when one wishes to establish a flexible balance of real forces. A federal type of solution would be for the organs to exercise the most important functions jointly. This would guarantee the rights of the Great Powers and also of the smaller States, but would make the international machinery very cumbersome and might be undesirable for general organisations responsible for the pacific settlement of international disputes, and is in any case only feasible in the few cases where it is possible to establish a federal structure.

(b) *Voting arrangements.* Some States may be given more influence than others through the system of voting.

Since State representatives represent their *governments* it is difficult to vary the number of representatives, each with one vote, allowed to each State. But a comparable result can be achieved by allowing certain territorial units to have their own representatives although they form part of one of the States already represented. This is done in most specialised organisations (UPU, ILO, WMO, etc.); if the bodies in question have neither separate interests nor an autonomous will this amounts to increasing the representation of one of the States. One may compare this solution as used in technical organisations with the membership of Byelorussia and the Ukraine, both States in the USSR, as separate members in the United Nations.

An alternative system usually adopted in economic organisations is simple weighting of votes, retaining the principle of one vote for each State.

It is also possible to vary the kind of majority required. At first decisions usually had to be unanimous; with some exceptions this was the case of the League of Nations (art. 5 of the Covenant). Administrative organisations such as the ILO and the UPU were readier to accept a majority voting system (namely two-thirds); it already existed in some organisations before the First World War, and rapidly became general. Certain organisations even use a simple majority for all resolutions. But this again is going too far, since if there is no 'weighting' the small States can dictate to the Great Powers. To avoid this a power of veto may be allowed which requires that certain States be included in the majority for the vote to be effective (as in the United Nations Security Council) or more positively that they can actually veto any suggestion (nomination of members of the High Authority of the European Coal and Steel Community, art. 10).

Extremely subtle voting rules are not the best way of achieving a delicate equilibrium. The expression of political forces in action is rarely refined and subtly framed rules are then simply not applied (for example, the voting rules of the special Council of Ministers of the European Coal and Steel Community, art. 28 of the Treaty). Moreover international organisations are still not strong enough to withstand bitter internal conflicts, especially between the Great Powers, and for this reason they try to get unanimous decisions or substantial majorities. Modern organisations based on co-operation pass all resolutions unanimously (all major decisions of OEEC and the Committee of Ministers of the Council of Europe).

(C) *Balance between States and the international administration*

In the history of international organisations the administration, mainly the international officials, at first had no direct political power; they were few in number and subject to the laws and supervision of the State where the organisation had its headquarters. Although they were not strictly speaking a 'power' they came to be a force separate from the States and it would be very interesting to see a sociological study of their origins and character. Their influence rests on the fact that they are permanent, have a fair measure of independence, and executive functions give them considerable scope. The history of constitutional law has shown that once the executive obtains control of the instruments of power and takes the initiative, it becomes supreme.

The position of the heads of the international secretariats is important from this point of view.

Documents generally use the term 'secretary' and 'secretariat', though sometimes 'director' (art. VI of the Convention of 1 July, 1953, setting up a European Organisation of Nuclear Research); the Havana Charter created a Director General and a Secretariat (art. 73, 84, 85); the International Sugar Agreement of 1953 created an Executive Director and a Secretary (art. 29); the Tin Agreement of 25 June, 1954, a Director and a Secretary (art. IV, A, § 6); but these divergencies are purely formal and on technical grounds.

The secretaries of all organisations are in charge of supply services —as well as liaison between the States (distribution of documents, etc.). They may also discharge more important functions varying from one organisation to another: (1) run particular departments on their own responsibility (other than administrative and financial), for example registration or custody of treaties; (2) prepare the resolutions of the organs; this can be important if the secretary has the right to initiate or refer business to these organs; (3) put into effect the decisions of the organisation; the freedom and responsibility left to the head of the secretariat give some idea of the discretion allowed him.

There are three types of secretariat, some more developed than others:

(1) Secretariats with subordinate functions; the secretariat 'assists' the organs of the organisation; the secretary general sometimes even has to get the approval of these organs for appointments to his staff. This was the position in the League of Nations (art. 2 of the Covenant); it is still the case in the Council of Europe (art. 10 and 37 of the Statute); in OEEC the Secretary has fairly limited functions under articles 15 and 16, but they have been increased in an Annex to the Convention.

(2) Secretariats which are 'organs' of an organisation with their own powers, entitled to enter freely into contact with other organs

and authorised to take some political initiative; for example the Secretariat of the Interallied Reparation Agency (art. 3 A of the Statute), and today the Secretary General of the United Nations (art. 7 and 99 of the Charter).

(3) Secretariats which have political responsibilities; the secretary is the administrative head of the secretariat but he has become a politician with functions similar to those of a minister. The title secretary should be changed for one more in harmony with his functions. The members of the High Authority of the European Coal and Steel Community have been in this position from the start and form what appears to be a genuine executive; they should probably drop the title of official. This type of system can only be made to work in organisations developing along federal lines.

Section III

FINANCIAL INSTITUTIONS

§ 1 GENERAL NOTIONS

We shall ignore here problems connected with organisations entirely occupied with financial affairs such as international banks, and limit this section to those questions of finance common to all organisations.

(A) *Expenditure*

There are two categories of expenditure:

(*a*) *Administrative expenditure.* All international organisations incur administrative expenses. When the first 'bureaux' were organised by one State on behalf of the others expenditure was technically an expenditure of the 'director' State; the latter was reimbursed by the other members of the organisation; but this method has practically disappeared today.

Some States 'render financial services' to organisations; thus Switzerland makes interest-bearing loans to the ILO and audits its accounts free of charge.

Ordinary public accounting techniques are applied to the expenditure of organisations: expenditure on staff and material, ordinary and extraordinary expenditure, etc. Extraordinary expenditure is, for example, needed for business sessions (the ILO where expenses are heavy and financed in a special way), or more generally is non-recurring expenditure such as investments in real estate (purchase of premises) (art. 8, § 2, Brussels Convention, 5 July, 1890).

(b) *Expenditure to provide services.* Some organisations, though by no means all, incur expenses by providing services (other than the sale of publications, for which there is no special system and which is not very important); if the receipts for these services cover expenditure the organisation becomes in some ways a *business organisation.* If the services are provided free of charge the organisation becomes an instrument for the international redistribution of wealth, since those who benefit do not provide all the money. If the organisation is authorised to make grants, it may through them create or control other international bodies and so will expand and decentralise its sphere of activity. This is financial federalism and is a result of the power certain organisations here to set up subsidiary organs (*infra,* p. 260).

(B) *Revenue*

The revenue of international organisations, like the revenue of States, comes from direct taxes, loans, charges, subventions, dues. But their relative importance is quite different.

As in a confederation, an international organisation's principal source of revenue are the *contributions of the member States.* This is interesting and will be dealt with separately.

Organisations are very rarely entitled to levy *direct taxes*; since it presupposes a direct exercise of authority over individuals. Only the highest type of organisation, approximating to a federation, can have rights like this.

Since most international officials benefit from very generous tax concessions, it has several times been suggested that the organisation should tax its own officials; but this does not mean much if this tax cannot take into account the official's total income, and this is not at present technically possible. A progressive tax has been levied by the United Nations on the salaries of its officials; the money so raised constitutes an extra source of revenue which reduces the contributions demanded from the States, and helps to offset the fiscal losses suffered by States as a result of the immunities granted to international officials. The present system favours the United States; it has refused to allow fiscal immunity to United States citizens who are international officials at the seat of the United Nations; the United Nations reimburses United States officials for the tax they pay.

It has been held that the deductions made by the European Coal and Steel Community from the firms under its jurisdiction are strictly comparable to a tax on production; this interpretation is economically correct but is debatable from the legal point of view.

Only a minute portion of the resources of international organisations comes from *charges* and *dues* (sale of publications, conducted
tours, etc.); on the other hand organisations whose main purpose is
to provide services may sometimes finance a large part of their
expenditure from this source of revenue. Thus the principal source
of revenue of international banks is the commission they levy on
their operations; the International Bank for Reconstruction and
Development (art. IV, section 4) has used this as an argument to
reject the tutelage of the United Nations.

Organisations may also use *loans* as a source of revenue. They
borrow either to balance their budget when their principal sources
of revenue are irregular (contributions of member States), or to
finance extraordinary expenditure (construction of buildings of the
seat of the United Nations), or when they need considerable capital
for their normal business (loans raised by international banks; loans
raised by the European Danube Commission to carry out major
works for navigability: it has a rather unsettled history).

(C) *Budget*

The administration of international organisations is dominated
by the budget, which estimates future expenditure and authorises the
raising of the revenue necessary to meet it. Further on we shall
examine the allocation of functions between the different organs; it is
partly a political matter (*infra*, p. 258). The budgets of international
organisations normally follow the traditional rules of public
finance.

Sums are allocated to specific items of expenditure but transfer
between items is generally permissible. Authority to do so is usually
the responsibility of a special body such as a permanent finance
committee rather than a matter for the budgetary organ.

The budget is treated as a whole, but some revenue is often ear-
marked for special purposes, particularly loans. The treasury of the
organisation frequently keeps separate accounts showing the use of
different funds (working capital fund); the methods used by certain
States to disguise budgetary expenditure are not practised in international organisations.

There is generally an annual budget, but some cover several years.
In fact the expenditure of organisations is stable and a stable currency
is used. Sometimes the budget is approved by organs whose meetings
are costly and infrequent. The FAO and UNESCO for example have
two-yearly budgets and WMO a four-yearly budget.

(D) *Finance and currency*

Most international organisations receive an advance credit to launch them when they are first set up; later the member States provide advances in proportion to their quota. Some organisations which conduct complex financial operations, like the banks or the European Coal and Steel Community, frequently hold balances in excess of their annual budgets.

The financial operations of international organisations are conducted in a particular currency: the gold franc for the European Danube Commission, the Swiss franc for the League of Nations, and the dollar for the United Nations. Another question is which currency is used for reserves, disbursements and the collection of revenue. Out-payments are usually made in the currency of the State in which the organisation has its headquarters; the League of Nations found its assets had appreciated considerably after the devaluation of the Swiss franc in 1936. Since some currencies are inconvertible arrangements are made to lower the payment of contributions in hard currencies.

§ 2 THE CONTRIBUTIONS OF MEMBER STATES

The main problem is to assess the contribution of each State; an incidental problem is to obtain the payments in arrears.

(A) *Assessing the scale of contributions*

Only in exceptional cases can States be expected to finance organisations on an equal footing; for instance where the sums involved are very small or the States are of equal size (International Commission of the Cape Spartel Light). It is equally difficult to leave the States free to decide their own level of contributions, unless the amounts are negligible. Thus the UPU, which has always had a small budget and many members, has drawn up a scale of contributions numbered 1–25, and States choose their own place in this scale. (The same system: Bureau of the Permanent Court of Arbitration, art. 29, First Hague Convention; Union for Protection of Works of Art and Literature.) The League of Nations, before amendment, linked its scale of contributions to the UPU system, but it proved impracticable for such a large organisation (art. 6, § 5, original draft of the Covenant).

To solve the problem some conventions have drawn up a scale of contributions or laid down the principles for assessing them; others have left this to the organisations.

Attempts have been made to determine objective standards for assessments. The basis for assessing the scale of contributions is, in some technical organisations, implicit in the purpose of the organisation itself: level of international trade (art. 9, Brussels Convention, 5 July, 1890; International Union for the Publication of Customs Tariffs); length of railway covered by the convention (art. 1, § 3, of the Regulations of the Central Office for the Transport of Goods by Rail); the importance of industrial interests (a vague formula adopted by ILO). Other organisations, sometimes for a broader purpose, take into consideration size of population (International Bureau for Weights and Measures, Pan American Union 1906–10, Council of Europe, art. 38 (b) of the Statute).

A new notion gradually emerged: national income as an indication of a State's capacity to pay. How accurately national income is assessed depends on standards of national accounting. It was still at an elementary stage when the League of Nations was set up: tax receipts, population and war damage were taken into account. Since then it has become very meticulous in modern organisations: 'Average net national income at factor cost over the last three years' (art. 7 of the Statute of the European Organisation of Nuclear Research). But some organisations take into account other factors besides national income, for instance ICAO uses the number of passenger miles per State. The United Nations amplifies the figures of national income as criteria by taking as well income per head of population, temporary dislocation of national economies arising out of the Second World War and the ability of members to secure foreign currency.

The scale of contributions is fixed after complicated discussions. It is agreed that the contribution of a single State shall never exceed 30% of the total; this rule was to safeguard the independence of the organisation and was decided in order to reduce the contribution of the USA which had risen to 40%. Richer States (Canada) have had the principle accepted that no member State shall pay a higher contribution per head of population than that of the State making the largest contribution (principle of maximum per head of population); the contributions of weaker States have been reduced. The heaviest burden is on the 'medium-sized' States, and they complain. (Report of the Committee on Contributions, General Assembly, 91st special session, No. 10A/2716; Liveran Report, Fifth Commission, A/2822.)

These are the contributions for some States to the United Nations: USA 33%, USSR 17.61%, UK 8.85%, France 5.9%, India 3.3%, minimum contribution 0.04%. *Seven States pay over 75% of the contributions.*

(B) *Payments in arrears*

Some international organisations have had to contend with substantial arrears in the payment of contributions; deficits increase, or alternatively the administration is forced systematically to over-estimate its expenditure, as the League of Nations did at first. There is no satisfactory solution to this problem. It is the political rather than the financial aspect which is important; it goes to show how far international organisations still depend on the goodwill of States. When payments have got too far behind most international organisations have finally made new agreements so as to recover at least part of the money.

If an international institution hopes to become universal the expulsion of the debtor State is not a satisfactory solution. The United Nations (art. 19 of the Charter) and other international organisations have instituted sanctions against debtor States: they have no right to vote while the amount of their arrears exceeds a given amount, except in the case of special authorisation if the failure to pay is due to conditions beyond their control.

Apart from special difficulties arising out of the insolvency of important member governments, or the so-called 'inactive' members of WHO (1949–53), about 90% of contributions are usually paid.

Financial contributions are an important problem, as they throw light on the paradoxical position of international organisations often administered by political majorities which do not pay the major part of the contributions. In the past several international organisations accepted the close relationship between finance and administration and arranged for contributions either in proportion to the services rendered by the organisation (art. 6, Protocol of 20 March, 1883, Paris Conference creating the Union for the protection of Industrial Property; art. 78, § 6, London Agreement, 18 July, 1879, Telegraphic Union, art. 30, § 3, 1 June, 1878, UPU); or the number of votes of the States (International Agricultural Institute, International Commission for Air Navigation, art. 34, § 12, of the Treaty of Paris, 13 October, 1919, etc.). These methods have disappeared now because the political aspect of organisations has become predominant (nevertheless the International Refugee Organisation only came into being when the convention had been ratified by fifteen States representing 75% of the contributions). But if international organisations have to increase expenditure, they must necessarily find different sources of revenue and a new system of State representation (cf. *infra*, for *voluntary* contributions).

§ 3 BUDGETARY ARRANGEMENTS

(A) *Approval of the budget*

The history of financial institutions shows that organs which approve the budget virtually always obtain political predominance.

An examination of international organisations confirms this. The strongest organ in the organisation approves the budget, and in the

I

present state of international relations this is the organ which most completely and directly represents the member States.

This is evident both in the statutes of international organisations and in the way institutions have developed where the constituent documents are silent. It is very rare for them to be so, but the Covenant of the League of Nations, for instance, laid down no rules in this domain. Although it had important powers the Council allowed the Assembly to seize control of the budget when in 1922 it drew up a regulation for the finances of the League of Nations.

Conversely, where the balance of power in an organisation makes it impossible to allow one organ to approve the whole budget the budget disappears to be replaced by a set of estimates for each department; for example, the case of the European Coal and Steel Community.

And so, both in the League of Nations and the United Nations, the Assembly or the General Assembly approves the budget (art. 17 of the Charter) and also lays down conditions of formulation and execution.

Sometimes the constituent documents of an organisation contain detailed budgetary provisions; but the budgetary procedure of the United Nations is a good example to take of the budgetary procedure of most organisations.

Each administrative department sends its estimates to the Secretary General; these he approves after any necessary modifications. He submits these proposals to the Advisory Committee for Administrative and Budgetary Questions, a subsidiary organ composed of independent persons responsible for advising the Assembly, which disregards its recommendations very rarely. Its *de iure* powers (authorisation of certain transfers) and *de facto* powers make this committee one of the most efficient institutions in the United Nations. Nearly all organisations have a similar body. The budget is finally examined by the Fifth Committee of the Assembly and then voted by the Assembly. Its execution is entrusted to the Secretary General, under the supervision of the Board of Auditors. There is a similar institution in every organisation.

The most important political aspect of budgetary procedure is the size of the majority required for approval. In the past it was agreed that the budget had always to be voted unanimously, with the proviso that if no agreement was reached the current budget should be extended for the next year (European Danube Commission). Nowadays a majority vote is usually allowed. In the United Nations a two-thirds majority is required (art. 18 of the Charter); similarly in the ILO and WMO, and in the Council of Europe (art. 20 (d) of the Statute, two-thirds majority of members present and voting and a majority of the representatives entitled to sit on the Committee of Ministers). In other organisations a simple majority suffices: FAO, WHO, ICAO, UNESCO. There are serious drawbacks to approving the budget by a simple majority when member States are equally represented but make substantially different contributions.

(B) *Effects of the budget*
Income and expenditure must be dealt with separately.

(a) *Income.* When they approve the budget members assume a legal obligation to pay the contributions assigned to them. The *national* organs which approve the national budgets are bound to make provision in the national budget of sufficient sums to cover their contribution. It seems quite clear that the decision of an international organisation binds a parliament, even though this is not easy to reconcile with certain theories of the relations between constitutional and international law. But it is also undoubtedly a serious political drawback for States which make high contributions.

There have been two defensive reactions to this: (1) An organisation's non-obligatory expenditure is met by voluntary State contributions; this is a form of financial federalism, and is most common in the field of technical assistance; (2) According to a general theory mentioned earlier certain decisions on financial matters only bind members who have approved them, and not those who vote against them or abstain (Council of Europe, Resolution of the ninth session of the Committee of Ministers, August 1951; European Organisation of Nuclear Research, art. VII, § 2 of the Statute).

(b) *Expenditure.* The legal significance of 'appropriations' must be as clear as it is in municipal law. It is generally no more than an authorisation to spend; it is not an injunction to spend, nor can it override any other authorisation that may be required. If the organisation has debts the organ which authorises expenditure is bound to make provision to meet them. (Advisory opinion of the International Court of Justice, 13 July, 1954, Reports, p. 59.)

§ 4 FINANCIAL FEDERALISM

Financial procedures are a particularly flexible way of linking or subordinating one institution to another. The key to the political and administrative activity is financial. The system of inter-relationships brought about by these financial procedures is known as 'financial federalism'. There are two general tendencies:

(1) General organisations seek financial control over specialised organisations.

(2) International organisations, working in reverse, try to decentralise financial business.

(A) *Centralisation in favour of general organisations*

Behind the multiplicity of international organisations lies a political origin, State sovereignty; the disadvantages, however, are principally administrative and financial. By splitting international administration up into autonomous units it increases costs and prevents rational organisation. When organisations are composed of widely differing groups of States nothing can be done about this except to achieve what co-operation is possible. But where several organisations have more or less the same members is it not possible to reach a more organic solution?

It was planned, rather prematurely and without much success, to regroup various European organisations round the Council of Europe. The United Nations Charter (art. 17, § 3, 57 and 58, 63 and 64) fixed principles covering the problem of relations between the United Nations and specialised agencies, but so far their representatives have reached agreement only in a limited number of cases; the IMF and the International Bank for Reconstruction and Development, with adequate financial resources of their own, have shown no eagerness to respond; the UPU and the ILO have agreed to send their budgets to the United Nations Assembly so that the General Assembly may have the chance to make recommendations; other specialised agencies have agreed to follow as far as possible the practices and forms recommended by the United Nations.

The problem of the administrative and financial unification of international organisations is still open.

(B) *Decentralisation*

Special problems arise when subsidiary organs are created with considerable funds and wide financial autonomy. Autonomy is often conditioned by the nature of the funds at their disposal; for example, the International Children's Fund, the Enlarged Programme of Technical Assistance, the agencies for reconstruction in Korea and for Palestine refugees (UN Korean Reconstruction Agency and UN Relief and Works Agency for Palestine Refugees in the Near East), and the special fund for refugees (UN Refugee Emergency Fund) administered by the Office of the United Nations High Commissioner for Refugees (Resolutions 639 VII and 728 VIII of the General Assembly).

The scope of these bodies and the facility with which they were set up are quite remarkable examples of the creative dynamism of large international organisations. Can we consider these subsidiary organs financially autonomous services, without individual international personality ? They are still developing, and must be described before being classified.

The International Children's Fund was created by a simple resolution of the General Assembly (Resolution 57 of 11 December, 1946); it succeeded UNRRA, inherited its credit accounts and is authorised to make and receive payments and to conclude agreements with governments. The governments propose programmes for the benefit of children, the Fund approves them and helps to carry them out under the responsibility of the government concerned, on condition that the latter contributes half the cost. The Fund lives mainly on the voluntary grants in aid from certain States; it is run by a Board composed of government representatives with an administrative director appointed by the secretary general and under the control of the Economic and Social Council. Protocol agreements with WHO have arranged the respective responsibilities of the two organs, the Fund being responsible mainly for providing supplies.

Organisations which wish to be more independent still can make grants to national organisations; they can collaborate closely with all types of organisations, some of them international but not governmental, others institutions of municipal public law or private law.

A single example will help: the International Children's Centre. It was created after discussions in the Council of Administration of the International Children's Fund (30 June, 1949), and the Executive Board of WHO, followed by a resolution of the Economic and Social Council (28 July, 1949). Finally, on 10 November, 1949, a decree of the French government recognised it as a *fondation d'utilité publique*. It is financed by grants from France, WHO and the International Children's Fund; its rules of procedure indicate that it is an international institution working in collaboration with international organisations.

The following figures give some indication of the extent of the problems raised by the finance of international organisations. In 1954 the budget of the United Nations was about 47 million dollars, that of the eight principal specialised agencies totalled 35 million dollars. The French law of 2 February, 1955, gives a list of the French contributions to international (or assimilated) organisations; the obligatory expenditure amounts to 3 milliard 380 million francs (to which must be added 437,000 dollars for ILO—1953 figures, 226,800 Swiss francs for ITU—1953 figures, and 47,000 Swiss francs for the UPU). In addition about a milliard in voluntary contributions to decentralised bodies.

CONCLUSION

THE LAW OF INTERNATIONAL
ORGANISATIONS

We have so far been considering the rules governing a particular aspect of international organisations. If we now turn to the *legal basis of those rules* we are struck by their variety and the departures from traditional international law.

It is tempting to regard the law of international organisations as an exclusively written law. Legal forms as advanced as international organisations are certainly based in part on written law, and especially on treaty law. But if custom is not important in the foundation of the organisations (except in exceptional cases like the Pan American Union), it plays an important part in their operation. It alone accounts for the remarkable development of certain aspects of this branch of international law.

The written law of organisations is evident in the new juridical terms used. Even the treaties setting up the organisations have peculiarities which have often been mentioned in relation to other collective acts: special terms, techniques of revision on a majority basis, limitation of reservations, etc. The extraordinary proliferation of agreements concluded by international organisations has confused even further the complex picture of international agreements between States. Although international conventions show increasing traces of legislative methods, the principal legal innovation is in international organisations' regulatory decisions. With these regulations one of the traditional traits of international law is changed; legislation, unlike conventions, is incompatible with a legal system based on co-ordination, and regulations are undoubtedly a minor form of legislation.

Nevertheless, we must not overestimate the changes international organisations have made in international law, for they work at different levels; for the most part in international terms, with relations with other organisations and States, but also in terms of the national law of the States concerned.

As the ICJ recalled in the Advisory Opinion on Reparation for Injuries suffered in the service of the United Nations, an organisation may act in terms of the municipal law of a State, for example, in employing a person according to local labour laws, or in taking out an insurance under local law. To give them an appropriate status in local law conventions explicitly grant international organisations legal personality inside member States, and national courts sometimes spontaneously recognise an organisation's legal personality. However, international organisations can make only limited use of this faculty; if they wish to conserve their jurisdictional immunities they must set up their own jurisdictions to settle disputes or go to arbitration. In this case local law may not be applied, but law peculiar to the organisation.

But when a body is given national but not international personality, such as the International Children's Centre, it is no longer strictly speaking an international organisation (unless States have recognised it as such). This is the position certain 'unions' used to be in when they were recognised as legal persons in municipal law before they were given international personality.

Certain juristic acts of organisations however are neither municipal law nor international law in the strict sense of the term, but are internal laws of the organisation itself: relations with its officials, relations with individuals who enter directly into contact with the organisation, relations with suppliers, and even some relations with member States not covered by traditional rules of internal law.

At the end of the Introduction it was shown that international law could be defined either by its character as a 'law of co-ordination', when this would be the basic characteristic of all its rules, or by the fact that the rules it laid down were applied to States. Writers who lay emphasis on international law as a purely co-ordinating function are hard put to it to explain the legal nature of the internal regulations of international organisations and the regulations binding the authorities of each State.

Their difficulty is even greater if we consider the relations between an organisation and its officials. It is now no longer a question of relations with States or problems of co-ordination, but quite simply a master-servant relationship. This is clearly the expression of a law peculiar to the organisation itself except in those cases where the organisation has expressly accepted the validity of local municipal law.

The question is far from being theoretical. If the Administrative Tribunal of the United Nations, when dealing with disputes between the organs and its officials, were considered to be an international tribunal, it could have been expected to apply the theory of the nullity of arbitral awards applicable to disputes between States. It did no such thing. The ICJ rejected this view in its advisory opinion of 13 July, 1954, on the grounds that the issue was a 'domestic dispute'.

Relations between an organisation and its suppliers are usually settled by arbitral clauses referring the dispute to the municipal law

of a particular State; but this clause may authorise the arbitrator to
apply rules which are not identified with any particular national
legal system; they might come to form a special body of rules for
the organisation.

In general the United Nations adopts, at least for its headquarters in New
York, a compromissory clause which refers disputes to the usages and interven-
tion of the American Arbitration Association. C. Eagleton, *International
Organisation and the law of responsibility*, RCADI, 1950, 76, 323.

The relations between international organisations and private
persons are very important indeed. The fact that they exist shows
that there is a transition from an international to a federal level.
When individuals come in some respects under the direct administration of an international organisation, it means that some kind of
'direct' relationship has been created, and this marks the beginning
of a federal order. Such relations are infrequent, but there are already
some examples.

If an international organisation has the right to exclusive jurisdiction within a
defined territorial area, it will have direct relations with a fairly large public. Thus,
the agreement of 26 June, 1947, between the Secretary General of the United
Nations and the Secretary of State of the United States gave the Secretary
General the power to make regulations within the headquarters district of the
United Nations; he has made such regulations with regard to conditions of
employment and trade and the exercise of the medical profession.

The international banks and organisations providing credit facilities for private
persons have had to define which body of law shall be applicable to these operations. In general loan agreements contain an arbitration clause, and they define in
detail the legal system which will apply to the agreements 'notwithstanding any
contrary clause in the laws, legislations or regulations of any State or its public
bodies'. Even when the agreements are to be interpreted by municipal law, the
law so applied no longer has its original aspect of being nothing but the expression
of the State's sovereignty. In this connection refer to loan contracts of the International Bank for Reconstruction and Development (Adam, *The loan agreements
of the International Bank for Reconstruction and Development*, RGDIB, 1951, no.1)
or to those of the European Coal and Steel Community (cf. particularly art. XVII
of the loan contracts).

Relations between the European Coal and Steel Community and the firms
under its jurisdiction are clearly federal in character and come under the internal
law elaborated by the Community itself.

CHAPTER THREE

The United Nations and the Principal Regional Organisations

To round off the two preceding chapters some account of the major international organisations is necessary. It will be limited here to a brief examination of the United Nations, the various forms of European organisation, and the other regional organisations.

Section I

THE UNITED NATIONS

§ 1 THE LEAGUE OF NATIONS AS A PRECEDENT

We have already described certain aspects of the League of Nations; an overall view will make for a better understanding of the United Nations which, although differing in many respects from the League, nevertheless bears definite traces of its predecessor.

(A) *Origin*

The Covenant of the League of Nations was a result of the 1914–1918 War. Formally, the text of the Covenant was inserted in all the peace treaties (except the Treaty of Lausanne in 1923); but the League of Nations was already in most respects divorced from the original conflict. The text and general philosophy of the Covenant are clearly Anglo-Saxon and particularly American in inspiration. President Wilson was its moving spirit, and the need to obtain the support of the United States Senate caused certain points in the Covenant to be emphasised. Although the defeated States were not founder members, the League of Nations was intended to become universal; there is no reason for regarding the system established by the Covenant as a

265

settlement imposed by victors. Its aims were coloured by American idealism, and its conception bears the stamp of Anglo-Saxon empiricism. The Conference rejected the French proposals, and based the whole structure on the free determination of States, working in co-operation. The Covenant left State sovereignty almost untouched; the League of Nations was a framework for international action of the States. Unfortunately the United States refused to ratify the Treaty of Versailles and signed a separate peace treaty with Germany; she never joined the League of Nations, and from the start her absence undermined its chances of success.

Nevertheless, the League of Nations was in fact a universal organisation. In addition to the founder members who became members by ratifying the treaty (30 out of 32), some States were 'invited' to become members by means of an annex to the Covenant which listed them; finally other States, among them all those defeated in the 1914 War, were elected members by a two-thirds majority of the Assembly. From 45 in 1919 the number of members reached 60 (only very small States and the United States excluded) but declined to 44 in 1939 after the political upheavals.

The decline in numbers was not because States were excluded as a sanction (applied only to Russia in December 1939), nor an automatic withdrawal when States rejected an amendment (art. 26, § 1 of the Covenant), but was due to States exercising their right under article 1 (3), to withdraw after two years' notice.

(B) *Structure*

The structure was relatively simple. The League had only two organs: the Council and the Assembly. The purpose of dual representation of States in two organs was to ensure certain States a privileged position and to have besides the Assembly a smaller body which might meet more frequently and work more effectively. But if the jurisdiction of these two organs and changes in the composition of the Council are considered it seems clear that the Great Powers were not given much advantage. Even though the Council had exclusive jurisdiction in some matters (expulsion of members, guarantee of territorial integrity, art. 10; observance of certain treaties), the Assembly had exclusive jurisdiction in equally important matters (admission of new members, election of non-permanent members of the Council, revision of treaties, etc., art. 19), and it easily acquired jurisdiction over the budget (*supra*, p. 258). Furthermore there was concurrent jurisdiction in the most important matters; e.g. the maintenance of world peace (art. 3, 4, 11 and 15 of the Covenant).

If, with two exceptions, it was always the Council which acted in this case, this was mainly for practical reasons and the Council and Assembly were always substantially in agreement. Finally, certain questions could only be decided by the Council of the League of Nations with the approval of the majority of the Assembly: amendments to the Covenant (art. 26), increase in the number of members of the Council (art. 4 § 2), appointment of the Secretary General and judges of the Court of International Justice.

At first the council contained a majority of representatives of the Great Powers (4 out of 9) but this position changed. The number of non-permanent members grew steadily while the influence of the permanent members decreased with the withdrawal of Japan and Germany, and later Italy: on the eve of the Second World War there were only three permanent members out of 14.

The Great Powers were not in fact given overwhelming influence in relations between the two organs.

Nor was this so in voting procedure. The Great Powers had no privileges. In general in both organs decisions were taken unanimously. This was strictly in accordance with the principle of co-operation, and it was not so paralysing as might have been feared. Politically it was difficult for a single State, other than a Great Power, to block a resolution; legally not all decisions had to be unanimous. Apart from individual and temporary cases provided for in peace treaties, the Covenant waived the unanimity rule in the following cases: all questions of procedure were decided by a simple majority (art. 5 § 2); in settlement of disputes the parties had no vote and the Council could —admittedly without important juridical consequences—approve the report by a simple majority (art. 15, §§ 5 and 7); the Assembly voted amendments to the Covenant by a qualified majority (art. 26); etc. In practice attempts were always made to evade the rule of unanimity as much as possible, in particular by considering abstention no obstacle to unanimity and by defining the term 'procedural questions' very broadly.

The permanent Secretariat presided over by a Secretary General must also be mentioned; but the Secretary General was not strictly speaking an organ of the League of Nations, since his role was purely administrative and strictly controlled (*supra*, p. 251). The Secretariat was the common administrative and financial basis of all the bodies attached to the League of Nations (*supra*, p. 211).

The Permanent Court of International Justice should be considered an organ of the League of Nations. It took the combined intervention of votes in the Council and the Assembly to overcome the obstacle of appointment of judges on which previous proposals had foundered. On the other hand, although the Court was unable to take cognizance of disputes to which the League was a party, it was several times called upon to give advisory opinions on the proper interpretation of the Covenant or peace treaties; the Court's connection with the League of Nations unfortunately prevented the United States from being a party to it.

§ 2 ORIGIN AND PHILOSOPHY OF THE UNITED NATIONS CHARTER

(A) *The United Nations and the Second World War*
On 1 January, 1942, the allied States at war with the Axis Powers signed a declaration at Washington which set out the aims of the common struggle; it is in this text that the expression 'United Nations' was first used.

In the Declaration by the United Nations, 1942, the term 'United Nations' stood for a certain number of States. The San Francisco Charter bears the official title 'Charter of the United Nations' and the text refers sometimes to the 'United Nations Organisation', sometimes to the 'United Nations'.

From 1944 onwards the allies laid the foundations of several international organisations. Two economic organisations, the International Monetary Fund and the International Bank for Reconstruction and Development, were set up in 1944; a universal political organisation took longer to prepare. It could not be the League of Nations, unfairly held responsible for the impotence of its members, to which the United States had never been a party, and from which the USSR had been expelled in 1939. Preliminary proposals were drawn up at Dumbarton Oaks after discussions between representatives of the United States, the United Kingdom, the USSR and China. The most delicate points were tackled at the Yalta Conference (February 1945). These proposals were submitted to an international conference at San Francisco (25 April to 26 June, 1945). The work was rapidly completed and ended with the signing of the Charter (111 articles) which came into force in October, 1945.

In appearance the Charter was less intimately connected with the war than the Covenant of the League of Nations. In reality its text had been discussed before the end of hostilities; its main provisions were laid down by the Great Powers, who clearly overshadowed all others at the Conference; moreover, the four sponsoring Powers,

UK, USA, USSR and China, invited only States at war with the Axis.

But the spirit which permeates the Charter is principally the result of wartime experience: agreement between the Great Powers could ensure world peace within the framework of an international organisation; without this essential agreement there was no point in trying to do anything at all.

The Charter differs markedly from the Covenant. The United Nations has far broader powers than the League of Nations. The powers of the Security Council under Chapter VII of the Charter show the organisation is not simply a framework for co-operation between States, but that it has a genuine legal power to make decisions and take practical measures, so that some writers have used the term 'supra-national' to describe its authority (Brierly, *The Law of Nations*, p. 98). But it can only have this authority if there is unanimous agreement between the Great Powers: this is the underlying assumption.

The United Nations has not become a universal organisation owing to differences between the USSR and the United States (*supra*, p. 225). Fifty-one States are original members of the United Nations, 9 others have been admitted under article 4 § 2, by a decision of the General Assembly taken by a two-thirds majority, on the recommendation of the Security Council. Twelve States have had their applications rejected by the Security Council. Neither Germany nor Japan has applied.

§ 3 THE STRUCTURE OF THE UNITED NATIONS

According to article 7 of the Charter the Organisation has 6 principal organs; a General Assembly, a Security Council, an Economic and Social Council, a Trusteeship Council, an International Court of Justice and a Secretariat. The structure is apparently more complex than the League of Nations. The new formula making the Secretariat an organ of the United Nations and the profound difference between the role of the Secretary General of the Organisation and of the League have already been noted (*supra* p. 251). The International Court of Justice is also an organ; the Permanent Court of International Justice had been in a comparable position. We shall explain later how the role of the Trusteeship Council is not very different from the Mandates Commission of the League of Nations. The vital differences occur in the respective roles of the Security Council (reminiscent of the Council of the League of Nations) and the

General Assembly (reminiscent of the Assembly of the League of Nations), and the existence of a new organ: the Economic and Social Council.

(A) *The Security Council*

(a) *Composition.* The Security Council has 11 members; 5 permanent members (China, France, UK, USSR, US), 6 non-permanent members nominated by the Assembly for two years, 3 being elected every year and not eligible for immediate re-election. In choosing them the Assembly pays due regard to their contribution to the maintenance of peace and to the other purposes of the Organisation, and also to equitable geographical distribution (art. 23).

(b) *Voting procedure* (*veto*). Article 27 makes a fundamental distinction between 'procedural matters' and 'all other matters'. The first only need an affirmative vote of 7 members, that is a simple majority. For the second the affirmative vote of 7 members must include all the permanent members. Every permanent member can therefore block any resolution of the Council with this power of veto.

Under these conditions the definition of 'procedural matters' is very important. But naturally the veto may also be exercised in deciding whether or not a matter is 'procedural' (double veto); this could only be avoided by having another organ empowered to decide the question, or alternatively by drafting a list of procedural and non-procedural matters. At the time of the San Francisco Conference the permanent members issued a declaration suggesting some examples and general principles, but this interpretation was not incorporated in the Charter.

The right of veto has been used very frequently in the Security Council and in serious cases has completely paralysed the Organisation.

The right of veto has been slightly modified in some ways. It has been agreed that to abstain is not to veto; this is now confirmed by United Nations practice. It has also been held that the Council can pass resolutions in the absence of a permanent member, and several resolutions were passed during the absence of the Soviet delegate between 13 January and 1 August, 1950, notably about the Korean War; but this view has been challenged. Article 27 of the Charter also restricts the right of veto by stipulating that a party to a 'dispute' must abstain from voting when the procedure for the peaceful settlement of disputes by the Council is in operation, or when the dispute is referred to a regional organisation. Unfortunately the Council's jurisdiction is defined in terms of 'disputes' and 'situations' (art. 34 et seq.); a permanent member only has to use its right of veto to prevent the Council from recognising that there is a 'dispute' and it can be sure of not losing its right to vote.

(c) *Functions and powers.* The Great Powers intended the Security Council to be the principal organ of the United Nations; this met opposition from the other States who insisted that the functions and powers of the Assembly be reinforced in the Charter. Later, when the USSR consistently vetoed resolutions over Korea, the Charter was interpreted so as to reduce the supremacy of the Security Council, but it is still by far the most important organ.

The Security Council owes its importance to the fact that, under article 24, it bears 'the primary responsibility for the maintenance of international peace and security'. This is the principal purpose of the United Nations; it takes precedence over all other considerations; however interesting its work may be in other fields its future depends on this factor. In addition, all major political decisions of the United Nations require the intervention of the Security Council in some form; the admission, suspension or expulsion of members is decided by the Assembly on the recommendation of the Security Council (art. 4, §§ 2, 5 and 6). The Security Council reinstates a suspended member with rights and privileges. The Secretary General is appointed on the recommendation of the Security Council (art. 97). In all these cases the 'recommendation' is virtually a decision which it is possible to veto (there is no veto in the election of members of the International Court of Justice—art. 10 § 2 of the Court's Statute). The Security Council is involved in the general revision of the Charter (art. 109); in this case there is no power to veto, but no alteration of the Charter under this article, or by way of amendment under article 108, can take effect if it is not ratified by two-thirds of the members of the United Nations, including all the permanent members of the Security Council.

The Council can take steps to preserve peace in two different ways: (1) First it can intervene in the pacific settlement of disputes by making recommendations on appropriate procedures or methods of adjustment, or on the terms of a settlement. Its field of action is therefore far wider than the methods allowed in the Covenant. These 'recommendations' have no binding force in law, but they can affect the Council's action when exercising those powers which constitute its second source of authority; (2) The Council may also, in the event of a threat to peace, breach of the peace or act of aggression, decide what steps shall be taken up to and including the use of armed force. Here the Security Council has infinitely greater freedom and powers than the organs of the League of Nations under the Covenant.

The Council has genuine powers of decision. Member States must carry out its decisions. Any international action then undertaken, if the occasion should arise, is undertaken *by* the Security Council, and member States make military forces available to it in accordance with special agreements (art. 43). It is assisted by a Military Staff Committee. The Charter leaves the Council entirely free to decide what action to take and it lays down no definition of aggression. The machinery for maintaining peace is therefore more political than legal; and for this reason it needs to be supplemented by regional machinery.

This is the theoretical position; in practice, the work of the Security Council has often been paralysed by the veto.

(B) *The General Assembly*

(*a*) *Functions and Powers.* The United Nations General Assembly was basically conceived as a vast forum where any question relating to the purposes of the United Nations could be discussed; but under the Charter the Assembly has fewer powers than the Council. It can discuss matters and make recommendations (with one major reservation to be explained later), but it is not once mentioned in chapter VII of the Charter relating to 'action' to maintain peace. Nevertheless the General Assembly has important powers and functions in other fields.

It is associated with the Security Council in important decisions such as admission, suspension or expulsion of members, appointment of the Secretary General and judges of the ICJ, and it has general functions which make it the real administrative and political centre of the United Nations in all fields except the maintenance of peace. All the United Nations organs are attached to the General Assembly, either because it appoints their members, or because it has some authority over the exercise of their functions; the Assembly elects the non-permanent members of the Security Council, and the Economic and Social Council, and the members of the Trusteeship Council who do not administer trust territories. The General Assembly initiates and co-ordinates the specialised agencies; the Economic and Social Council operates 'under the authority' (art. 60) of the General Assembly, and is no more than the authorised agent and expert adviser of the Assembly. The same is true of the Trusteeship Council (art. 85). Finally, the Assembly has under its

authority the whole United Nations administration by the fact that
it approves the budget (art. 15, 17 and 101).

One can understand how, with these important functions, the
General Assembly has been called on to develop the part it plays
in the United Nations.

(*b*) *Composition and procedure.* The Assembly consists of representatives of all the member States, and each delegation has one vote.
It is a large body, organised in the way assemblies usually are: an
annual session (supplemented if necessary by special sessions), its
own officers, committees, etc.

Decisions of the General Assembly are in principle made by a
majority of members present and voting. But a two-thirds majority
is required for 'important questions'; they are enumerated in article
18 and additions can be made to this list by a simple majority.

(C) *Economic and Social Council*

It consists of 18 members elected by the General Assembly for
three years and renewable by one-third each year; each member of
the Economic and Social Council has one representative and decisions of the Council are made by a majority of the members present
and voting.

The Council is under the authority of the General Assembly and
does not seem to have power to do more than make recommendations. In reality its role is to centralise and stimulate all the international institutions connected with the United Nations (in particular
the specialised agencies). Some non-govermental organs have been
given 'consultative status', which means that they can maintain close
and continual contact with the Council. Its work is mainly to prepare
conventions, enquiries, consultations and all kinds of reports: it is
assisted by expert committees consisting of government delegates
and by a large secretariat.

(D) *Trusteeship Council*

This body discharges the functions of the United Nations concerning certain colonial territories. It is therefore part of a broader system
involving other organs of the United Nations which will be explained
later.

The composition of the Trusteeship Council is laid down under
article 86. The members are States, not, as in the League of Nations
Mandates Commission, independent persons. It must contain: (1) the
permanent members of the Security Council and any other States

administering trust territories, members as of right; (2) as many other members, elected for three years by the General Assembly, as may ensure that the number of States which administer trust territories is equal to the number of those which do not. The principle is one of equal representation combined with guaranteed membership of the Big Five.

The Trusteeship Council carries out very precise functions under the authority of the General Assembly.

(E) *International Court of Justice*

Its judicial functions take the form of: (1) advisory opinions at the request of the Security Council, the General Assembly or any organ of the United Nations or any specialised agency so authorised by the General Assembly; these opinions are not legally binding; (2) judgments which bind States; private persons and international organisations cannot be parties in cases before the Court.

The procedure for appointing members of the Court is this: candidates are nominated not by governments but by national groups as prescribed by the First Hague Convention instituting a Permanent Court of Arbitration. These national groups, after consulting the highest national judicial and academic authorities, nominate a number of candidates equal to double the number of seats to be filled, with a maximum of four names. The Secretary General prepares a list of the persons nominated in this way and the Security Council and the General Assembly vote independently by absolute majority to elect the members. Those who receive an absolute majority in both bodies are declared elected. If a seat remains unfilled after three meetings, a joint conference consisting of representatives of the General Assembly and the Security Council puts forward a name which is submitted to both bodies for their respective acceptance; if this fails, the members of the Court already elected fill the vacant seats by selection from candidates who obtained votes in either the General Assembly or the Security Council.

The members of the Court are elected for nine years and a third of the seats fall vacant every third year.

(F) *Secretariat* (cf. *supra*, p. 251)

§ 4 THE GENERAL WORK OF THE UNITED NATIONS

The work of the United Nations is directed towards two general purposes: the maintenance of peace, and economic and social progress.

(A) *Maintenance of peace*

The United Nations has dealt with a great many questions, 'disputes', 'situations', 'cases', as they are variously termed in United Nations parlance. These questions have been more or less satisfactorily cleared up. What would have happened if the Organisation had not existed? One cannot know with any certainty. United Nations practice suggests that it is mainly a framework for negotiations and a platform for influencing world opinion—in so far as it exists—and States not yet committed. But the United Nations does not carry very much political weight outside the States which are members.

The Security Council has many times been paralysed by the exercise of the right of veto. It had the best and most decisive results in matters which did not involve a direct conflict of interests between the Great Powers. For instance, it intervened to stop hostilities between the Netherlands and Indonesia which ended with the birth of the new State.

Under chapter VI of the Charter (Pacific Settlement of Disputes) the Assembly is only empowered to make recommendations, and art. 12 restricts this power. 'While the Security Council is exercising in respect of any dispute or situation the functions assigned to it by the present Charter, the General Assembly shall not make any recommendation with regard to that dispute or situation unless the Security Council so requests.' Moreover, any member may bring a dispute to the attention of the Security Council; the Security Council's jurisdiction in this field is clearly broader than that of the Assembly.

Nevertheless, the Assembly has had occasionally to play some part, either because the Security Council refrained from taking action as in the so-called case of the Spanish régime which in 1946 led to a rupture of relations between Spain and the international organisations attached to the United Nations and also between Spain and some member States; or because a matter has been directly referred to the Assembly, and its intervention was successful. The best example of this is the Palestine Question; the Assembly's intervention ended hostilities between Israel and the Arab States, but the latter did not recognise Israel, the City of Jerusalem is still divided in half by an absurd demarcation line, the interests of the Great Powers in the Middle East are not safeguarded and the area remains on a war footing. In this question the General Assembly acted jointly with the Security Council.

The fact is, the General Assembly is not technically suited to the task it has had thrust on it; it does not meet often enough and it has too many members. But the inadequacy of the Security Council through excessive use of the veto has led to work being devolved where possible to the General Assembly to make up for it.

The Assembly is empowered to create 'subsidiary organs' to assist it in the pacific settlement of disputes; under this heading it set up, for example, the Palestine Commission, a special United Nations Committee on the Balkans, the United Nations Temporary Commission on Korea, etc. Resolution III of the Assembly of 13 November, 1947, created an interim committee popularly known as 'Little Assembly'. This body has important functions: to convoke the Assembly, to make enquiries at headquarters and on the spot with the consent of the States concerned.

But the role of the United Nations faced with a breach of the peace was best seen over the question of Korea.

On 25 June, 1950, fighting broke out between North and South Korea. The Secretary General of the United Nations requested and received information from a United Nations Commission set up by the Assembly in 1947 to study on the spot the reunification of Korea. At the request of the United States he also immediately summoned the Security Council. In view of the information it had received the Security Council declared that an act of aggression had been committed and called upon North Korea to withdraw her troops. This decision was only taken owing to the absence of the Soviet delegate. This is the only occasion so far that, due to fortuitous circumstances, the Council has been able to put into effect chapter VII of the Charter on enforcement measures. On 27 June the Council called upon member States to come to the aid of the South Korean Republic. By 7 July, 32 States had responded to this summons; that day the Security Council formed a Unified Command of United Nations forces and asked the United States to appoint the commander, authorising those forces to use the United Nations flag. The USSR contested the validity of these decisions, and on 1 August, after an absence of six months, her representative resumed his place in the Security Council of which he was the President. A battle of procedure started then in the Security Council and it took a month of debating to reach an agreement on the agenda and from then onwards the Security Council was virtually paralysed. The Assembly took up the matter in September, 1950, and it formed a new commission on Korea with broader terms of reference than its predecessor. At the same time, on 8 October, a resolution was put before the Assembly which it passed on 3 November, 1950; this resolution is usually referred to as the 'Resolution on Uniting for Peace'. Its intention was to create a nucleus of collective security outside the Security Council; if the Council failed to perform its duty when there was an act of aggression, the Assembly was convoked; in order to provide a sound basis for its intervention, it depended on two permanent committees, the Peace Observation Commission responsible for following the evolution of a situation in any region in a state of tension, and the Collective Measures Committee responsible for preparing in advance plans, including military measures, to preserve peace and security.

It was clearly intended to set up machinery able to take the place of the Security Council, and it should be noted that there is nothing in this comparable to the Council's power of decision: it is more a matter of co-ordination; this resolution had very few practical consequences. The USSR and her allies and many authors have challenged its legality under the Charter.

The United Nations is in principle in a very different position from the League of Nations when faced with a conflict. Its powers for the pacific settlement of disputes are mainly political and do not bind members as long as, in the opinion of the Security Council, there is no threat to the peace. If the Security Council *does* consider peace is threatened then it *can* act very vigorously, and impose a solution. The League of Nations involved fewer but more precise legal obligations for the pacific settlement of disputes but enforcement was left to the discretion of its members. In practice there is not all that much difference; minor conflicts are put down or avoided altogether, and the others depend on the attitude of the Great Powers; this is unavoidable in the present state of the world.

The one sure sign of the importance of the United Nations is the importance parties in disputes attach to neutralising it or winning its favour.

(B) *General activity in the economic and social field*

The United Nations has no power of decision and can only act indirectly: studies, information, proposals, etc. It arranges exchanges of views and gradually brings out common interests; when no common interests emerge it seeks to reduce disagreement. This task has resulted in international agreements of very varied importance. Some agreements set up the specialised agencies, but they were, for the most part, created within the framework of the United Nations or were attached to it. Other agreements were in the form of general conventions. But United Nations action is best seen in simpler agreements, often devoid of any legal procedure; they may be settled within or through bodies set up by the United Nations. For instance, the major economic commissions established by the General Assembly (Economic Commission for Europe, Economic Commission for Asia and the Far East, Economic Commission for Latin-America), have made praiseworthy attempts to find a basis for agreements even in apparently restricted fields. Some of these agreements simply state a common approach to a problem in a minute. An agreement on the classification of coal arranged by the Economic Commission for Europe is not of major importance but several agreements of this kind may prove useful and gradually convince States that something always comes out of carefully prepared exchanges of views, and this is a step forward. It is impossible to go into details of the United Nations work in this field, but it may be useful to state once again its general policy (*supra*, p. 81). The United Nations, like the League of Nations, has to expand by eliminating the barriers erected by States (tariffs, quantitative restrictions, subsidies, all kinds of discrimination, bulk-buying or government purchasing). Neither IMF nor GATT has achieved very much in this respect. It has also sought to regulate the market for the most important raw materials by encouraging increased government intervention; important results have been achieved for wheat, sugar and tin. Problems of credit and economic development have proved more difficult still. The world's needs for capital are immense, but the risks are too great for private capital, and public capital is limited and often undesirable. The United Nations has been able to mobilise State capital (principally American) through the International Bank for Reconstruction and Development; it makes loans to States or with State guarantee; but it has not been able to meet the situation in face of the need. There is virtually no international movement of private capital, since it requires guarantees against arbitrary State action which it has been impossible to give. The 'International Finance Corporation' created as a second string to the International Bank may perhaps bring some improvement; but the situation is still very disquieting. Gifts can only be used as a method when universal organisations dispose of considerable resources; so far gifts have only been on a bilateral or at least a regional basis (American Aid).

On the other hand free aid, in the form of expertise rather than capital, has grown up in the United Nations in the form of technical assistance. This is very important and should be examined more closely (§ 5).

United Nations economic activity is in sum dominated by two factors; the painful formulation of common interests in fairly narrow fields, and the fundamental problem of the enormous gulf between different levels of economic development.

The same factors appear in the social field. The United Nations has taken up and extended the work of the League of Nations in the fight against natural disasters, disease and crime (drugs, traffic in women and children, obscene publications); public opinion is easily convinced of the existence of common interests. The general movement for improvement in public health in the post-war world can be measured by the work of WHO and the extent of its powers. But in the world as a whole the order of priority is determined by the unequal condition of States. The fact that UNESCO spends much time developing the free exchange of information and culture can hardly interest countries where neither information nor culture exists. The same might be said for the work of ILO; there is nothing wrong with the idea: improvement in the economic and social conditions of workers can only be achieved on an international level; but how is it that the greater part of its work is not directed to the social conditions of workers in countries where there are regular famines, that is in over two-thirds of the world? Indeed, the various forms of assistance to children, mainly distributed through the International Children's Fund, go principally to children in underdeveloped countries.

Only United Nations work for refugees is on a different footing: apart from the difficult work accomplished in Palestine, particularly for the benefit of Arab refugees, United Nations action on behalf of refugees is principally concerned with old European countries; The International Refugee Organisation, which succeeded UNRRA, has in turn been replaced by the Office of the High Commissioner for Refugees.

§ 5 UNITED NATIONS ACTION REGARDING NON-SELF-GOVERNING TERRITORIES AND TRUST TERRITORIES

The Charter has adopted and enlarged upon the principles of the Covenant of the League of Nations as regards colonisation. There is a legal distinction between non-self-governing territories, trust territories and strategic areas.

(A) *Non-self-governing territories*

The Charter contains a declaration regarding 'non-self-governing territories'. Article 73 lists the general duties of States which 'have to assume responsibilities for the administration of territories whose peoples have not yet attained a full measure of self-government'. Among these duties is an obligation 'to develop self-government, to take due account of the political aspirations of the peoples and to assist them in the progressive development of their free political institutions.'

The only 'institutional' obligation in this article is that of 'transmitting regularly to the Secretary General, for information purposes, subject to such limitations as security and constitutional considerations may require, statistical and other information of a technical nature, relating to economic, social and educational conditions in the territories for which they are respectively responsible'.

An authoritarian interpretation has allowed the General Assembly to graft on to this provision real control of the administration of non-self-governing territories. The General Assembly set up a Special Committee to examine information (1946) composed on the same basis of equal representation as the Trusteeship Council, and has gradually extended its field of action by inviting it to send the Assembly reports and recommendations. The specialised agencies collaborate with this Special Committee; the administering States must reply to requests on an increasingly extensive range of subjects (for example, how the Declaration of Human Rights is put into effect). The United Nations itself claims to decide the meaning of the term 'non-self-governing territories' and also whether it applies to any given territory.

The Special Committee has therefore become an instrument for controlling the administration of certain territories, which means that it applies solely to certain States.

(B) *Trust territories*

The purposes of the trusteeship system are similar to those for the non-self-governing territories, although they are stated more explicitly. In addition, they insist on 'equal treatment in social, economic and commercial matters of all Members of the United Nations', and also equal treatment in the administration of justice. These principles are in part inherited from the old system of the 'open door'; they must be read in conjunction with the more concrete provisions of trusteeship agreements, which make it a condition of this equality that the beneficiaries accord most favoured nation treatment to trust territories.

This system applies to three groups of territories:

(1) *Territories held under mandate;* Nine territories in this group have been placed under the trusteeship system; South-West Africa has not

been placed under this system by the Union of South Africa. In an advisory opinion of 11 July, 1950, the International Court of Justice considered that there was no legal obligation to place mandate territories under the trusteeship system, but obligations assumed under the mandate system continued despite the disappearance of the League of Nations, and the General Assembly of the United Nations has inherited the League's 'right to supervise'.

(2) *Territories detached from former enemy States;* only Somaliland has been placed under this system in an agreement dated 2 December, 1950; Italy was appointed trustee assisted by an international advisory council.

(3) *Territories voluntarily placed under the trusteeship system;* there are no examples.

According to a rather obscure provision in article 79 the terms of the trusteeship system were to be 'agreed upon by the States directly concerned' and approved by the General Assembly. No agreement has been reached on the interpretation of the expression 'States directly concerned' and the 'agreements' have simply been approved by the General Assembly.

The Charter provided that the administering authority might be not only a single State but several States or the Organisation itself; in fact trusteeship is always assumed by one State, except for the island of Nauru placed under the joint trusteeship of the UK, Australia and New Zealand.

United Nations control is exercised by means of:

(1) Examination by the Trusteeship Council of a report submitted annually by the administering authority based on a questionnaire drafted by the Trusteeship Council.

(2) Examination of petitions from the inhabitants of trust territories in consultation with the administering authority.

(3) Periodic visits to the territories.

These functions are in principle exercised by the General Assembly and under its authority by the Trusteeship Council.

The political questions which have raised most difficulties are administrative and economic unions between trust and neighbouring territories, the date of termination of the trusteeship system, and the precise legal status of trust territories.

(C) *Strategic areas*

Changes in strategy and colonial problems have emphasised the interest which the Great Powers have in controlling certain military bases. At the end of the Second World War the United States possessed several bases which she has kept or substituted by others. It was quite natural to establish similar strategic bases for the military organisation to be placed at the disposal of the Security Council; this was the purpose of articles 82 and 83 of the Charter. In fact the system has only been applied so as to further the interests of the United States; she has obtained trusteeship of the strategic area constituted by the Pacific Islands formerly held under mandate by Japan. The main difference between ordinary trusteeship and trusteeship over a strategic area is that the functions of the General Assembly are transferred to the Security Council which can call upon the assistance of the Trusteeship Council for questions which do not concern the strategic use of the area. The basic objectives of the two systems are the same: the trusteeship agreement over the Pacific Islands has reduced third-party rights and the control of the United Nations.

§ 6 TECHNICAL ASSISTANCE

(A) *General considerations*

(a) Notion and forms. The expression 'technical assistance' is new but the idea behind it is not. It may be defined as assistance given in the form of advice, skill, or more generally the dissemination of knowledge, excluding financial aid or primarily material gifts.

In principle it is *free of charge*; and is a preliminary to more extensive practical work to be carried out later.

From this point of view it closely resembles private business. When buying important supplies or carrying out large-scale works, the buyer normally receives technical assistance from his prospective contractor in the form of advice, studies, recommendations, etc.

In international relations technical assistance is arranged directly between States, or else distributed through an international organisation.

Although technical assistance is essentially preliminary to other work it is often entirely for its own sake in international affairs. This is quite explicable. Gifts of money or materials represent a net loss for the donor. Technical advice only costs the donor the price of the incidentals: travel, living expenses, samples, etc., and it generally adds to the donor's stock of knowledge and expertise. Of all gifts, therefore, technical assistance is the least onerous. In a technological civilisation a State has a strong political interest in being reckoned among those in a position to give useful technical assistance.

But technical assistance involves a certain risk for the assisted State; it reveals facts about that State's situation, commits it in the future to a particular source of supplies and gives the assisting State a general influence in internal affairs. All relations on an unequal footing lead to the domination of one party by the other, and this may sometimes be to the detriment of an assisted State.

Technical assistance, provided and supervised by an international organisation, is therefore of great historical importance; it is one of the foremost examples in our day of 'economic relations free of charge'. It is part of the effort to free colonisation from the stigma of domination; at the same time it promotes a further expansion of the international organisation, which is called upon to intervene in an unusually direct and far-reaching way in the internal administration of States.

No proper consideration can be given here of technical assistance on a national basis, often coupled with considerable financial aid (relations between a State and distant or backward territories) or on a bilateral basis (several agreements between the United States and South American States). We must also omit the interesting forms of international technical assistance provided on a regional basis; these would include relations between the popular democracies, and the Colombo Plan which provides for assistance to Asiatic countries within the Commonwealth.

(b) *Technical assistance through international organisations.* Technical assistance distributed through international organisations was part of the work of League of Nations, although it did not use the word. It is provided for in the constituent documents of the specialised agencies, in particular ILO, WHO, FAO, UNESCO and ICAO. Moreover the principle of technical assistance is laid down in article 55 of the Charter.

The United Nations tackled the question of technical assistance from the start but took effective steps in two stages:

First the Assembly's Resolution 200 (III) of 4 December, 1948, made appropriations in the budget for the Secretary General to use to provide some forms of technical assistance; at the same time it laid down certain general principles to be followed:

(1) Teams of experts to advise governments on their programmes of economic expansion;

(2) Scholarships for the nationals of underdeveloped countries to enable them to become qualified experts;

(3) Training of technicians on the spot in underdeveloped countries;

(4) Financial aid to governments to enable them to obtain staff, material and technical supplies.

Later an International Institute of Public Administration was created, attached to the Organisation with substantial credits to extend technical assistance to social services.

All these activities have their own appropriations (about one and a half million dollars) and a special service, the Technical Assistance Administration, organised within the General Secretariat.

In a speech to the United States Congress on 20 January, 1949, President Truman mentioned the United States' intention to put a 'bold new programme' into operation for the dissemination of technical knowledge. President Truman alluded to the limited nature of the government's financial resources, but he considered that the dissemination of technical knowledge (which is inexhaustible) would later on attract private capital. Internationally this programme led to what is known as the Expanded Programme of Technical Assistance (EPTA) by virtue of Resolution 222 (IX) of 15 August, 1949 of the Economic and Social Council and 304 (IV) of 16 November, 1949 of the General Assembly. Its main point is that it is financed by *voluntary* and direct contributions from governments. It amounts annually to some 20 million dollars and it raises especially important problems of international administration.

(B) *The major problems of international technical assistance*

(*a*) *In general*. These problems are political in origin, financial and administrative in practice.

At present international organisations can never meet the needs of technical assistance out of their ordinary budget. Some organisations approve their budget by a simple majority vote, which enables States wishing to obtain technical assistance to inflate the sums allocated for this purpose. On the other hand technical assistance brings together people of different countries; technical experts are nationals of a particular country, assisted students study in foreign schools and

universities, etc. In short technical assistance establishes contact
between the donating and receiving States and brings together one or
more international organisations.

The divergent interests of all these groups have to be reconciled.
The States providing the money insist on taking an active part in the
management of technical assistance in order to make sure that it is
handled properly and to draw some credit in the extension of its
influence which is the real counterpart to the gift. States which
benefit wish to safeguard their internal autonomy and their political
independence ; and they should naturally make every effort to see that
the aid is used efficiently. They are reasonably expected to furnish
information, receive persons and advice, make their own financial
contribution and see that their economic expansion proceeds
smoothly and efficiently. Clearly technical assistance undertaken on
the scale of the United Nations and the specialised agencies involves
several international organisations. Economic growth and the struggle
against underdevelopment have many aspects but are closely in-
terrelated. Famine and epidemics must be dealt with together, to
take what is unfortunately the most frequently recurring example.
Technical assistance is therefore administered through several
specialised agencies working in collaboration, or by several decentralised bodies known as subsidiary organs within the United
Nations. There is a great temptation to set up a new international
body to federate the efforts of existing services ; would not a single
autonomous body be better able to administer the large voluntary
contributions which the States have to be asked for? But it may be as
well not to build up too large a bureaucracy. The same problem
arises at the local level. To provide technical assistance experts are sent
to the assisted State, training centres are set up, pilot schemes,
propaganda, tours, etc. Only scholarships involve nationals of the
assisted States travelling to the donor. It is hard to imagine that the
various forms of assistance provided by various organisations should
remain decentralised.

In economic terms technical assistance implies a belief that the
course of economic development can be determined *scientifically*. So
far the assisted countries have been in such a desperate social and
economic condition that the problem has unfortunately been grossly
over-simplified. But it will not always be so, and some problems
arise which cannot be solved objectively by technical experts, but
only by *political decisions*. There may be a conflict between the
Organisation and the beneficiary State. On economic and humanitarian grounds an organisation will always direct efforts first to

agricultural production and the elimination of unnecessary middle-men in the distribution of food products; but political power lies in rapid industrialisation, and this may be preferred even at the expense of human lives.

Difficult problems are involved; and even when the principles are clear it is a delicate matter to put them into effect. Some account will be given of the Enlarged Programme of Technical Assistance, which is by its size the most interesting form of technical assistance.

(b) *The Enlarged Programme of Technical Assistance.* EPTA operates through inter-governmental conferences, the Technical Assistance Board, the Technical Assistance Committee and the Resident Representatives.

The inter-governmental conferences decide the extent of voluntary contributions from the States; the first was held in 1950; the size of the collective effort was fixed at 20 million dollars, the United States being responsible for 60% of this sum. The other States participated either from conviction or for reasons of prestige; the USSR and Poland joined in in 1953, Byelorussia, the Ukraine and Czechoslovakia in 1954. The sums are either deposited in currency in a special fund run by the Budget Bureau of the United Nations, in gifts, in kind or otherwise, provided directly by the donor. One difficulty arises because the fund is financed by voluntary contributions from the States written into their annual national budgets, but an annual rate of contribution does not correspond to the demands of planning within the framework of the economy of the assisted States. This is a common difficulty even in national planning; the same thing happened with Marshall Aid. The Technical Assistance Board contains the General Directors of the specialised agencies, presided over by a senior United Nations official. It is the co-ordinating body.

The Board co-ordinates the work of the specialised agencies, and ensures that EPTA does not duplicate other forms of technical assistance provided outside the framework of the United Nations. At first it reflected the independence of the specialised agencies, but this has changed.

The Technical Assistance Committee is the intermediary between the Board and the permanent organs of the United Nations; the Security Council and the General Assembly.

It is composed of representatives of the member States from the Economic and Social Council. This is not very logical. One would expect it to be composed of representatives of the States contributing to EPTA.

There are Resident Representatives in the assisted States, appointed by the Chairman of the Technical Assistance Board; in principle they represent the specialised agencies collectively in the 27 States at present assisted, although some of them have their own agents. The role of the international expert varies with each country and even with each service. Each assisted country makes its own arrangements for the experts to work with the national administration.

Most countries look upon the experts simply as consultants, a source of knowledge and information. The expert is attached to a national official who alone is responsible for taking decisions and putting the programme into effect. Other States make the expert a more or less integral part of the national administration. For example they set up a bureau within the national administration composed of both international experts and national officials ('servicio' formula for administration of American assistance in South America). Sometimes the experts are seconded to an official position in the national administration (agreement between the United Nations and Bolivia in 1951).

In any case the presence inside a country of international services and sometimes international undertakings means there are direct relations between the international organisation and individual 'users' of services provided by the organisation; it is as if there were international public services operating. Legal problems, especially the question of legal liability, can arise from this situation in a very complex form and are only just beginning to be studied.

There are as yet no hard and fast guides to action. In principle, assistance is only granted on a State's request addressed to the relevant specialised agency or the Secretary General of the United Nations. On the basis of their requests aid is distributed according to a system of priorities. But although this doctrine was reaffirmed by the Economic and Social Council (session of 29 June, 1954 to 6 August, 1954) it does not adequately explain what really happens; there are negotiations and contacts with the international administration from the moment the detailed programmes are submitted in support of the request. In the first instance EPTA funds were allocated to the specialised agencies on a percentage basis (29% FAO, 23% UNO, 22% WHO, 14% UNESCO, 11% ILO). Since 1954 the Technical Assistance Committee representing the governments has played a more active part and has tried to allocate assistance on the basis of more carefully worked out programmes.

If technical assistance were to become a permanent form of

international relations it would help to solve by international means the problem of underdeveloped countries. It would profoundly alter international relations and lead to a great expansion of international organisations.

Section II

THE EUROPEAN ORGANISATIONS

There is no point in tracing the history of European organisations prior to the end of the Second World War. On the one hand, Europe's pre-eminent place in the world centred all efforts towards world organisation on her. On the other hand, the Concert of Europe, the first outline of an organisation, has already been explained (*supra* p. 55). The only notable attempt at a European organisation as distinct from a world organisation was the French proposal of M. Briand known as European Union; it came to nothing.

In a speech to the League of Nations on 5 September, 1929, the French Foreign Minister proposed to link the European States by a 'sort of federal bond'. A Memorandum of 1 May, 1930, was rather more explicit, stressed economic matters and provided for a very rudimentary organisation. In reply to the Memorandum only the Netherlands accepted the prospect of limitations on her sovereignty; the United States declared that she would consider a complete economic union as directed against herself.

Since 1945 many European organisations have appeared; they vary in object, nature, geographical distribution of their members, and general purpose. The principal efforts for European organisation since 1945 have been influenced by the hostility between the USSR and the United States. Eastern Europe is fairly closely integrated with the USSR in political, economic and military affairs. This is well-known, but it can be left on one side since not much is known of the way it works and the structure is rather informal. Some organisations connected with Europe are, on the other hand, as much 'Atlantic' as European. This alone explains the extraordinary chaos of European organisations and uncertainty about their future.

European organisations fall into three categories: economic co-operation, politico-military co-operation, integration.

§ 1 ECONOMIC CO-OPERATION

The organisations to be examined are the Economic Commission for
Europe (ECE) at Geneva, the Organisation for European Economic
Co-operation (OEEC) and smaller unions.

(A) *Economic Commission for Europe*

It is a subsidiary organ of the United Nations. It is therefore completely dependent on the United Nations and has no autonomous
powers. It simply provides a convenient forum for meetings and study
groups unrestricted by the usual diplomatic conventions. The Europe
of ECE is the Europe of the United Nations, that is geographical
Europe comprising the States of both Eastern and Western Europe;
the United States also takes part in its work. The Commission has a
large secretariat of over 150 international officials as well as operational services. Since 1947, through specialist committees, commis-
ions and groups of experts, the ECE has tried to facilitate agreements
in all fields, for example coal (except prices) and transport, particularly
road and rail. It has been responsible for some very interesting
technical studies and some useful results. It has been hampered by the
attitude of the USSR.

It sponsored an agreement between railway networks for a 'wagon pool'. This
is an operational matter based on the use of foreign rolling stock; instead of each
wagon being strictly accounted for and returned, a periodical balance is kept, and
this assumes that rolling stock is to some extent interchangeable. (Agreement 1
May, 1951, between France and Germany, extended in 1953 to Denmark,
Switzerland, Benelux, Austria and Italy.)

(B) *Organisation for European Economic Co-operation*

When Marshall Aid was proposed it assumed that the beneficiaries
would come to some understanding between themselves. It was
easier for them to bargain collectively with the United States than
individually. As opposed to what happened to the United Nations
Technical Assistance, the international organisation does not stand
as the donor but as beneficiary, at least in part. Moreover this idea
harmonised with the United States' desire to rationalise distribution
and its conviction that the European States would unite to form a
single common market.

But the institutions established did not go all the way to achieve
this object. American aid had its origin in annual national laws
voted by the United States Congress and bilateral agreements between
the United States and the assisted States. The only condition the

K

United States attached to this aid was that the assisted States should co-operate together. This did not allow the United States to insist on European unification. Only later, when aid was granted in some measure collectively (European Payments Union), did the United States bring some slight pressure to bear on European States to form a closer union.

OEEC, set up at the time of United States aid (1948), could only act administratively in the field covered by this aid, but it was useful in some ways. In origin however it had much broader aims. Apart from working with the American authorities and discreetly and efficiently allocating Marshall Aid between its members, OEEC did some useful work in allocating materials in short supply (1950–52), in co-ordinating to a certain extent national reconstruction plans, and in arousing interest in problems of productivity. But its most important task was to try to re-establish convertibility. It sought gradually to abolish quantitative restrictions (freer trade); and this was closely bound up with a system of international payments between European countries. The European Payments Union, founded in 1950 and renewed each year, made multilateral payments possible through a clearing house run by the Bank for International Settlements at Basle, with credits from American Aid or allowed by member States. By concentrating on currencies and not territories, the European Payments Union included in the settlement area all territories using a particular currency; through the sterling area it affects the whole of the Commonwealth, except Canada.

Questions about export bounties are also referred to OEEC.

OEEC includes 17 States plus the United States and Canada, represented since 1950 by observers. Switzerland is a member but has not received American Aid. It has the classical structure: a Council made up of all members, an Executive Committee of 7 members which any member State can attend when it is concerned with a question under discussion, and a Secretary General. Its function is to co-ordinate. Decisions of the Council must be unanimous (art. 14); but this rule is mitigated by the fact that in many economic matters one State alone cannot use a right of veto. Moreover the Convention of 16 April, 1948, setting up the OEEC modifies the rule for unanimous decisions in several ways:

(1) 'The abstention of any members declaring themselves not to be interested in the subject under discussion shall not invalidate decisions which shall be binding for the other members'; this provision was made to accommodate Switzerland;

(2) The organisation may agree to abandon the unanimity rule for special cases;

(3) The organisation can set up subsidiary bodies and these may draw up proposals by a simple majority vote; in fact the Council adopts these proposals unanimously.

The OEEC has done some useful work; all the same it must not be forgotten that the economic unity of Europe in 1956 is far from what it was in 1928 and *a fortiori* in 1913.

(C) *Partial Unions*

This covers less ambitious efforts at unification, some covering a small number of States, some concerning only a limited economic field.

In the first group is Benelux which joined the Belgium-Luxembourg Economic Union with the Netherlands in one economic system.

The principle was decided on 21 October, 1943, but was only realised gradually step by step; the customs convention of 5 September, 1944; the Hague Conference of 1946 which distinguished five stages: tariff union, customs union, fiscal union for indirect taxes, lifting of all quantitative restrictions, complete economic union. The Hague Protocol of 14 March, 1947, set up 4 permanent organs. In fact Benelux has only just passed the stage of tariff union.

Various proposals for customs unions under various names were studied round about 1949.

Some organisations cover only one commodity or one service. Some organisations are the only practical result of an original proposal for integration which failed. For instance, in 1950 an advanced form of integration was envisaged in the field of transport, but European States were eventually content to set up, in the Brussels Protocol of 17 October, 1953, a European Conference of Ministers of Transport whose status as an international organisation is doubtful (*supra*, p. 216); the only notable feature of this Conference is the inclusion of Spain and Portugal. Even less successful was the project for a 'pool of agricultural products', which only survives in the form of a conference held under the auspices of OEEC.

On the other hand it is impossible to overestimate the importance of one organisation of a special kind, the European Organisation of Nuclear Research (Agreement of 15 February, 1952, and Convention of 1 July, 1953). It is unique in that it is an industrial undertaking whose main purpose is to set up laboratories for nuclear research; a task beyond the capacity of small States. The members of the European Organisation of Nuclear Research are Belgium, Denmark, France, the German Federal Republic, Greece, Italy, Jugoslavia, the

Netherlands, Sweden, Switzerland and the UK. The seat of the organisation is in Switzerland; but the organisation carries out no research of a military nature and in the event of war Switzerland may call upon it to suspend operations. This kind of organisation opens up new fields for international organisation, less formalised and more constructive than other examples quoted.

The European Organisation of Nuclear Research is an inter-governmental undertaking. Other similar undertakings would be possible for work which all countries agreed could not be entrusted to private enterprise. When, as frequently happens, the work is part of private enterprise, the problem takes a different form: European States could encourage, by financial, fiscal and arbitral guarantees, joint European capital projects by companies with a special status responsible for large-scale development operations either in Europe or overseas. There are already several examples of this: cf. the Council of Europe publication *Compagnies Européennes* (AS/EC(4)I, Strasbourg, 30 May, 1952), which has examined this problem.

§ 2 POLITICO-MILITARY CO-OPERATION

The various attempts at European organisation in this field follow closely on one another; they will therefore be examined in historical order.

(A) *Brussels Treaty*

In view of the events which followed the Moscow Conference (1947), particularly events in Czechoslovakia and Berlin (blockade by the Soviet authorities), the UK, France and the three Benelux States signed this treaty; it is similar to a pact of mutual assistance in the event of armed aggression as well as a pledge of co-operation in economic, social and cultural matters. The preamble still envisaged the possibility of German aggression. The treaty was inspired by fear of war. In the British fashion it only set up organs for co-operation: a consultative Council where Foreign Ministers should 'consult together' on the application of the treaty. A permanent commission in London, composed in the traditional way of resident ambassadors and a senior UK civil servant. Social and cultural committees and a permanent military commission, set about giving effect to the treaty, notably by setting up a Supreme Allied Command.

This organisation has undertaken a number of enquiries and studies and arranged social and cultural conventions, and made useful contacts. But this is only one side; it was set up with a second purpose. From the military point of view an organisation containing France, the UK and the Benelux countries was too narrow; from the start they sought to bring in the United States and Canada, and this was the genesis of the Atlantic Pact (4 April, 1949). As the European countries became aware of the general feeling that a broader union covering all fields was desirable, the framework of the Brussels Treaty had to be enlarged to associate other States; and so the Council of Europe was set up (5 May, 1949).

(B) *Atlantic Pact*

This treaty is essentially a pact of mutual assistance in the event of aggression. The States undertook to 'maintain and develop their individual and collective capacity to resist armed attack'. This provision meant there had to be an organisation. But it is—in the text of the treaty—as elementary as possible: a council, on which all parties are represented, considers matters concerning the implementation of the treaty; article 9 authorises the council to set up such subsidiary bodies as may be necessary. On the basis of this text a flexible and increasingly complex organisation has been built up, comprising integrated military commands, a civil organisation for financial and economic questions with an international secretariat which alone comprises over 600 officials.

The North Atlantic Treaty Organisation (NATO) therefore controls enormous security forces; but it has its paradoxical side.

After the accession of Turkey and Greece in 1951 and before the accession of Germany and Italy, it contained 14 States: Belgium, Canada, Denmark, France, Greece, Iceland, Luxembourg, the Netherlands, Norway, Portugal, Turkey, the UK and the USA. Sweden's policy of neutrality has kept her out; Spain, closely bound to the US by other detailed agreements, has taken very little part so far in European politics. All the States of Western Europe belong to NATO. But the guarantee provided in article 6 of the treaty does not cover the whole territory of the members, but only covers an armed attack against the territory of the countries in Europe or North America, including islands under their jurisdiction within the North Atlantic area north of the tropic of Cancer, Algeria and Turkey. The treaty also covers attacks against members' armed forces within those territories, in the Mediterranean or the North Atlantic area. In short not all the territory of the member States is protected and the treaty is based entirely on strategic considerations which makes it rather precarious. One may well wonder whether it should be studied as a European organisation.

It follows logically from its nature that in law the organisation involves no transfer of sovereignty; decisions of NATO organs are unanimous; they do not appear to give effect to powers transferred to NATO; they are only recommendations and the States take such measures as they think fit to implement them in their own countries. The details are not simple and there are several curious legal sides to the system of an integrated allied command. In fact the actual political importance of NATO is in contrast to the completely voluntary and therefore precarious nature of its legal foundations. The example of the Commonwealth has shown that when there is a real interdependence of interests solidarity does not have to be embodied in a closely integrated organisation. The North Atlantic Treaty Organisation rests on the lasting political interdependence of its members. As long as this continues the powers of the organisation in matters of general policy will probably continue to grow.

(C) *Council of Europe*

The Statute of the Council of Europe, as formulated in the treaty of 5 May, 1949, almost a month after the conclusion of the Atlantic Pact, was the result of a compromise; one view upheld by Great Britain was that the new organisation should be strictly intergovernmental, closely following the traditional ties of co-operation; the other view, represented by France and Belgium, wanted it to contain the dynamic element provided by a parliamentary assembly. The Council of Europe comprises a Secretariat, a Committee of Ministers and a Consultative Assembly. It has a very general jurisdiction with military affairs (not very strictly interpreted) excepted, but in this vast field the Council can only make proposals and recommendations which do not bind the governments. The work of the Council of Europe is that of a permanent diplomatic conference; it drafts conventions to be submitted to the governments. But closer examination of its organs shows the Council in a different light, mainly because of the existence of the Consultative Assembly. At first it was under the close control of the Committee of Ministers and the governments; it only communicated with the Committee of Ministers which controlled its agenda and it met for a month each year unless specifically convened at the request of the Committee; the members of the Consultative Assembly were representatives 'appointed in such a manner as the government of that Member State shall decide'. A subsequent reform of the Statute (22 May, 1951) and modification in practice gave the Assembly more autonomy: control of its own agenda, possibility of meeting in sessions on the initiative of the President after agreement with the Committee of Ministers, communication with national parliaments, etc. The

new Statute also confirmed the existing situation by stipulating that
the Assembly should be composed of representatives of each member
State 'elected by its parliament or appointed in such manner as that
parliament shall decide'.

The characteristic feature of the Council of Europe is that it has
an Assembly of national members of parliament. The representative
character, in the parliamentary not the international sense, is modified
by the method of appointment, but by its origins, its methods of
work, its reactions, the Assembly is a parliamentary institution, the
first on a European plane. Perhaps the positive results of the Council
of Europe's work are less important than the creation of a European
political milieu which has shown vitality, competence and an
undoubted dignity.

The work of the Council of Europe has covered a great many
subjects, from the most general aspects of European policy to highly
technical questions. Particularly important was a European Convention of Human Rights signed on 4 November, 1950, which
entered into force on 3 September, 1953. This Convention is in a
way the logical conclusion to the condition for membership of the
Council in article 3 of the Statute: 'members must accept the principle . . . of the enjoyment by all persons within their jurisdiction of
human rights and fundamental freedoms'.

The rights guaranteed by this convention are formulated more
precisely than in the Universal Declaration of Human Rights. They
are also guaranteed very differently. The Convention set up a Commission of Human Rights. States can refer any case to the Commission and the Commission tries to arrange an amicable settlement.
If this fails it drafts a report which is sent to the Committee of
Ministers and the Committee pronounces by a two-thirds majority
on the violation of the Convention and if necessary on the measures
to be taken. There are two other devices which States may use if
they agree: petitions by private persons to the Commission, and
petitions to a European Court of Human Rights reserved to States
after the Commission has failed to find a solution. Not all States have
agreed to accept these methods of petition.

The following States belong to the Council of Europe: Belgium,
Denmark, Eire, France, Germany, Greece, Iceland, Italy, Luxembourg, the Netherlands, Norway, Sweden, Turkey and the UK. The
Saar is an associate member. The Council had an important political
part to play in helping the Saar to evolve along lines which were
acceptable to the countries concerned. (Van der Groes van Naters
Report.)

(D) *Western European Union*

After the French National Assembly had rejected proposals for a European Defence Community, the Paris Agreements of 23 October, 1954 settled (with provision for reaching a joint agreement with the USSR in the event of general negotiation) the general position of Germany in relation to the Western Powers, the termination of the occupation in Western Germany, the accession of Germany and Italy to NATO and radical changes in the Brussels Treaty. The military balance within NATO was modified by accepting German rearmament; proposals contained in the EDC project were reintroduced to moderate the change; the forces and armaments of the Federal Republic of Germany were limited; the UK undertook to maintain military forces of a certain size on the continent. An agency for the control of armaments was created; its purpose was to control the level of armaments limited by the agreements and the level of stocks of certain types of armaments determined by a majority decision of the Council of the Western European Union. The agency is only one of the services of the Union and is entirely under its authority.

The agreements also modified the Brussels Treaty which had fallen into abeyance, and created the Western European Union, which has seven members, Germany and Italy having joined the five original parties.

The structure is slightly stronger than the original Brussels Treaty. The Consultative Council was given the title 'Council of Western European Union'; it can set up such subsidiary organs as shall be deemed useful. It seems that it can take 'decisions', but unless expressly provided these decisions only have the legal force of 'recommendations'; in principle a vote has to be unanimous, but there are a number of cases of limited interest when it can pass resolutions on a majority vote; official quarters consider the system is 'in some respects supranational'. In view of the progress of European institutions since the conclusion of the Brussels Treaty, a new Assembly was created; it included the representatives of the Brussels Treaty Powers at the Consultative Assembly of the Council of Europe. The Agreements briefly state that the Council of Western European Union shall furnish it with an annual report on its activities, especially in respect of the control of armaments.

Western European Union is more absorbed with military problems than the Brussels Treaty Organisation in 1948. The Council of Europe of 1949 has not disappeared and it encourages general collaboration on a wider field than Western European Union. The principal military role belongs to NATO, as article IV of the new Brussels Treaty mentions. Western European Union is therefore a politico-military structure purely to meet the needs of the moment. The agreements reiterate the contracting parties' wish to foster 'the progressive integration of Europe'.

Other particular unions must be mentioned. One unites the four Scandinavian States in a union; contacts are kept as informal as possible, at parliamentary and ministerial level; it is known as the Northern Council (Sørensen, *Le Conseil Nordique*, RGDIP, 1955, p. 63). The other union is of Greece, Turkey and Jugoslavia in the Balkan Alliance (Ankara Treaty, 28 February, 1953, and the Bled Treaty, 9 August, 1954); apart from a secretariat it comprises a Permanent Council of Ministers and an Assembly of parliamentary delegates.

§ 3 INTEGRATION

(A) *General and historical remarks*

The term 'integration' is used in diplomatic practice to signify agreements and administrative machinery to form an organisation with powers of decision in important matters, entering into direct contact with individuals and free from direct government control. Whether the term 'integration' or 'supranational institution' is used, it is certain that such an organisation is more federal than the traditional international institution.

There is one example of this kind of organisation: the European Coal and Steel Community, set up by the Treaty of 18 April, 1951, more usually referred to as the Schumann Plan. From the beginning it included Belgium, France, the German Federal Republic, Italy, Luxembourg and the Netherlands. The UK refused to take part in negotiations opened on the basis of the French declaration of 9 May, 1950; in 1954 she only agreed (*supra* p. 240) to be loosely 'associated' with the Community.

The Community marked a step towards integration which spread to other economic sectors, but which was political in origin. After the declaration of 9 May the 'pool' idea, as it was inaccurately called, came into favour; there were proposals for an agricultural pool, transport pool, electricity pool, health pool, etc. Most of them did not get past the theoretical stage; others were the subject of interminable preparatory conferences; none came to anything; events in Korea upset the world economic balance and diverted attention.

However, indirectly it provoked another attempt at European integration.

After the 5th session of its Council (15–18 September, 1950), all members of NATO, except France, came out in favour of German rearmament. Following a speech in the National Assembly by M. René Pleven on 24 October, 1950, France put forward a new plan for a European Army attached to the political institutions of a United Europe. This proposal was received rather coolly by the United States and even by some European countries. A conference of experts met in Paris at the beginning of 1951 ; five member States of the European Coal and Steel Community attended it, including the Netherlands who sent an observer. Towards the end of the year the United States and the UK gave support to the proposal and a treaty was signed on 27 May, 1952, establishing a European Defence Community to include the member States of the European Coal and Steel Community. But to counter objections and to keep to the policy of the Schumann Plan, the governments, in September 1952, at the first meeting of the Common Assembly of the European Coal and Steel Community, invited the members of that Assembly to hold a special sitting to consider and submit proposals for a European political community to the governments. This proposal was formally submitted to the government representatives at Strasbourg on 10 March, 1953. It was received without enthusiasm in a speech by the President of the Special Council of Ministers. This date marks a change in the policy of European integration. The proposals for a political community were modified at general inter-governmental conferences. On 30 August, 1954, the French National Assembly refused without discussion to consider the treaty setting up a European Defence Community. The policy of integration was therefore halted and the problem of German rearmament was solved by the Paris Agreements within the framework of the resurrected Brussels Treaty.

(B) *The European Coal and Steel Community*

(a) *Economic features.* This Community is based on a 'common market' within which there is free movement of coal and steel. To obtain this result powers have been conferred on organs of the Community, and member States have had to accept fairly strict obligations; the unification of a limited 'economic sector' can only work with certain expedients. The States have retained their jurisdiction in some very important fields such as transport, social affairs, by-products (electricity, fertilizers), certain raw materials (non-ferrous metals), taxation, foreign trade. They are forbidden in general to discriminate, and indirect measures (particularly financial) help to counteract factors which would seriously distort competition. But there is no doubt that to succeed this common market must be extended to other products and other activities. The treaty itself provides for measures of 'general harmonisation', for transport for example; these must be the prelude to unification on a wider scale. This process of expansion is the economic technique of unification by sector.

The 'common market' is based on the free movement of goods and reflects the liberal outlook which, as has already been seen, lies behind modern federations. But liberalism must be defined and controlled, kept within limits and given a course to follow. The firms concerned are subject to rules and controls whose purpose is to ensure fair competition (prohibition of discriminatory practices, cartels and price-fixing). Competition is, in the course of events, softened to a point where its effects harmonise with the rhythm of other economic and social affairs. The social results of unbridled competition, in particular unemployment, are where necessary corrected. The economic activity of all the industries concerned is subject to continuous direction and not only during a slump; indirect methods are used (information) as well as an active policy of controlling investment through guaranteed loans. There have been protests against this economic planning which is considered contrary to the spirit of the treaty; in fact the Community has used its powers in this domain very cautiously. On the other hand it has been suggested that the economic unification which is the aim of the Community, will have no decisive effects until it gets beyond the stage of encouraging domestic transactions and proceeds basically to reform the whole system of production. Both points of view are correct, and it will take time to find a satisfactory solution.

Nevertheless the Community is by no means passive in its approach to forming a common market; it has considerable powers and these are of a nature to be exercised by organs which clearly differ from any other international organisation, European or otherwise.

(b) *Juridical features.* The Community has specific federal characteristics: the member States have granted it important powers, in particular powers to make regulations, to levy dues from the concerns under its jurisdiction, to make inspections, and to have some of its decisions enforced almost automatically within the member States. It is in direct contact with the concerns under its jurisdiction, they are in the real sense of the word administered by it.

Its most original feature is that it is managed by an executive body, the High Authority, independent of the member States and, in the event of a vote of censure carried by a two-thirds majority, politically responsible to a Common Assembly similar to the Consultative Assembly of the Council of Europe. Although the governments have some part in choosing members of the High Authority (it has complex rules which leave room for co-optation), they are not government representatives; they must be independent of all public or private interests. The governments intervene in the Community through a Special Council of Ministers; this Council has some control over the major decisions of the High Authority and must try to bring into line the economic powers which the governments have retained; but unlike similar bodies it can decide many matters by a majority vote.

A Court of Justice rounds off the political structure of the Community. The Court has jurisdiction over appeals by a member State or by the Council for the annulment of decisions and recommendations of the High Authority on the grounds of lack of legal competence, substantial procedural violations, violation of the treaty or of any rule of law relating to its application, or abuse of power. The undertakings concerned and their associations therefore have access to the Court.

The outline of a European Political Community drafted by the *ad hoc* assembly clearly shows the direction a system like the European Coal and Steel Community might take. The natural development of the Assembly's powers would lead to a parliamentary system if it could count on public opinion.

Section III

OTHER REGIONAL ORGANISATIONS: AMERICAN ORGANISATIONS

Outside Europe only the American continent has an extensive general organisation; this last section will be devoted to it; we shall simply mention the following regional organisations: the Arab League, the various organisations set up by the treaties of mutual assistance and security in the Pacific and South-East Asia, the South Pacific Commission and the Caribbean Commission.

What has been said above (p. 223) on decentralisation within the universal international organisations should be borne in mind.

The Arab League was created in Cairo on 22 March, 1945, to link the Arab States; at present its members are Egypt, Iraq, Jordan, Lebanon, Libya, Saudi-Arabia, Syria, Yemen. It relies on the co-operation of the member States and comprises a Council, Committee and a Permanent Secretariat. It has an important political role, but despite events in Palestine no integration has taken place. It has made useful studies of regional aspects of certain problems, for example the drug traffic.

ANZUS: On 1 September, 1951, the United States, Australia and New Zealand signed a treaty of security or mutual assistance at San Francisco; a Council was formed of the Foreign Ministers or their representatives; this Council has met infrequently but the military representatives have held several meetings to set up the machinery for military co-operation as applied in the treaty.

SEATO: On 8 September, 1954, at Manila, Australia, France, New Zealand, Pakistan, the Philippines, Burma, the UK and the USA signed a treaty of collective defence for South-East Asia. Article 5 instituted a Council of Foreign Ministers or their representatives to make unanimous resolutions, a permanent council sitting at Bangkok composed of diplomatic representatives of the member countries in Siam and a Siamese delegate, and three working parties of military advisers, economic experts and one for co-operation in the struggle against subversion and infiltration.

The *South Pacific Commission* was created by a conference of 6 February, 1947, at Canberra, and includes Australia, France, the Netherlands, New Zealand, the UK and the USA. It has advisory powers in all matters affecting economic and social development of the non-self-governing territories administered in that region by the signatory States. The Commission is assisted by a Conference, a Secretariat and auxiliary bodies.

The *Caribbean Commission* began as a wartime body, the Anglo-American Caribbean Commission, created in 1942; it rests on the Washington Convention of 30 October, 1946; its programme is similar to the preceding Commission: its powers do not go beyond the field of co-operation. The Commission is assisted by a permanent Committee, a Secretariat and auxiliary bodies.

(A) *General features of inter-American Organisations*

Circumstances favour regional organisation in America; common origin, language, culture, aspirations and needs are strongly marked in the American continent; from Alaska to Patagonia natural conditions have features in common. Closer inspection modifies these favourable circumstances. Distances are immense, populations isolated from each other, the only land route between North and South is the Pan American Highway. Relations between States have often been difficult because of territorial claims and political problems caused by the internal instability of the Governments. As always States are most willing to act together when threatened from outside; the American continent therefore draws together when danger threatens from another continent. It is no longer a question of the old colonial powers, but indirect dangers are to be feared from economic imperialism or subversive activities in countries which rely on immigration to expand their population. Furthermore, the continent as a whole lacks the internal balance which it would have if the States were of more or less equal strength; the presence of the United States is a factor in American relations which alternately attracts and repels the other countries.

This explains some of the special features of the international organisation of the New World.

In addition to a joint organisation covering Latin-America and the United States there are smaller regional organisations.

The Central American Republics have several times tried to build up a political organisation; the Central American Court of Justice has remained famous. Today some limited organisations still exist in Central America. An Organisation of Central American States was created by the San Salvador Charter of 14 October, 1951. Colombia, Ecuador, Panama and Venezuela, which were one State from 1824 to 1830, set up an economic and customs bloc with the Quito Charter of 9 August, 1948.

Until the Second World War there was no particular urgency about creating a really efficient organisation. Hence the procedure by which the American States have built up their organisation. Without formally signing treaties the Pan American Conferences signed 'resolutions' and 'declarations' which became the basis of the American organisation. The legal nature of these 'resolutions' has been questioned; some have been subsequently approved by the governments, but on the whole the process was to accept them as customary rules. The basis of the American organisation has therefore always been very flexible.

Until the Bogotá Charter, organisation was rudimentary. Periodical conferences (formed by the diplomatic representatives), a Commercial Bureau and a steering committee, were for a long time the only organs of the Union of American Republics. At Lima meetings of Foreign Ministers were decided on if the continent was threatened; during the war these meetings tried to formulate the basis of a policy of neutrality and later of common defence. Only when faced with proposals for world organisation did the American States decide to define the basis of their security in a proper treaty (Treaty of Rio de Janiero, 1947) and a joint organisation (Bogotá Charter). The importance of inter-American customary law must not be underestimated, nor the numerous conventions of all kinds signed since 1928; many of these however have not become effective for want of the necessary ratifications.

(B) *The Bogotá Charter*

Prepared by the Act of Chapultepec, 6 March, 1945, the Bogotá Charter provided the American continent with a more formal organisation. The Charter contained rules and principles defining the character of international relations in America; it also created the Organisation of American States. It took over all the organs previously created and tried to maintain the former Pan American Union; the latter still had its Council and a Bureau and their functions were considerably extended. The Charter also added new bodies based on the United Nations Charter. But however wide the new organisation may be, it remains entirely based on co-operation. The Organisation of American States, which came into force in 1951, comprises:

(1) The Inter-American Conference, supreme organ which meets every 5 years, unless convoked with the approval of two-thirds of the States;

(2) A Meeting of Consultation of Ministers of Foreign Affairs, which meets to study problems of an urgent nature; it is assisted by an Advisory Defence Committee;

(3) A Council made up of special envoys or diplomatic representatives accredited to the country in which the Council has its seat; it is a research, advisory and executive authority; it is responsible to Pan American Union and is assisted by three councils (economic and social, jurists, cultural);

(4) Pan American Union, the central and permanent organ, formed from the former Commercial Bureau, henceforward acting as the General Secretariat.

BIBLIOGRAPHY

INTRODUCTION

DE VISSCHER, C.: *Théories et réalités en droit international* (Pédone, Paris, 1953).

DUPRÉEL, E.: *Sociologie générale* (PUF, Paris, 1948).

KELSEN, H.: 'La technique du droit international et l'organisation de la paix' (*Revue de droit international et de législation comparée*, 1934, p. 9).

KELSEN, H.: *Law and peace in international relations* (Harvard Univ. Press, Oxford, 1942).

LAUTERPACHT, H.: *The function of law in the international community* (OUP, 1943).

POLITIS, N.: *La morale internationale* (La Braconnière, Neufchatel, 1943).

RUYSSEN, T.: *Les caractères sociologiques de la communauté humaine* (RCADI, 1939, pp. 67, 121).

SCHINDLER: *Contribution à l'étude des facteurs sociologiques du droit international* (RCADI, 1933, pp. 46, 233).

SOROKIN, P.: *Society, culture and personality. Their structure and dynamics. A system of general sociology* (Harper, New York, 1947).

PART ONE

ALVAREZ, A.: *Le droit international americain* (Pédone, Paris, 1910).

ARON, R.: *Les guerres en chaine* (Gallimard, Paris, 1951).

BASDEVANT, J.: *Règles générales du droit de la paix* (RCADI, 1936, pp. 58, 471).

BOURQUIN, M.: *Pouvoir scientifique et droit international* (RCADI, 1947, pp. 70, 335).

BRIERLY, J.: *The law of nations* (OUP, 1946).

CHENG, B.: *General principles of law as applied by international courts and tribunals* (Stevens, London, 1953).

COLBY, C. H.: *Geographical aspects of international relations* (Chicago Univ. Press, 1938).

DE LA BRIÈRE, Y.: *L'organisation internationale du monde contemporain. et la papauté souveraine, 1885–1930* (ed. Spes, 2nd ed. 1934,3 vols.).

DEUTSCH, K. W.: *Nationalism and social communication* (Wiley and Sons, New York, 1953).

DONNEDIEU DE VABRES, H.: *Le procès de Nuremberg devant les principes modernes du droit penal international* (RCADI, 1947, pp. 70, 481).

FISCHER, L.: *The Soviets in world affairs, 1917–29,* vol. I (Princeton, 1951).

GÜGGENHEIM: *Traité de droit international public.*

HARVARD LAW SCHOOL: *Law of treaties. Research in international law* (AJ, supplement, 1935).

JENKS, C. W.: *The interpretation of municipal law by the Permanent Court of International Justice* (BYBIL, 1938, p. 67).

JENKS, C. W.: *Les instruments internationaux à caractère collectif* (RCADI, 1939, pp. 69, 451).

JONES, F. C.: *Japan's new order in East Asia, its rise and fall, 1937–45.* Issued under the joint auspices of the Royal Institute of International Affairs and the Institute of Pacific Relations (OUP, 1954).

KELSEN, H.: *The communist theory of law* (Stevens, London, 1955).

LAPENNA, I.: *Conceptions sovietiques de droit international public* (Pédone, Paris, 1954).

LAUTERPACHT, H.: *The so-called Anglo-American and continental schools of thought in international law* (BYBIL, 1931).

LAUTERPACHT, H.: *International law and human rights* (Stevens, London, 1950).

LISZT, F. von: *Droit international* (French trans. Pédone, Paris, 1928).

NUSSBAUM, A.: *A concise history of the law of nations* (Macmillan, New York, 2nd ed. 1954).

PALMER, N. D., and PERKINS, H. C.: *International relations. The world community in transition* (Stevens, London, 1954).

PHILLIPSON, C.: *The international law and custom of ancient Greece and Rome* (Macmillan, London, 1911, 2 vols.).

POUTHAS, C.: *Le mouvement des nationalités en Europe dans la première moitié du XIXe siècle* (Centre de documentation universitaire, Paris, 1945).

RENOUVIN, P.: *Histoire des relations internationales* (Paris, 1953).

ROUSSEAU, C.: *Principes généraux du droit international public,* vol. I (Paris).

ROYAL INSTITUTE OF INTERNATIONAL AFFAIRS: *The problem of foreign investments* (OUP, 1937).

ROYAL INSTITUTE OF INTERNATIONAL AFFAIRS: *Atomic energy, its international implications* (London, 1948).

SCHACHTER: *The development of international law through the legal opinions of the United Nations secretariat* (BYBIL, 1948, p. 91).

SCHWARZENBERGER, G.: *Power politics. A study of international society* (Stevens, London, 2nd ed. 1951).

SOROKIN, P.: *Russia and the United States* (Stevens, London, 2nd ed. 1950).

STONE, J.: *Legal controls of international conflict. A treatise on the dynamics of disputes and war law* (Stevens, London, 1954).

TCHIRKOVITCH: *La règle de non-discrimination et la protection des minorités* (RGDIP, 1951, p. 247).

TER MEULEN, J.: *Der Gedanke des internationalen Organisations in seiner Entwicklung* (Hague, Nijhoff, 1917, 1929, 1940).

TINBERGER, J.: *International economic integration* (Elsevier, Amsterdam, 1954).

TOBIN, H. J.: *The termination of multipartite treaties* (Columbia Univ. Press, 1933).

TOYNBEE, A.: *Survey of international affairs* (OUP, 1920–1939).

UNITED NATIONS INTERNATIONAL LAW COMMISSION: *Laws and practices concerning the conclusion of treaties* (United Nations, 1952, vol. 4).

VANDERPOL, A.: *La doctrine scolastique du droit de la guerre* (Pédone, Paris, 1919).

VAN HEUVEN GOEDHART, G. J.: *The problem of refugees* (RCADI, 1953, pp. 82, 265).

VAN KLEFFENS, E. N.: *Sovereignty in international law* (RCADI, 1953, p. 82).

VAN VOLLENHOVEN, C: *Les trois phases du droit des gens* (Nijhof, Hague, 1919).

WALTERS, F. P.: *A history of the League of Nations* (OUP, 1952, 2 vols.).

WRIGHT, Q.: *The world community* (Chicago Univ. Press, 1948).

ZIMMERN: *La crise de l'organisation internationale à la fin du Moyen Age* (RCADI, 1933, pp. 44, 319).

PART TWO

AUFRICHT, H.: *Principles and practices of recognition by international organisations* (AJ, 1949, p. 679).

DE LA BRIÈRE, Y.: *La constitution juridique de la Cité du Vatican* (RCADI, 1930, pp. 33, 115).

DUROSELLE, J. B.: 'L'évolution des formes de la diplomatie et son effet sur la politique étrangère des états' (in collective work, *La politique étrangère et ses fondements*, Colin, Paris, 1954).

LAUTERPACHT, H.: *Recognition in international law* (Macmillan, Cambridge, 1948).

MANSERGH, N.: *The multiracial commonwealth* (RIIA, London, 1955).

MAREK, K.: *Identity and continuity of States in public international law* (Droz, Geneva, 1954).

MEADE, J. E.: *Problems of economic union* (Allen and Unwin, London, 1953).

PASTUHOV, V. D.: *A guide to the practice of international conferences* (Carnegie, Washington, 1945).

PILOTTI, M.: *Les unions d'états* (RCADI, 1928, pp. 24, 445).

SATOW, E.: *A guide to diplomatic practice* (London, 3rd ed. 1932).

STUYT, A. M.: *The general principles of law* (Nijhoff, Hague, 1946).

TI CHIANG CHEN: *The international law of recognition*. Preface by Brierly (Stevens, London, 1951).

TUNC, A. and S.: *Le système constitutionnel des Etats Unis d'Amerique* (Domat-Montchrestien, Paris, 1953-4).

UNESCO: *La technique des conférences internationales* (UNESCO, SS/3, 16 April, 1951).

WEHBERG, H.: *La guerre civile et le droit international* (RCADI, 1938, p. 63).

WEHBERG, H.: *L'interdiction du recours à la force* (RCADI, 1951, p. 78).

WHEARE, K. C.: *The Statute of Westminster and dominion status* (OUP, 5th ed. 1953).

PART THREE

AUFRICHT, H.: *Guide to League of Nations publications. A bibliographical survey of the work of the League, 1920-1947* (Columbia Univ. Press, 1951).

BASTID, S.: *Le droit des organisations internationales* (Les Cours de droit, Paris, 1951-2).

BEER, G.: *Regional organisations, a United Nations problem* (AJ, 1955, p. 166).

BENTWICH, N., and MARTIN, A.: *A commentary on the Charter of the United Nations* (Routledge and Kegan Paul, London, 2nd ed. 1951).

BONNEFOUS, E,: *L'Europe en face de son destin* (PUF, Paris, 1952).

DUNCAN HALL, H.: *Mandates, dependencies and trusteeship* (Stevens, London, 1948).

FRANKENSTEIN, M.: *L'organisation des Nations Unies devant le conflict coréen* (Pédone, Paris, 1952).

GOODRICH and HAMBRO: *Charter of the United Nations, commentary and documents* (Stevens, London, 2nd ed. 1949).

HAMMARSKJÖLD, A.: *Les immunités de personnes investies de fonctions internationales* (RCADI, 1936, pp. 56, 110).

HILL, M.: *The economic and financial organisation of the League of Nations* (Carnegie, Washington, 1945).

ISMAY, LORD: *NATO, the first five years, 1949-54* (NATO, 1955).

JENKS, C. W.: *Co-ordination in international organisation, an introductory survey* (BYBIL, 1951, p. 29).

JENKS, C. W.: *Some constitutional problems of international organisation* (BYBIL, 1945, p. 11).

JIMÉNEZ DE ARÉCHAGA, E.: *Voting and handling of disputes in the Security Council* (Carnegie, New York, 1950).

KELSEN, H.: *The law of the United Nations* (Stevens, London, 1950, supplement 1951).

KOO, WELLINGTON.: *Voting procedures in international political organisations* (Columbia Univ. Press, 1947).

KOPELMANAS, L.: *L'organisation des Nations Unies* (Sirey, Paris, 1947).

KULSKI, W. W.: *The Soviet system of collective security compared with the western system* (AJ, 1950, p. 453).

MARTIN, A.: *Sécurité collective* (UNESCO, 1952).

POTTER, P. B.: *An introduction to the study of international organisation* (Appleton Century Crofts, New York, 5th ed. 1948).

PUIG, J. C.: *Les principes du droit international public americain* (Pédone, Paris, 1954).

RABSHOFEN-WERTHEIMER, E. F.: *The international secretariat* (Carnegie, Washington, 1945).

RAY, J.: *Commentaire du pacte de la Société des Nations* (Sirey, Paris, 1 vol., 4 supplements, 1930–35).

REUTER, P.: *La Communauté Européenne du Charbon et de l'Acier* (Librairie générale du droit et de la jurisprudence, Paris, 1953).

RICHES, C. A.: *Majority rule in international organisation* (John Hopkins, Baltimore, 1940).

ROYAL INSTITUTE OF INTERNATIONAL AFFAIRS: *Documents on regional organisation outside Western Europe, 1940–49* (RIIA London, 1940).

SABA, M. H.: *Les accords régionaux dans les accords de l'ONU* (RCADI, 1952, pp. 80, 635).

SAYRE, F. B.: *Experiments in international administration* (Harper, London, 1919).

SCHWEBEL, S. M.: *The Secretary-General of the United Nations* (Harvard Univ. Press, 1952).

SHARP, W. R.: *International technical assistance programs and organisation* (Public administration service, Chicago, 1952).

SØRENSEN, M.: *Le Conseil de l'Europe* (RCADI, 1952, pp. 81, 121).

STAMP, D.: *Our undeveloped world* (Faber, London, 1953).

UNITED NATIONS: *Agreements between the United Nations and the specialised agencies* (New York, 1952).

UNITED NATIONS SECRETARIAT: *Handbook on the legal status, privileges and immunities of the United Nations* (UN legal department ST/SG/3, 1953, X2).

VAN ASBECK, F. M., and VERZIJL, J.: *United Nations textbook* (Leiden, 2nd ed. 1954).

WHITE, L. C., and ZOCCA, M. R.: *International non-governmental organisations, their purposes, methods and accomplishments* (Rutger, New Brunswick, 1951).

WOOLF, L. S.: *International government* (Brentano, New York, 1916).

YUEN-LI-LIANG: *What is an international conference?* (AJ, 1950, p. 333).

INDEX

Figures in bold type indicate major references to the subject.

International Trade Organisation
(ITO), 213, 216, 219, 239
International Union for the Publi-
cation of Customs Tariffs, 208
Investment, 59, 74, 75, 80, 277, 297
Israel, 144, 224, 239, 244, 245, 260,
275, 279, 301

J

Jurisdiction, of States, **97**, 181, 183,
232
of international organisations,
220, 228, 232, 237
Justice, international (*see* Arbitration; *also* International Court
of Justice)

K

Korea, 239, 260, 271, 276

L

Labour (*see* International Labour
Organisation)
Lacunae (*see* Non liquet)
Law, international, 19, 24, 64, **85,**
107, **114**
general principles of, **133**
natural, 45, 50, 66
of international organisations,
262
of nations, 187
public European, 55, 65, 155
League of Nations, **58,** 61, 126, 174,
210, 224, 225, 235, 242, 244,
249, 251, 255, 257, **265**
Liberalism (*see* Capitalism, Trade,
Investment)
Loans (of international organisations), 254

M

Mandates, **60,** 179, 269, 280
Manilla Pact, 216
Marshall Aid, 81, 289
Mediation, 172
Migration, 59, 73 (*see* Population,
Refugees)
Military organisations, **220** (*see*
NATO)
Military Staff Committee of UN,
272
Morocco, 148, **181,** 184, 207
Moscow Conference, 212, 292
Most Favoured Nation clause, 62,
88, 111, 164

N

National income, 69, 256
Nationality, 98, **143**
Nations, 50, 63, 71 (*see* MFN clause,
United Nations)
Non-discrimination, 62, 86, 278
Non-intervention, 62, 100, 145
Non liquet, 100, 135
Non-self-governing territories, 273,
279
North Atlantic Treaty Organisa-
tion (NATO), 216, 220, 224,
238, 245, 248, 303, 306, 308
Northern Council, 163, 297
Nuclear Research (*see* European
Organisation of)

O

Officials, international, 241 (*see*
Agents)
Open door, 43, 59, 280
Organisation (*see* International
organisation)
Organisation for Communications
and Transit, 212